WHEN FATHER AND SON CONSPIRE

WHEN
FATHER AND SON
CONSPIRE

A Minnesota Farm Murder

by JOSEPH AMATO

Iowa State University Press / Ames

Joseph Amato is Professor of History and Director of the Rural Studies Program at Southwest State University, Marshall, Minnesota. Among Amato's writings are *Ethics: Living or Dead?*, *Guilt and Gratitude: The Study of the Origins of Contemporary Conscience*, and *Death Book: Terrors, Consolations, Contradictions, and Paradoxes*.

© 1988 Iowa State University Press, Ames, Iowa 50010

Composed by Iowa State University Press
Printed in the United States of America

First edition, 1988

Library of Congress Cataloging-in-Publication Data

Amato, Joseph Anthony.
  When father and son conspire: a Minnesota farm murder / by Joseph Amato.
    p.   cm.
  Bibliography: p.
  Includes index.
  ISBN 0–8138–1974–1
  1. Murder—Minnesota—Case studies. 2. Jenkins, James. 3. Jenkins, Steven. 4. Fathers and sons—Minnesota—Case studies. 5. Agriculture—Economic aspects—Minnesota. I. Title.
HV6533.M6A46   1988
364.1′523′097762—dc19
                                                87–24535
                                                  CIP

DEDICATION

TO Adam Bavolack, who first interested me in the law; Kevin Stroup, whose intelligence and enthusiasm sustained my interest in this work; and all of you who in one way or another helped me write this work.

CONTENTS

I PERCEIVE these families as Greek tragedies without God. They seemed destined to misery even catastrophe because they were locked in by their past and by configurations of love, hate, anxiety and sham which became established in their homes, rigid as walls.

JULES HENRY, *Pathways to Madness*

WHOM the gods would destroy, they first make mad.

EURIPIDES

IF A SON shall ask bread of any of you that is a father, will he give him a stone? or if he ask a fish, give him a serpent?

LUKE 11:11 (*King James*)

FOREWORD

THIS is a multilayered account of a murder. It deals with the story we were told a few years ago, about the murder of two bankers by indebted farmers, father and son. This story is about the farm crisis, undeniably tragic in itself. With a bit more probing, the story also involves the agricultural poor, who kept a dream of farming but existed in a special, marginal layer within rural Minnesota society, from school days onward.

Above all, however, this is a story of family collapse and of a deviant male culture built on militarism and intense, distorted emotions. Professor Amato paints in a way a classic tragedy. He also deals with a number of recognizable features of American male culture in our time—issues of emotional expression and targeting, of the consequences of family disruption, and of the frequent absence of clear standards in father-son relations. Yet this is, as well, a case of deviance, in which common problems and values are refracted through a grotesque mirror. The story in this final sense is a unique one, even as it weaves together strands from a wider psychological tapestry. At all its levels, this is a powerful and gripping contribution to contemporary history, based on prodigious research and even greater insight.

PETER N. STEARNS
Carnegie-Mellon University
Pittsburgh, Pennsylvania

PREFACE

WE like stories. Some say God does too and that is why he created us. We tell stories to know ourselves and to hide from ourselves, to love and to lie, to prosecute and to defend. Individuals are stories. Families are stories. Friendships are stories. Religions are stories. We live and die by stories. Stories, it seems at times, are all we have—are all we are. At times it seems the only important difference is the difference between a good story and a bad story.

Perhaps holding this view is the price I paid for having worked too long and too closely on the story of a Minnesota father and son who, in the fall of 1983, killed two bankers and fled from southwestern Minnesota to Texas. (Four days later, the son surrendered to the law and then led police to his father, who was dead.)

Storytelling is not the subject of this work—at least, it was not meant to be when I started to tell the story of this unusual father and son who conspired and killed together. (Paradoxically, the father and son could have been no closer together nor any farther apart.) However, in trying to tell their story, I realized how much storytelling forms the tissue of human understanding, action, and relations.

As I prepared this work, I discovered that stories filled the father and son's family before it came apart and that stories kept the father and son together. The stories—the tales, myths, and lies they told each other—made possible their crime and sealed their fates.

In turn, the crime caused others to tell stories. There were the stories the prosecution told to convict the son of the killings and the stories the defense told to spare him. And, too, there are all the stories we—the survivors—must tell each other to understand the actions of this father and son. Perhaps above all else, we tell our stories to mend what their actions tore apart, to chain the beast they unleashed.

The son never confessed to killing the bankers, nor did he tell the world a story that silenced all other stories. In his silence, stories thrive. Here I tell my story and also recount many of the other stories that belong to families, communities, courtrooms, the press, and publications.

I do wish here to answer the question I often heard while writing this work and that I hope to hear less after its publication: "Why should you, an academic writer who only occasionally dabbles in popular writing, write about a contemporary murder?" The answer could be no more simple: the murder took hold of me.

Like most people in southwestern Minnesota, I was fascinated by this father and son who murdered and fled together. Like others, I was captivated by uncertainty. I did not know which of the two did the killing nor whether the father killed himself or was killed by his son. The actions of this father and son begged a story.

WHEN FATHER AND SON CONSPIRE

The Story and the Silence

On the morning of September 29, 1983, on an abandoned farm in southwestern Minnesota, two bankers were killed. The owner of the Buffalo Ridge State Bank, Rudolph Blythe, and his first loan officer, Deems Thulin, arrived early that morning at the farm to prepare for an appointment with a prospective buyer. The farm had stood empty for the last three years since the previous owner had left the farm. The prospective buyer, who had phoned the previous afternoon, had called himself Ron Anderson.

Following the gravel farm road up to the garage which stood directly behind the farm house, Blythe and Thulin discovered a trespasser on the farm. Parked in front of the garage was a white pickup with Texas plates. Blythe and Thulin searched the house. As they began their search of the yard, Blythe's wife, Susan, arrived at the farm to trade cars with her husband. Blythe sent Susan to the nearby town of Tyler to call the county sheriff to come and help evict the trespasser. Because of the Texas plates, he told Susan he suspected the trespasser was James Jenkins, the former owner, who had abandoned the farm, beating Blythe out of his mortgage payments as well as approximately thirty cows that had been given as collateral.

Blythe never guessed the trespasser and the prospective buyer, Ron Anderson, were one and the same. If Blythe had guessed, he and Thulin would have known they had been lured into a trap.

Moments after Susan left, Blythe and Thulin were dead. The first loan officer, Deems Thulin, a Vietnam veteran, was killed by a single shot through the neck. He was found dead at the passenger's side of the bank car. The car door was open. His legs were in the car; his body was out of it. The owner of the bank, Rudolph Blythe, a veteran too, was killed as he fled. He was wounded at the driver's side of the bank car. He fled from there, around the side of the house, down the incline of the large front lawn. He had just about reached the county road when he was cut down by a volley of rifle shots.

Two sets of spent rifle shells, found at different ends of the farm, and a distinct trail left in the weeds revealed the path of the murderer. He had fired his first volley of shots from the corner of the back shed at the two bankers as they reached their car. From there, where the front edges of the granary and chicken house were closest, the murderer had run through the high weeds to Thulin. Then, from the dead body of Thulin, the murderer had pursued Blythe around the farm house. From the crest of the front lawn, he had fired a second volley of shots, which had killed the fleeing Blythe as he entered the ditch.

Only moments after the shooting, a passing off-duty deputy spied something at the road's edge. It was Blythe's body, marked out by his bright yellow slicker. As the deputy stopped and turned his vehicle to return, a white pickup containing two men came rushing out of the farm road, heading in the opposite direction. The driver—the shorter of the two—wore a wool hat.

Before either the sheriff or the ambulance crew arrived, Susan Blythe returned to the farm to find her husband dead in the ditch. Susan stood in the ditch, cursing Jenkins.

The sheriff put out an all-points bulletin on Jenkins and his son, who was known to be living with his father, James Jenkins, forty-six, and his son Steven, eighteen, became the objects of a nationwide search.

James and Steven Jenkins fled in their white pickup, disappearing into a fog that engulfed the region that morning. Several hours later they reappeared at Luverne, Minnesota, forty miles to the south of Ruthton. There, at Harvey's Gun Shop, they purchased additional .30-caliber ammunition, which the store owner cautioned them was illegal for hunting. At Schutz's OK Hardware, they purchased shotgun shells and a flashlight.

Minutes later, on the outskirts of Luverne, a Rock County deputy recognized their vehicle as one described in the all-points bulletin. Cautiously, he began to follow them. They quickly turned off the highway. They stopped and fired at the deputy. Afraid of being ambushed, the deputy did not pursue them beyond the hill from which they had fired at him.

The father and son again disappeared into the fog that shrouded the area for the next several days. There was no sign of them until four days later, on October 2, when Steven surrendered to the police in Paducah, Texas.

Steven led the police to a nearby abandoned farm where he and his father, who had refused to turn himself in, had spent their last day together. Steven claimed his father had been alive when Steven left him. Near the entrance to the farm, Steven and the police found his father dead. A good portion of James Jenkins's face and head had been destroyed by a shotgun blast.

The sole survivor—a boy who had just turned eighteen—was in custody. People expected that now questions could be answered and the story of the father's and son's deeds would be told.

The brutal killings, the son's surrender, and the father's apparent suicide all begged for a story to explain them. Questions about the father and son were inevitably asked: Who were they? Why had they killed two bankers? Had they gone to the scene of the crime intending to kill them? Had they wanted to kill anyone else? What had their flight been like? There were also questions about the fate of the bankers: Why had they met their end, in that way, on that day? Not easily forgotten was the fact that the bankers were young and that they had wives and children.

One of the law's first questions was, Who had shot? Only one of the Jenkinses had killed the bankers: either the father or the son had done it. Who was the murderer? From this question, other questions followed: Had each equally wanted and planned to kill that day? Had the one who shot been the one who was most responsible for the killing?

Some assumed that Steven was the murderer, thus raising questions about the father's death itself. Some early newspaper accounts wrote "suicide"; others wrote "apparent suicide." Did James Jenkins despair over what he and his son had done or what he had tempted his son to do? Conjecture invited conjecture.

If there had been a pact between the father and the son to declare the son innocent in the eyes of the world—a supposition made by many—why hadn't the father left a suicide note? At least, he could have telephoned the police with his confession, some remarked. Why had the father abandoned his son to stand trial alone? The father had involved his son in murder and then—as many told the story—deserted him.

Anything the mind could conjure between the father and son seemed possible. Perhaps the father had proposed a dual suicide pact, and the son had declined. Maybe the son had killed the father in order to go free.

A father and son had killed two bankers, and later the father had been found dead. Beyond this, people could repeat facts and ask questions, make conjectures and tell one another stories. But all had to wait for Steven, who alone survived, to tell his story.

STEVEN'S STORY

THE FIRST NEWSPAPER photographs taken of Steven in custody showed a young man who looked like a captured war prisoner. Steven was approximately five feet ten inches tall, thin, gaunt, and dark. A shadow seemed to cover his face. Sporting a short crew cut, he was dressed in military fatigues. He wore a tee shirt. Steven had tattoos on both arms. On his right arm—telling the world he was a serious soldier—he had a skull with a beret. On his left arm—revealing both the hunter and the boy he was—he had a picture of Sylvester the Cat pursuing little Tweety-Bird.

The police search of his father's pickup, which Steven had driven to the station, harvested a collection of weapons and military goods. The police found, among other things, two walkie-talkies, a bayonet, a .410 shotgun with bayonet affixed to it, a pistol, a considerable number of shells, and an M-1 carbine. All the weapons—whose quality suggested an owner with only enough money to occasionally canvass an army surplus store—belonged to Steven.

Steven appeared to be wrongly cast for a part in a farm story. Contrary to the stories of several reporters from outside the region, he simply did not look like a farmer's son. Far more than appearing to be a typical eighteen-year-old son of a farmer, he resembled some kind of soldier—a prisoner of war, a revolutionist, a survivalist, anything but a typical farmer's son.

Thelma Hall, dispatcher of the Paducah police, told the Bureau of Criminal Apprehension (BCA) that Steven had walked into the station on October 2 at 6:30 P.M. Her first impression, given his military dress and appearance, was that he was AWOL. "He had come to turn himself in. And I said, 'What for?' And he said that he was an accomplice in a murder case."

"He cried a great deal," Thelma Hall continued. "I think that he was scared. Ah it's just like a child . . . coming in, telling a grownup he had done wrong." She "consoled him just like I guess any mother would. I can't stand a child that's crying."

For the first time, Steven told the essentials of his story to Texas Ranger Leo Hickman: Steven claimed his and his father's intention had not been to kill anyone. They had only wanted to rob and scare "the bank people."

According to Steven, they had arrived at the farm at 8:30 A.M. Surprised by the arrival of the banker's car, Steven and his father had run and hidden, his father taking the M-1 and he, the shotgun. Hidden behind the garage, Steven had heard someone holler, "He's got a gun!" Then he had heard a volley of shots. He had emerged from behind the garage to see an unidentified man lying on the passenger side of the banker's green station wagon.

Steven did acknowledge that after stopping in Luverne for additional shells, he had fired three or four shots at the pursuing police vehicle before his gun had jammed.

Hiding by day and driving by night, Steven and his father had arrived in Cottle County, Texas, where they had spent their first night in the truck before proceeding to a nearby abandoned farm, just four miles north of Paducah, on which only a garage stood.

Steven then described how he and his father had spent their last day together. They had neither money nor food. They spent time in the shade of the empty garage. Steven said he had decided he wanted to give up, whereas his father did not. According to Steven, as summarized by Texas Ranger Leo Hickman, his father said he was not going to jail but that Steven could surrender if he wanted to. However, according to Hickman, James further told Steven, if Steven turned himself in, James was going to commit suicide. His father helped Steven push the pickup out of the sand and said that he was going to commit suicide.

Steven added that the last time he had seen his father, James had been sitting on a cement slab near the empty garage. He had the 12-gauge shotgun with him. Officer Hickman said that when they returned with Steven to the abandoned farm and discovered the body of James, Steven became "extremely upset and hysterical."

The next evening Steven retold his story to Officers Robert Berg and Michael O'Gorman of the Minnesota BCA. The middle-aged officers—O'Gorman from Mankato, the older and larger of the two, and Berg from Worthington—pressed Steven as hard as they could, using what tricks of interrogation they had learned. With no hesitation, Steven admitted that all the weapons found in the truck were his, that the murder weapon (the M-1 carbine) was his, and that he had taken it to the scene of the crime. Additionally, Steven acknowledged that he had practiced shooting the weapon at dummies dressed like humans. He did not flinch when saying he had fired shots at a pursuing police vehicle. But to the murders of the bankers themselves, Steven would not confess, however insistent Berg and O'Gorman were.

For Steven, it was his father, not he, who had reasons to kill the banker Rudolph Blythe. Blythe had—according to Steven—taken away one farm from his father, and Blythe's bad credit references were denying his father a chance to have another farm. His father, in Steven's words, "wanted to grab and really scare the shit [out of him]."

Steven persisted in saying he had taken the shotgun, not the M-1, and had run behind the garage. "I stayed right there. . . I didn't know who was shooting . . . where the bullets were going." When he had emerged, meeting his father at the pickup, his father had thrown him the keys and told him to drive.

Through their October 4 interrogation, Officers Berg and O'Gorman tried to crack Steven. They told him that whether he pulled the trigger or not, "you are just as guilty in the eyes of the law." They challenged his story. O'Gorman told Steven there was no way his father could have done the running and shooting that the murders required. O'Gorman could not—nor did he believe any jury would—believe that Steven's father had run a hundred yards from the corner of the hog barn, where the first volley had been fired, to the front of the house, where the second volley—which cut Blythe down—had been fired.

"I don't want to browbeat you into saying something that didn't go on out there," O'Gorman continued, "but put yourself in the place of the jury. . . . They're gonna look at you, a young man of your stature and your health condition and your record with that gun, the amount of practice with that gun, and they're going to look at your father with his stature, his age, and the amount of practice that he had with the gun—now twelve people are going to see, are going to sit there, and have to make a decision."

They pushed Steven. They suggested he shared his father's hatred of Blythe. They suggested his father had pumped Steven up against Blythe. They told him his story made no sense. The first shots had been taken from too far away for them to have planned robbery or assault. It made no sense to have brought Rudy out to the old farm to rob him. O'Gorman pushed harder against what he took to be the implausible character of Steven's story: "When you talk about motive of what has gone on in the past, as far as he feels that Rudy . . . jewed [*sic*] him out of the farm some way or another, and then brings him back to kill him on the farm he screwed him out of. That makes sense, but not to stick him up. Or to scare the hell out of him."

Berg and O'Gorman insisted Steven must have heard something out there. He had to have heard more than shots. Steven persisted in saying he knew nothing. He had not seen anything; he had not heard anything. At one point Steven replied, "I ducked down. I was trying to keep from pissing my pants."

As they approached the conclusion of their interrogation, Berg and O'Gorman put all the pressure they could on Steven. Berg queried Steven about "the pact" that he had made with his father. "Your senses were coming back. You realized that you couldn't get away with it . . . , that you had to turn yourself in. Wasn't it at that point that you reached an agreement? That agreement being that you'd put the blame on your dad." Steven replied, in a voice which often trailed off, becoming inaudible. "I didn't shoot."

Officer Berg tried another line of attack. "I think you owe it to your dad, no matter what he told you . . . before he decided to commit suicide. . . . I think you deserve . . . [to] send him to his grave with a clean bill of health." Steven interrupted Berg: "You want me to take the blame. . . . I didn't kill anybody."

Officer O'Gorman sought to follow Berg's line of interrogation: "But I am telling you this, Steve . . . that if you are not telling us the truth, you are going to live with it the rest of your life. I tell you it will eat you alive. Especially where your father is concerned."

Despite Steven's denials, O'Gorman, a large man, turned up the heat. He told Steven that maybe he was out for revenge, that he was "a little abnormal", "a little bit out of the ordinary" with all his interest in military stuff. "Your father says we are going out and scare somebody . . . and if something clicks, Steve, in your mind and you've got the gun and start pulling the trigger . . . once the first shot's fired, you can't call it back. It's Johnny-bar-the-door at that point. That is why I say I think things got out of hand out there that day. There could've been an argument . . . and you could have stepped in."

O'Gorman concluded by returning to his most powerful appeal to Steven's conscience. "Four people knew what went on out there that day. Out of the four people, right now three of them are dead. . . . One person knows, and if . . . you send your father to the grave, even though you have got an agreement with him, it's going to eat you alive. . . . It'll haunt you the rest of your life. All I ask is the truth, Steve. Nothing more, nothing less." In the videotape taken of Steven's confession, it appeared to the BCA officers that he was on the verge of breaking at this point; he didn't.

Steven's reply, which trailed off, was: "Why would I turn myself in if I did . . . ?" To the question why would he have left his father out there on the farm to commit suicide, Steven answered: "I want to go back and . . . I couldn't leave Mom and Grandpa and Grandma. How much longer is this going to take?"

O'Gorman and Berg, no doubt sensing that they had failed to break Steven, made one last effort. They asked Steven why he had gone along with his father on such an illogical plan to rob Blythe. Berg asked: "Give me some logical reason why you went there with your dad . . . when you knew it wasn't going to work . . . if you left him [Blythe] there alive?"

Steven replied: "I have got a responsibility, okay?" What was Steven's responsibility? Was it to do whatever his father wanted? Was it to keep the promise he had made to his dead father? Was he pledged by his father's death to the story of his own innocence? Or did Steven's responsibility have another source? Good soldiers don't tell the enemy the truth.

Steven had not broken. Steven, a boy who had just turned eighteen, had told the world the story he wanted to.

Steven's story, however, was not worthy of the known facts. Not by passion nor by detail was it equal to the lives of three men. Steven had not provided the crime with even the core of its minimal story.

The silence of Steven's story was the vortex out of which many other stories arose. There was Steven's own story to the grand jury, which added only a few details to his earlier testimony. In turn, there was his lawyer's story to the court. With the help of a psychiatrist, his lawyer tried to make the case turn on a matter of his father's duress. There was also the prosecution's story. With extensive investigatory work and the special testimony of Susan Blythe, the prosecutor sought to convict Steven of first-degree murder. Also, there was that final story the jury told itself regarding Steven's guilt or innocence.

Most intriguing of all the stories, however, were the stories that James and Steven told each other. Their stories took them to the farm, led one of them to shoot, commanded their flight, and defined their last hours together. Their stories were inseparable from their lives and their fate.

Their stories, above all else, were family stories. They were about how they had lost their farm, their home, and the wife and mother of their family. They were stories about how lonely they were and how unjustly the world had treated them. Finally James and Steven Jenkins told each other a story about revenge, which led them to do what fathers and sons rarely do: kill together.

It takes a very strange father and son to conspire to kill and to join in murder and suicide. This is a story of such a father and son.

CHAPTER ONE

The Place and First Stories

After that he was alone
and I was alone.
Few friends came: he invited none.
His two-story house he turned
into a forest,
where both he and I are the hunters.

—ROBERT BLY, *"My Father's Wedding," Selected Poems*

THE PLACE THEY CALLED HOME

SOUTHWESTERN MINNESOTA was the home of James and Steven Jenkins. Its land, its farms, its villages, its people and their ways formed the corner of the world with which the Jenkinses were familiar and at home. They could not separate what they felt, knew, experienced, and hoped for from this region, which for thousands of years had belonged to the tall grass prairie and has for the last century—since the white people settled—formed part of the northernmost edge of the great midwestern Corn Belt.

The wind blows freely and constantly here. The wind averages at least ten miles an hour; only on the ocean coasts does it blow as strongly. Still days are unusual and often are preludes to serious storms. Only in the tree-filled river valleys, in the center of villages and cities, or amidst the most dense groves that surround the farms on their north and east sides does one escape the force of the wind. At times the wind seems malicious. It is the primary accomplice of hailstorms, gigantic thunderstorms, tornados, and blizzards—of all that makes the climate one of extremes. On the coldest winter days, the wind joins snow and cold to make blizzards that kill. The worst blizzards, in a matter of hours, bring a foot of snow blown by seventy-mile-per-hour arctic winds, which send temperatures plummeting to forty degrees below zero. Everything shuts down. Nothing can be seen. Settlers told tales of how they ran ropes from their houses to their barns so they would not be lost when going outside. During the worst blizzards, like the one in the spring of 1975, cattle are driven out of their pens into open fields, which come to resemble a stormy ocean of frozen waves. The nostrils of the beasts get covered with ice as their breath turns snow to water, which in turn becomes ice, and in a while they are suffocated. In the spring of 1975, farmers found herds of dead cattle in their fields. It was estimated that twenty thousand cattle were lost in the great blizzard of January 1975. After such blizzards, even those who have never known how lonely the prairie was for its first settlers join the plaint of an old Polish settler to the area: "O God, why have you cast me out on these winds?" Little interrupts the wind's crossing here.

The world is big here; views are large. There is endless sky above. Below—where seas of natural tall grasses once stood—now stand fields of corn and soybeans. Here the world is tented by the sky above. One truly sees the sun's daily and seasonal passings, the movement of the evening skies, and the annual migration of the geese, ducks, and pelicans.

Not much breaks the horizon here. There are river valleys that, in the spring, form great and small green veins on the great black soil. Occasional lakes, which are large and always shallow (rarely deeper than ten feet), dot the landscape. Marshes and sloughs still abound here. Once, before drainage turned so much of the low lands into land suited for agricultural production, the area teemed with animal life, especially wild fowl, which—with the tall prairie grass itself—defined the region.

As one moves west across Minnesota through Lyon, Lincoln, and Pipestone counties toward the South Dakota border, one encounters hills. This higher ground of glacial moraine, called the Buffalo Ridge, makes a drop from Florence (a small village in western Lincoln County) to Marshall (county seat of Lyon County) greater than the drop of the Mississippi River from St. Paul to New Orleans.

Breaking the horizon are farmsteads. Sometimes one, two, and even three farmsteads per square mile appear as if they were symmetrically placed. More often, they appear irregularly as if seeded by the wind. Each farmstead has a character of its own, with its different groves, hedges, houses, sheds, barns, and grain storage bins placed in different positions around the farm site.

Until the present farm crisis, the number of metal grain bins—especially the tall, new, blue ones—were an indisputable sign of wealth. They meant the farmer had a lot of grain and enough cash to wait out the market to get a good price. Also showing farm prosperity, some farmsteads featured brand new homes (sometimes a big one-floor ranch home rather than the more traditional two-story ones) and farm yards filled with equipment. Eighty-thousand-dollar tractors and hundred-thousand-dollar combines were common implements on richer farms. Today, prosperous farms stand in dramatic contrast to poor and abandoned farmsteads, which in richer counties and times were plowed under or left only partially standing to house farm helpers and their families or machinery.

Also interrupting the horizon are the solitary country churches. Most have a cemetery adjacent to the church building. Often the cemetery is surrounded by a row of pines. Most of these churches have high steeples, which declared to the world immediately around them, as well as to ancestors and friends in their distant homelands—mainly Norway, Sweden, Germany, or Holland—that the builders of these churches had made something of themselves. They had succeeded on this prairie—in America. Lutherans of different synods, Presbyterians, and Catholics (the latter built no churches out in the countryside) comprise the three main faiths of the region.

Every six or seven miles along a main road—which is a paved state or county highway—there is a small village of less than a thousand people. Sometimes these villages have less than a hundred inhabitants. Villages mark the horizon with their church steeples, grain elevators—which form rows of silver vertical blocks—and always a water tower. The elevators, water towers, and steeples uniquely stamp each horizon and thus provide each village with its own distinctive gyre.

Yet often the traveler sees only sameness here. The great openness and the immensity of the prairie can appear flat and boring. The imposing grid of straight roads, the predictable measure of 640 acres (one square mile) and its parts (320 acres—a half section, and 180 acres—a quarter), lead the traveler to see only repetition. When the corn is mature, nothing relieves that sense of sameness. The frequent fields of soybeans, the occasional feedlot, and the regular succession of villages alone spare the traveler the sense of being surrounded by an endless curtain of corn.

Yet the traveler misses how the countryside, patterned like a quilt, is of great diversity. Each grove holds a different family, a different homestead. Each is filled with old machinery and memories of old struggles that radiate the past. Each county has a different history. In one county, agrarian radicalism was fostered, and consequently it still tends to vote Democratic and to provide its share of protesters at farm rallies; whereas another has always put its mark on the conservative side of the ballot. Different counties—different townships for that matter—conceal different ethnic patterns of settling, holding, and transmitting land. Norwegians, for instance, leave the land or trade it for white collar and educational opportunities for their sons and daughters; whereas regional Germans (Catholic, Lutheran, or Presbyterian) and Catholic Belgians and Dutch rarely relinquish their hold on the land. Accordingly, their numbers grow in the countryside, while those of other groups diminish.

One of the most striking and paradoxical differences between the counties is that some are more rural than others. The more rural a county is here, the poorer it is. Some of the counties in southwestern Minnesota not only lack a city of 5,000 or more, but they are almost entirely comprised of smaller towns and villages and farms. Without exception, the history of these towns since 1950 has been one of population loss and decline. In these counties, schools have been closed or merged. Villages have lost their population, stores, and leaders. They no longer function as whole communities. Signs of poverty in the villages and the countryside abound—empty store fronts, uncared for and deteriorating houses, abandoned farmsteads surrounded by discarded machines and rusted cars that have not run for the last ten to fifty years. The relative need for social services has increased, while the tax base for such services has diminished.

Such a poor, rural county—in fact by almost every measure the poorest and most rural county in southwestern Minnesota—is Lincoln County, where the murders occurred and where James Jenkins spent a good portion of his life trying to make himself into a somebody. Lincoln County, with 531 square miles, has a population of 8,000. Norwegians, Germans, Poles, Danes, Dutch, English, and Irish form the mixed ethnic communities of Lincoln County. Having almost no industry, Lincoln County is mainly comprised of small dairy and grain farms and a handful of villages and towns. The largest town, Tyler—predominantly Danish—has a population of 1,400. The county seat, Ivanhoe—predominantly Polish—is the second smallest county seat in Minnesota with its population of 750.

There is not a single traffic light in Lincoln County. When Ivanhoe's only hardware store—a Coast to Coast—went out of business recently, the empty store was turned over to the production of a new crop for the region: mushrooms.

Poverty, which showed so clearly in the life of James Jenkins, is visible throughout Lincoln County. Poverty is not new to Lincoln County. Poverty in Lincoln County, while exacerbated, is not the result of the present farm crisis. Since the settlers came to this land dominated by Buffalo Ridge—whose height shortens the growing season and denies needed summer rainfall—Lincoln County has been one of the region's poorer counties. Since the 1950s, numbers have told a story of decline: dwindling population, more old people, and fewer young people.

Despite its natural beauty and abundant signs of its people's pride in themselves and in their communities, numbers themselves tell something of Lincoln County's poverty. Its median income of $12,668 is the lowest in Minnesota; whereas its neighbor county to the east, Lyon County, has a median income of $21,077. Lincoln County's poverty rate of 22 percent is the state's second highest. (A family of four is considered in poverty if its annual income is $10,650 or less.) Even though it has an unemployment rate of only 6.4 percent, county statistics assert that 70 percent of its workers are economically disadvantaged. A recent Harvard study of poverty in America ranked Lincoln County as the "hungriest county" in the state and as 47th in the nation.

The people of Lincoln County have their pride: only 13 percent of those eligible for food stamps have enrolled in the program. There is a shared sense that people want to make it on their own, out on the land. They take pride in their communities, schools, churches, and villages. This pride can manifest itself in a strong spirit of independence, as it did in James Jenkins, or it can express itself in cooperation and community. In Lincoln County, there is a strong history of cooperation and of collective farm protest.

But pride will not disguise the fact that in Lincoln County things for most people have been going from bad to worse. Too many people have been failing on the land and in the villages for parents to do anything other than counsel their children to leave. "There is no future here for you."

In a recent article in the *Minneapolis Tribune*, by Paul Levy, Minnesota Commissioner of Agriculture Jim Nichols spoke nostalgically of broken dreams: "There was an old saying when I was growing up in Verdi [a Lincoln County village of 55]: 'It may not be God's country, but you can see it from there.' All that has changed. . . . Nowhere is the depression more evident than Lincoln County, Minnesota. The dreams are gone."

In the same article, Arco grocery store owner Erling Pedersen spoke of the town he had known since he was a boy: "Now everybody's gone. We used to have 250, maybe 300 people here. Now there is less than 100. The railroad used to go through here. Years ago we had a creamery, two stores, a pool hall, a barber shop, meat market, two cafes, three or four places that sold gas, an implement dealer, our own telephone office and power plant, a school. *We used to have young people here!*"

Just outside of Lincoln County, south on County Road 7, four miles from where the murders occurred, is Ruthton. Ruthton, located at the northernmost edge of Pipestone County (named for the rock quarried there for the Indians' famous peace pipes), is another small southwestern Minnesota village experiencing decline. Like all the region's villages, Ruthton is a railroad town. Its origin was in its service to the surrounding farms.

Old timers recall Ruthton as a prosperous village of 500 along a main east-west railroad line. Ken Toft, recorder of deeds at the Lincoln County Courthouse, remembers better days when, back in the 1940s, Ruthton had a lumberyard, all three kinds of farm implement dealers—John Deere, International, and Allis Chalmers—a GM car dealer, three grocery stores, three hardware stores, one doctor, one dentist, a creamery and two other places which bought cream, three filling stations, a home appliance store, a newspaper, a drug store, a restaurant, a bank, a butcher, a Lutheran church, a Methodist church, a movie theatre, a couple bars, and yet a few other stores.

Now Ruthton is a village of only a few hundred people and a couple of blocks of stores, several of which are empty. At one end of main street, along the abandoned railroad tracks, one sees a deserted cooperative creamery. Once the pride of Ruthton and the proof of its cooperative values, the creamery has long been deserted and is now surrounded by randomly growing vegetation and discarded machines.

Along main street itself, there is on one side a grocery store, an abandoned store, a closed laundromat, an old time bar–pool hall (which off and on has a serious problem with mice), an American Legion Hall, the Woodstock telephone office, and the Buffalo Ridge State Bank.

It was this small but newer brick building that Rudolph Blythe purchased in the middle 1970s and on which he cast his and his family's fortune. As the town's banker, he hoped to realize his dream of helping to transform an underdeveloped region.

On the other side of the street, there is a small and still-functioning bowling alley, Lindy's Lanes; a newspaper, *The Buffalo Ridge Gazette*; a senior citizens' center; a store that doubles as a library and an upholstery shop; and Alene's Restaurant. In his last year on the Ruthton farm—his marriage coming undone—James Jenkins spent a considerable amount of time eating alone at Alene's. He often ate all three meals there. His habit of ordering steak for breakfast led Alene to remark that "James was a man with a worker's salary and a champagne appetite."

With some pride the people of Ruthton still can claim having their own independent elementary school and high school (which, however, were to be paired in 1987 with the school districts of nearby Tyler and Russell); two churches, Peace Lutheran Church and the United Methodist Church; and the repainted old Mason's hall. Also, the town has a central park, which has the characteristic cannon and military honor plaque with the names of many war dead.

Along main street, between Alene's and the newspaper office, there is a small lot with a plaque commemorating Ruthton as the 1975 state class B football champion and as a 1981 participant in the state basketball tournament. In 1985 and 1986, Ruthton's nine-man football team made it to the first round of the state tournament. Athletic teams—on which neither James nor Steven Jenkins played—are exceptionally important throughout southwestern Minnesota. Here, probably like everywhere else in rural America, athletic teams as much as anything focus the community's pride. Their successes are offered to prove that their towns are still winners—still able to compete in a world that they sense is passing them by.

While Ruthton had experienced violence before, nothing comparable to the Jenkins case had ever happened there. For many, it was a blight on the town's reputation. Why should Ruthton, they asked, be identified as the place of the murders? They pointed out that the murders occurred on a farm four miles away, that James Jenkins was not born here, and that he and his family did not live in town nor attend Ruthton's schools.

But the murdered bankers did come from Ruthton, and the killings drew national attention. All sorts of reporters made their way into Alene's for the daily special and then over to the *Buffalo Ridge Gazette* for background information. Like it or not, because Ruthton was the closest place on the map, it became nationally known as the site of the murders.

Word of the murders swept through southwestern Minnesota like a blizzard. Within an hour of the crime, local radio stations carried news of the killings, and James and Steven were named as suspects. Within five hours of the murders, the people of the region heard that a deputy had been fired at. Later that day, they heard James's mother appeal to her son to turn himself in.

Doors were locked that had not been locked for years. Relatives and friends called loved ones, warning them not to drive home or, if they were going to, not to stop along the way. Helicopters and planes flew overhead until the fog made it impossible for the police to continue their search. Everyone wondered when and where the father and son would reappear.

Some people had special reasons to be afraid. The Buffalo Ridge bank closed. Susan Blythe went into hiding. Darlene Jenkins's friend Louis Taveirne had reason for concern as did other bankers and loan agents who had had unfavorable dealings with James Jenkins.

Anyone, especially if alone on a farm, could conjure up the presence of the Jenkinses. People could easily imagine a white pickup coming up their gravel roads. With just a little imagination, they could see two dark figures prowling in their groves, out behind their sheds. The local sheriff, Abe Thompson, was inundated with hundreds of calls from around the state, claiming possible sightings of James's white pickup. In the region itself, the sheriff made several stake-outs.

Revealing the power the crime exercised over the people of the region, people still ask, "Where were you when you first heard of the killings?" Even as fear subsided—as it did steadily each day after the crime—interest remained exceptionally high. With each new piece of information, questions and conjectures multiplied. For the people of southwestern Minnesota, this was the crime of the century.

News of the crime filled the connective tissues of the region—the towns, schools, courthouses, churches, cafes, pool halls, and bars. Wherever people talked here, the crime became the topic of the day.

Almost everything that happens here is taken personally. The great majority of people, especially those on farms and in smaller villages, are familiar with and assume themselves to be connected to everything else—if not by relationship, then by history, knowledge, and proximity. A common attitude prevails: this is our home; what happens here pertains to us.

Some knew the farmstead where the murders occurred. Others had relatives or friends just down the road from it. Still others knew the Jenkinses' families, who had been in the region for a couple of generations. In one way or another, the majority of people in the region knew of and personalized the crime.

James and Steven Jenkins were fairly well known. They had spent their entire lives here. They had lived in the small communities of Lynd, Arco, Tyler, and Ruthton, as well as in Marshall for a short while. Most recently, the father and the son had lived on a farmstead near Hardwick after their return from Texas. James's parents had lived for more than thirty years within a mile of Florence, which is located on the extreme western edge of Lyon County, adjacent to Lincoln County, and which is one of the highest points along the Buffalo Ridge. Florence has a population of 55.

THE FARM CRISIS CONNECTION

ESPECIALLY AMONG TROUBLED FARMERS of the region, the Jenkinses were endowed with a kind of nobility for killing the bankers. The idea of a father and son avenging the loss of their family farm had an irresible moral attraction. Over generations, a family invests itself in a farm: every pile of rocks, each building, and every discarded object in the grove tells the story of a family's investment of its life in the farm. No farm, the embodied work and love of a family, should be lost to any bank.

In some of the very first articles, the suggestion was made that the Jenkinses may have had reasons for their actions. Ruthton mayor LeRoy Burch was quoted in the *Marshall Independent* (October 1, 1983): "James is a hard worker who loved to milk cows, but didn't have the money to buy cattle. Every time he tried to get a loan, the references in town referred him to the bank, and they shut the door on him."

A neighbor who lived across the road from the scene of the crime was reported to say in the *Worthington Daily Globe*, "Rudy was a nice guy, but he was putting a lot of pressure on farmers." In the same article Glenn Lindahl, owner of the Ruthton bowling alley (which is directly across from the Blythe bank), while commenting on Rudolph Blythe's large civic contributions, ventured to say: "He lent money to people he should not have lent money to." Many remarked that Blythe was awfully tough on his borrowers.

There were abiding myths that seemed to take James Jenkins's side against Rudolph Blythe's. James Jenkins was a farmer. He wanted to make his living from the land. He wanted to milk cows, to have a place in the countryside—to fulfill what might be considered the minimal good of living off of the earth by the sweat of one's brow. James's dream was the American myth of the independent farmer.

If a myth such as this lent James nobility, negative myths

about bankers villanized Rudolph Blythe. According to such myths, money buys and sells human suffering. Bankers are the priests of money. They benefit from the exchange of human fortunes. Bankers live off of the lives of others. They are indifferent to the land and to its people; their profits hurt, destroy, and even kill.

Dressed in myths like these, Rudolph Blythe was denied all moral stature. In killing him, James Jenkins—it could be said—acted in self-defense; he did nothing unjust.

So the killings brought into play the moral myths of the farmer and the banker. The combination of the positive myth of the farmer and the negative myth of the banker made certain that James Jenkins would receive a sympathetic hearing in many quarters. In addition, specific conditions at the time made the moral story of the good farmer striking back at the bad banker seem appropriate.

At the time of the crime, things were not good on the farm. High interest rates, low prices for grain, and steeply declining land values resulted in a growing number of farm foreclosures. Talk about real and suspected foreclosures was heard everywhere. Auction signs for farms were plastered on restaurant bulletin boards throughout the region. Everyone knew a farmer in trouble; everyone who paid any attention to such matters suspected others were on the verge of bankruptcy. Almost every town had a farm implement dealer or two who had failed—"gone belly up" to use the popular local expression. Up and down main street there was a growing consensus, although often made only grudgingly, that times were getting mean.

It was commonly said that the old timers' warning had been right: when everyone had said "grow, grow, grow," the old timers had warned, "The depression will come again; there is always need for a fire to clean things out." The price of land had tripled and even quadrupled during the 1970s, raising the price of the best land from $500 to $1,500 and $2,000 an acre and even a little higher here and there in the region. The same land now had declined in value by 40 percent and more, leaving farmers without equity to borrow the money they needed to cover operations. Dependent on grain prices, they were operating at a loss or without any significant profit. So everywhere in the region there was talk of hard times; in fact, a year after the crime, state officials predicted the loss of 10,000 farms—30 percent of Minnesota farms—in the next few years. Talk was still not specific about which types of farmers were in trouble. It remained general, dramatic, and moral as the farm crisis began to take form in 1983.

At farm rallies throughout the Midwest, in article after article, in sermons and pastoral letters, the word was put out: the family farm is in trouble.

With increased frequency, there was a call for a moratorium on farm loans. In Minnesota, as well as in Iowa and the Dakotas, farmers stopped farm sales by moral persuasion, by fixed bids of a penny or a nickel, and by force. Eventually open protest and violence convinced the federal government that it was time to put a moratorium on loans.

Given the dimensions of the farm crisis and the accompanying belief that something should be done, it was natural that some viewed the murders as a result of the crisis. The additional assumption was made that James Jenkins was one of the first victims of the crisis to hit back. He was understood to be acting prophetically.

Two stories in particular predisposed people to think of James's crime as an act of farm protest. In 1983, a statewide protest group, Citizens Organizations Acting Together (COACT), had begun actively protesting farm foreclosures throughout Lincoln County. Lincoln County Sheriff Abe Thompson was mistakenly quoted as saying that James was among the protesting farmers at one such protest.

Also in the minds of many in 1983 was Gordon Kahl of the Posse Comitatus. This radical, armed, political sect, with little enclaves scattered throughout the rural upper Midwest, preached resistance to federal taxes and authority. In the process of resisting arrest in North Dakota, Gordon Kahl and his son Yorivon killed two federal marshals and wounded a third. Yorivon was captured and Gordon Kahl fled, thereby becoming the object of a nationwide search that lasted for three months. In June 1983, he was killed in a shoot-out in Arkansas that cost the life of another federal marshal.

In the eyes of many who were sympathetic to farmers and their right to resist, James and Steven Jenkins were transformed into agrarian rebels. The people with the most active imaginations deciphered a new rebellion taking form in the countryside. As in the 1930s—with the struggle against farm foreclosure—and the 1960s—marked by the dumpings associated with the National Farmers Organization (particularly active in Lincoln County)—the farmers were seen as again rising up. James and Steven Jenkins were seen as the beginning of a new rural rebellion.

Several regional farm advocates were quick to exploit the murders by issuing warnings to any and all who planned to repossess farms. One such advocate was Jim Langman, who was the local president of the American Agriculture Movement, which had filled Washington with tractors a few years before. It was Langman's farm that the recently founded Groundswell movement (with the help of Jesse Jackson) had chosen to defend against foreclosure in the spring of 1985. Jim Langman offered this interpretation of the killings: "A farmer is a human being, and a human being is an animal; if you beat at him, poke at him, and take everything away from him, he's going to turn and bite back." Langman continued: "I think the slayings were symbolic and should send a message to the nation that lenders have to work things out on a long-term basis." He did concede it was "unfortunate that the bankers were caught in the middle."

An important local COACT leader, Eric DeRycke—who was also a lawyer who once helped James Jenkins with his debts and later appeared for Steven Jenkins's defense—was quoted by the *Worthington Daily Globe* as saying that the murders were "spite for the foreclosure." He went on to caution: "The job of the lender is going to become extremely dangerous because of the foreclosures we're seeing."

This kind of interpretation quickly found its way into local and national presses. The crime was promptly interpreted to be at the eye of the farm crisis. Because of the crime, southwestern Minnesota had found its way into the pages of the *New York Times*. (The last time southwestern Minnesota had "earned" such national attention was forty years before when 10,000 farmers, led by the Farm Holiday movement, shut down the Swift plant and the whole city of Marshall, Minnesota, by disarming the city's police in 1934.) "The killings," declared the *Times*'s article, "appear to be by far the most violent outburst yet in connection with the threatened or actual eviction of many of the nation's farmers. Foreclosures and tight farm finances are each extremely emotional issues across the Middle West, whose agricultural sector is still reeling from the effects of the recession. . . ."

The day after the murders, Andrew Malcolm, *New York Times* Chicago Bureau Chief, set out for Ruthton. He had just completed a lengthy set of articles for the *Times*; and that very morning he and his boss, David Jones, national news editor, had agreed that Malcolm would return to the subject of "the major social, economic, and structural changes under way all across the nation's *heartland* [emphasis added], especially the mounting financial difficulties being encountered by farm families and businesses. . . ."

Right from the start, Malcolm chose to find in that "fatal farmyard confrontation, the manhunt, and the resulting trial," the story of "the deep changes happening slowly in so many communities important to the *country's soul* [emphasis added]." It was that story which he unswervingly followed from his first filings on the murders, throughout the trial, until the recent publication of his book, *Final Harvest.*

The story he chose to tell—with the close collaboration of Susan Blythe, the banker's widow—was that the murders were ultimately the result of a violent collision between a hard-working farmer, who wanted to be back on the land, and a well-intentioned young banker from the East, whose bank had fallen on hard times. In the preface to his work, Malcolm affirmed his position that the murders were a microcosm of the farm crisis—tied to, in his words, "the underlying changes haunting the heartland."

While many from the press and from the farm protest movement tried to tie the murders to the growing farm crisis, forceful and contradictory evidence rapidly accumulated, suggesting that the murders didn't belong to the story of the farm crisis at all.

The most stunning and immediate evidence was the singular truth that no father, farmer or not, would take his son to kill—exposing his son to either death or to life in prison—unless something was very wrong with him and with his relationship to his son. How was anyone to believe that a farmer, who cared about his animals and wanted a farm and home, would take his son with him to kill—or would allow or order his son to murder two men? Whichever of the two shot, this story was undeniably a story about the irrational doings of an unusual father and son. It was not an economic and cultural story about a farming crisis in the Midwest. This was a family story.

The military appearance of the son at the time of his surrender made the irrational character of the crime clear. Whoever Steven was, he was more than a farm boy who hunted now and then.

There was additional evidence suggesting that the psychological story eclipsed any social or economic story. James and Steven Jenkins did not belong to any political organization. They were not tied to either the Posse Comitatus or the local COACT group.

Several things about the Jenkinses' farm itself undercut those who wanted this to be an archtypical farm story. First, the farm was not the Jenkinses' family farm. The Jenkinses had only lived on it for a few years. It had not been in the family for generations. It did not embody a family's work, hopes, and history. Additionally, when the Jenkinses left the farm three years before the crime, the farm was not in the process of being repossessed nor had it been repossessed. The Jenkins family was not pushed off the land. They left the farm by their own will. With the marriage in its final stages of disintegration, the family had actually abandoned the farm. Up to the time of their departure, they had successfully made payments on the farm, which they had deeded to the bank to obtain sufficient operating capital.

In fact, James had quit farming when agriculture in Minnesota and the Midwest flourished. With good prices and the rapidly inflating price of land, "almost any damn fool could have made it in agriculture," a local lender commented. Only the most speculative, the least fortunate, or the least competent did not.

If anything, the murders of Blythe and Thulin were a violent act of commemoration. James and Steven Jenkins used the murders to punish others and themselves for the family they had lost.

By comparison with the size and scale of successful farms in the region, the Jenkinses' ten-acre, sixty-cow dairy farm had never been a viable operation. (A ten-acre dairy farm is not, and never has been, the size or type of farm that constitutes a viable family farm in the Midwest.) From the beginning, the Jenkinses' farm had been a marginal farm; it had been numbered among those farms that were highly likely to fail. In the long term, without the best of luck and with both James and his wife working—his wife, Darlene, worked full time—their farm had no future.

The fact that James had undergone a series of repossessions prior to the leaving the farm further weakened his claim of being an injured, innocent farmer. Bad business decisions, debts, and economic failure marked James's whole adult life. His wife, his daughter, his father—almost anyone who knew him well—testified in one way or another that James was "a man who screwed up about everything he tried." He was, by most accounts, a "dead beat," "a loser," "someone you lent to at a risk." "He could always turn gold into shit," one person remarked.

On October 1, 1983, a *Worthington Daily Globe* reporter indicated that, in the primary region the bank served, "only the Jenkinses' and another farm were recently foreclosed. The bank hasn't obtained any farm land in the last ten years in this region, according to land transfer records in Pipestone and Lincoln counties." Even though troubled banker Rudolph Blythe had been pushing his debtors harder than ever before as his small bank was caught in the squeeze of high interest rates and declining farm values, there was no proof Blythe had been involved in widespread foreclosures.

Only a week after the crime, leaders of Minnesota banking organizations were already expressing their confidence that James Jenkins was neither Robin Hood nor the vanguard of a new farm movement. They denied that the killings symbolized the tension and the plight of American farmers. As early as October 6, Norbert McCrady, executive vice president of the Minnesota Independent Bankers Association, told the press, "This is an isolated incident. I think 99 percent of the farmers upset over what's going on out there with foreclosure," Mc-Crady continued, "wouldn't even let the thought of murder run through their minds."

On October 7, 1983, the *St. Paul Pioneer Press* attacked the front-page article in the *New York Times* that linked the killings to economic conditions in the American Midwest. The *Times*, according to the *Pioneer Press* editorial, had read far too much into "a single tragic, but isolated, incident." "The Jenkinses' farm operation," the editorial continued, "was small, part time, and virtually foredoomed James Jenkins to failure as he tried to run a full-size dairy farm on only nine or ten acres. If revenge was his motive, his was a personal vendetta, and had nothing to do with the economic woes of midwestern agriculture. To suggest the killings were an outburst in connection with the threatened or actual eviction of many of the nation's farmers," the editorial went on, "is to suggest that farmers include ambush and murder among the weapons with which they seek to stem the tide of such evictions and foreclosures. That is nonsense and gravely insulting."

The character of the crime itself impugned much of the story's romanticized status. The Jenkinses had killed, but were not killed. They had not shot in self-defense nor in a shoot-out. They had killed one more man than they had intended. They had killed both men while their victims were fleeing. Rudolph Blythe, the man they wanted to kill, had been chased down and shot in the back. Furthermore, they had murdered without announcing their intention. They had killed without explaining themselves or their actions to the world. They killed without an apparent plan of escape. Their flight had not ended with "a shoot-out" nor with a statement about the injustice they suffered or the vengeance they wrought. Instead, they wrote the conclusions to their crime with the apparent suicide of the father and the tearful surrender of a boy dressed like a soldier.

If James and Steven Jenkins were to be idealized as victims and rebels—the personification of the agonizing condition in the "heartland"—reality had to be seriously distorted. A convoluted story had to be told.

Their crime reeked with irrationalism. The character of the crime indicated that what James and Steven Jenkins had done was anything but reasonable or because of the farm crisis. As local people who knew them stated from the start, this was a strange father and son.

Of course, their irrationality need not be considered absolutely unique and separate unto itself. No one's craziness is altogether free of culture, class, circumstances, and time. James and

Steven were members of a broken family. They belonged to a class and an area of the rural poor. The father sustained himself on common dreams of the independent American farm, and his son fed himself on the cultural fantasies found in survivalist magazines. When we seek to tell their story, we discover it does not turn on their representing the American heartland. Instead, their story is a tragic family story of a father and son who conspired and killed together.

CHAPTER TWO

The Father

Let no man think lightly of evil, saying in his
heart, it will not come nigh unto me. Even by
the falling of waterdrops a water-pot is filled;
the fool becomes full of evil, even if he gather
it little by little.

Dhammapada

GROWING UP POOR IN THE COUNTRY

CLASS, marriage, and character are among the things
that determine an individual's fate. James Jenkins had
no choice about the world into which he was born.
He belonged to the class of the rural poor, that class in
the countryside which is always in an economic crisis. For them
there are never really good times. They never quite have
enough. They are never secure about their place on the land.
Life for them is a constant struggle. Not acknowledging the
unforgiving laws of the changing countryside, or unwilling to
give up their place, the members of this class hang on to that
existence. They remain when circumstances insist they leave.

To belong to this class, as James did, means sharing a fate
with poor rural people in the Midwest, as well as in the South
and West and even the East. The land is where their memories
and hearts are. The places they call home are in decline. Most
often the rural poor farm marginal lands—lands with too much
sand and clay, lands shaped by hills and gullies, lands more fit
for grazing or wildlife than for cash crops, lands where railroad
companies long ago abandoned the tracks. If they are able to
continue farming at all—instead of having to drive a truck,
work at an elevator, repair machines, or something else—they
farm to survive. They work smaller pieces of land; they work

with machines discarded by their neighbors ten and twenty years before; and both husband and wife often need second and third jobs. They live amidst broken and rusted things.

To be members of this class is to be without enough money—and thus to suffer more than their share of hurt, pain, and insult. There is insult especially for those who proudly seek to keep themselves off of the public welfare rolls.

To be among the rural poor often entails doing without those things others would have for themselves: forgetting about the dentist when one's tooth aches, ignoring the trips and vacations one's neighbors take, and never getting a new car. Unlike their richer country neighbors—the farm families who benefited from electrification and improved crop prices in the 1940s—the countryside's subsistence farmers do not live well.

Their sheds and buildings are run down, decayed, and even collapsed; they stand on vacant, wind-blown lots or amidst untended groves of dying and dead trees. The dwellings they live in vary, but in greatest number they are trailer homes or older houses that almost always need paint and lack insulation. They lack the wall-to-wall carpeting, modern kitchens, finished basements, and recreation rooms of their well-to-do neighbors. In some cases, their houses are still without indoor plumbing, central heating, and electricity.

The country poor are never quite at home where they live. Their poverty threatens the independence they cherish. Every day they are at war with broken things, unexpected bills, and emotions that aren't easy to manage. Always beckoning for their surrender are welfare, alcoholism, and despair. Though they work as hard as they can, the rural poor still find themselves living on the margins of the land—neighbors to those who have made it.

Trying to make it in the countryside drives some crazy. While some finally achieve that high state of wisdom or imperturbable fatalism which allows them to say, "Another day of rain, another day of rest," others go crazy from working, loneliness, insult, failure, and anger. Their will is thwarted again and again. They grow progressively angrier. This madness is not altogether theirs alone—it belongs to generations of their class who have tried to make it on the land. This craziness is a sad, proud, tragic thing.

James was born into the country's poor. James's parents never had much. Only in 1948 did Nina and Clayton Jenkins—who had previously rented and share-cropped land in the region and had originally come from the Worthington area—purchase their own eighty acres of land. Located less than a mile south of Florence, the land cost them $8,500. In 1952, for the price of $3,200, they added eighty more acres of farm land—half of which was slough and which in 1965 they sold to the Department of Natural Resources as a wetland for $4,400. While still retaining the right to live on the family farmstead, in 1985—the year of their golden anniversary—they sold their farm for $52,200 on a contract for deed; the final payment for it was is to be made in 1995.

What Nina and Clayton had, they worked hard for. The land they farmed was not good land; it was hilly and sandy compared to land farther to the east in Lyon County. Their land was at nearly the highest point in southwestern Minnesota. They farmed the land as best they could—without the use of the newest machinery and always foregoing fertilizer and pesticides that larger and richer farmers used. Like other smaller farmers, they relied on more than their crops to survive on the land. Clayton and Nina tended their garden and had their ten or twelve cows and a few pigs and chickens. For a number of years Nina Jenkins—who, in the words of one neighbor, "was good at meeting people"—worked at the Coast to Coast store in Tyler.

Clayton and Nina Jenkins were both known and liked where they lived. They did their share of visiting back and forth. Clayton liked to socialize and enjoyed playing cards. Pinochle games in nearby Tyler were a regular pastime for him, according to one of his old-time neighbors. Clayton and Nina pitched in to help neighbors too. "They were good neighbors, . . . the nicest guys around," according to Gordon Stafne, a long-time acquaintance from the 1940s and 1950s.

Nina and Clayton were always proud that they were independent. They never accepted public assistance.

They were not belongers. Several remarked that the Jenkinses just weren't church-goers. One neighbor, Carl Johnson, remarked, "They used to have an affliation with the Methodist church, but Clayton said all they [the church] ever wanted was money." Clayton and Nina may have attended an occasional Farm Bureau meeting, but, when asked if they were joiners, Johnson remarked that the Jenkinses were not intersted in farm organizations or politics. "When the cup was passed in the neighborhood, they were not big contributors."

James, their only child, was, according to Johnson, "the most important thing in their lives." James was brought up working hard. Pulling rocks, threshing, baling, milking—he did the chores a farm boy does.

James's life centered around the farm, not school or town. One neighbor recalled that James did not have friends or date. He kept to himself. To the best of several teachers' memories, James was not involved in anything—not choir, sports, nor theater. In the school yearbooks for the two years he attended Tyler High School, James appears only once: in a picture, at one side of the back row, of the Future Farmers of America Club.

James was interested in machines. He worked well with them. Remarks like "he could fix machinery like no one in the area," "he was real handy," "he could about fix any piece of machinery there was," and "best welder around" were commonly made about James. He was a skilled wood-worker, remarked a relative who recalled a set of end tables and some bowling pin lamps James had made.

One old-time neighbor remarked that "James wasn't interested in farming. He was more interested in pulling apart cars and selling them. He even had a junk lot up on the hill at the entrance to their farm." James's first business venture involved selling used machines and parts from his father's farm.

James alternated between owning farms and working with machines. Not counting a four-year, stateside stint in the National Guard in the late 1950s, James went back and forth between these two vocations with almost predictable regularity from the time he quit school until he made his final effort to start a farm in 1983.

James also went back and forth between employment for others and self-employment with nearly equal regularity. Having failed in one major effort to own and operate his own heavy road and agricultural machines, James found himself in a painful dilemma: if he was to make his living working with machines—for which he had considerable talent—he would have to work for someone else. He could only be his own boss on his own farm; but never once, over any period of time, did he succeed in farming.

MARRIAGE AND FAILURE

MARRIAGE DID NOT FREE James from the class of the rural poor and its marginal farmers. Indeed, his marriage to Darlene Abraham confirmed his place in the countryside.

Darlene, born in 1940 (three years after James), was brought up on a farm just outside of Arco, Minnesota—another declining village with a population of approximately 100 people. (Since the Second World War all the young people, according to local grocer Erling Pedersen, had fled Arco; Pedersen himself seems to regret his return to the village after the war.)

Unlike James, Darlene finished high school. While not a school leader, she attended school events. In the Ivanhoe senior high yearbook, *The Aquila*, for the years 1955 to 1959, it is noted below Darlene's picture that she participated in the girl's choir and the mixed choir; and during her senior year she worked on the school paper and the yearbook.

She was known by former classmates as a quiet person who, while occasionally going to school events, did not date much. One girlfriend—who knew her for many years before and during high school—remarked, "Darlene was a loner. She didn't date . . . didn't go to dances or games." This same friend said Darlene rarely expressed her emotions and that she had never seen Darlene in any pronounced emotional state.

One of her high school classmates noted that Darlene was clean and neat—"not all the kids were then," he added. She dressed uniquely at the time by wearing jeans and corduroy shirts. "She," he noted, "had her head screwed on right." Another commented, "While most of the girls only wore jeans on Friday, Darlene wore them every day."

Darlene came from the same social class that James did. Her family worked 160 acres of land just south of Arco in the neighborhood of Dead Coon Lake. Their land, which had been in their family for a long time, was not particularly good land. It was swampy in many parts. It had been in the family since 1880, when Gottlieb Abraham, born in Germany in 1833, homesteaded 160 acres. The land passed from Great-grandfather Gottlieb, who died in 1904, to Grandfather Henry Abraham.

In 1934, the Great Depression temporarily cost the Abrahams their farm. Henry was unable to make payments on his 1926 mortgage ($9,382 to be paid at 6 percent annually). The Abrahams lost their place on the land—all 200 acres of the family's land were sold in 1934 at a sheriff's sale to the Metropolitan Insurance Company. However, in November of that year, Henry repurchased the land from the Metropolitan Insurance Company.

Henry died in 1960, leaving his land to his wife, Martha. She died in 1971; and upon her death, Reuben, the third of her four children, received approximately an additional 100 acres.

After several years of trucking in North Dakota and Nebraska and working at Hardwick, Minnesota, Reuben returned in 1953 to work the family farm, according to one neighbor. Reuben and his wife were hard workers who kept to themselves, according to another neighbor. While they were said to be hospitable, they were not outgoing. In the words of one old neighbor, "They were enjoyable people, but they weren't minglers." The mother, who was a school cook at Hardwick, was an excellent cook, making it a pleasure to be invited to their place.

Like the Jenkinses, Reuben and his wife played no significant role in farm or community organizations. They were not church-goers. They tried the church in Arco a few times, according to this neighbor. They occupied themselves with making a living and raising their four children: Eugene, Lavonne, Darlene, and Lugene.

The Abrahams were independent people. While they used credit, they did not receive welfare checks. One neighbor remarked, "They worked hard, but never progressed. Others passed them by." According to this neighbor, they continued to live the old way. "They used an old rubbish burner for heat." According to another neighbor, "They didn't have an indoor toilet as long as they stayed on the farm."

According to county records, in 1978 Reuben sold the 115 acres that remained to him (having previously sold the other portion to a neighbor). He received $64,000, or approximately $550 an acre. (This sale, which later fell through, occurred at a time when prices were the highest they had ever been. Good land in the vicinity of nearby Marshall reached $2,000 an acre.) After the sale, Reuben and his wife Laura lived in a modest home in nearby Lake Benton.

Darlene and James had one thing in common: their origin in the same class of marginal and subsistence farmers. Even if they were not attracted to each other when they first met, when James first brought over his combine to harvest her father's fields in 1960, Darlene and James did have things in common. Having lived on subsistence farms, they both knew what not having enough was. They knew the necessity of hard work. They knew what a struggle it was to be independent. They had to be proud of how generations of their families had struggled to stay on the land and off government rolls. They may well have shared the resentments that the poor often harbor against the rich, on the one side, and against people on welfare, on the other.

James and Darlene had other things in common. Neither was considered to be exceptionally social in school, nor did teachers and classmates judge them to be outstanding students. Neither, apparently, wanted any more schooling, nor did they have compelling ambitions "to see the world." Both knew only this region, and they chose to stay in it—even though James went away for a short stint in the National Guard and Darlene worked for a summer one hundred miles away in Mankato, Minnesota. What probably shaped their marriage most decisively was the fact that they shared the dream of their class: one day, through their hard work, they would own something and be somebody.

James already owned some machines. He had some ambition and ideas. Darlene had never been afraid of hard work. She could handle machines, all sorts of them. Together they hoped they would accomplish what their parents had—and a little more.

James and Darlene were married on April 1, 1961. James was twenty-four; Darlene, twenty-one. They were married in a small, home ceremony in Florence, Minnesota, by Lutheran minister Reverend Allen Erickson.

After twenty years of marriage, James and Darlene called it quits. They had not realized their dream. Aside from having two children and never accepting a welfare check, they had fought a long and losing battle to secure a place on the land and in the community.

In addition to being a mother and farm wife, Darlene had worked to keep the family afloat. She not only helped run the farm and drive the farm machinery, but she also did whatever was necessary to try to make her rural family survive. She worked at a variety of jobs. Eventually, with the children in school, she began to work full time, adding as much as $12,000 a year to the family's income. Her first full-time job was with an electronics firm in Canton, South Dakota. Then she worked at Bayliner Boats in Pipestone. She also worked for Louis Taverine at his landfill in the Pipestone vicinity; she did cleaning for Erik DeRycke's law office; and she worked full time at Schott Electronics in Marshall. Between these jobs, Darlene worked on a number of the two- and three-day farm jobs which come and go with every farm season.

James had worked hard too. No one ever faulted him for not working hard, but many questioned whether he worked sensibly and toward a good end. He never provided the family with economic security and stability. James never stayed at a job for very long; even when he was on a job, he would eventually assert his independence by quitting or getting fired for refusing to follow instructions.

James almost always had a scheme in his head. In one instance, his employer on an earth-moving job found that in a ten-hour-a-day job, James was only working a few hours. He helped himself to his employer's gas and spent the majority of his time "ramming around" the countryside on his own projects. James believed himself to be a man of importance.

In another instance, the same employer offered James the chance to remove and replace fence posts along a road he contracted to improve near Madison, South Dakota. He offered James $12,000—the amount of the subcontractor's bid. James snapped up the job, which provided needed cash and had the additional advantage that only a few of the farmers along the road really wanted the posts replaced. For weeks, Darlene and her two teenage children did the work, augering and pulling out the posts and, in one case, resetting the posts which stretched along one side of a feedlot. James never appeared at the scene of work.

After selling used machines and parts from the hill in front of his father's farm, James's next effort to find a career followed one path that is common to small farmers who seek to supplement their income or to find an alternative to farming. He established himself as an owner and operator of farm and road machines, which allowed him to rent out equipment or to contract to do any number of farming or construction jobs. In 1959 he purchased two small lots in Florence; in 1964 he added a third and a small part of another. On the first lots he built a Quonset hut in which he had among his inventory of second-hand machinery, at one time or another, a baler, a combine, a chopper, a blade, and a bulldozer. Also, as bizarre as it seems, James put inside the Quonset hut a very small house in which he and Darlene lived. (It was less than twelve feet high, permitting it to be moved in through the door of the Quonset hut.)

In 1967—with a three-year-old daughter and two-year-old son—James was unable to meet the payments, which included a significant amount owed to the Caterpillar Company and $3,000 on his 1964 mortgage owed to the Farmers and Merchants State Bank of Ruthton. Clayton gave James the money to avoid prosecution by the Caterpillar Company. Clyde Pedersen, the owner and president of the bank—which was the bank Rudolph Blythe was to purchase ten years later— foreclosed on him. James moved the very small house out of the repossessed Quonset hut and set it on another lot in Florence.

In February 1974, after working at a variety of short-term jobs in southwestern Minnesota and South Dakota—which included welding for the Burlington Northern Railroad—James and Darlene returned home and purchased a 148-acre farm for $38,000. In April of that year, they took two additional mortgages on their new place: a first mortgage for $5,000 and a second one for $31,000. While the value of the place itself more than doubled during this period—which was almost universally prosperous for farmers—good economic times did not smile on James and Darlene. James sold their place on October 31, 1977, for $104,000; however, from 1973 to 1977, five judgments of debt totaling nearly $5,000 had been filed against James.

Darlene resigned herself to having a full-time job to supplement the family income.

These were hard times, and James and Darlene were surrounded by creditors. One creditor recalled that ten years earlier he had rented 150 acres of land west of Arco to the Jenkinses. James consistently failed to pay the rent, always giving an excuse for why he had not paid and promising he would pay soon. Many times, according the creditor, he sought James out at home. All James's vehicles would be in the yard, but no one would answer the door. He believed the Jenkinses were hiding inside. When fall arrived and the creditor saw James—who had only made one small rent payment in the late spring—energetically harvesting corn and beans from the rented land, the creditor grew nervous about his money. Again James made excuses. With the aid of the sheriff, the creditor put a lien on James's crops at all the local elevators. One day shortly thereafter, the creditor saw James and Darlene on the road. With his wife in the car, the creditor pursued the Jenkinses "at speeds up to ninety miles an hour," catching up with them just as James and Darlene reached their place. The creditor stopped Darlene on the front lawn. She swore at him for stopping her and for pushing so hard for his money. The creditor replied that he had no choice since James always "lied to him." James returned and struck the creditor on the shoulder. They took each other by the shirts and began to tussle until the creditor pinned James. Meanwhile the wives exchanged insults. A week later James paid the creditor, who always remained leery of James, fearing James would do him no good.

In 1977, James and Darlene purchased the ten-acre farm on which the murder occurred. They purchased it for $21,500, having put down $3,000. To borrow money to purchase animals and improve the house, James assigned their interest in the farm to Buffalo Ridge State Bank in 1979. (Apparently Blythe and his board, who made the loan to James and Darlene, misplaced or disregarded the file of bad loans which former banker Pedersen, like any banker, had kept and—as a matter of course—had passed on to Blythe.)

Set back on the lot, standing on the top of a slight rise from which it overlooked an ample lawn with a few large trees, this two-story house could have been the Jenkinses' dream home. It had three bedrooms upstairs, one downstairs, an ample living room and dining room, and a sun porch. It had a touch of elegance with French glass doors and glass door knobs.

James worked hard to please Darlene and to make this new place their home. New carpeting was put in the downstairs; the bathroom upstairs was outfitted with new bathroom fixtures; and rooms were painted, including Steven's (which, according to one neighbor, was dark blue with orange squares, circles, crosses, and other abstract designs). James made considerable do-it-yourself electrical improvements in the basement. He put in a new well.

In the barn, too, James busied himself renovating and improving things. A neighbor said James made the barn "just beautiful, spectacular." He went so far as to light the barn with fluorescent lights. Darlene too must have worked hard during this period, for besides doing her household chores she worked in Pipestone at Bayliner Boats, cleaned Erik DeRycke's law office, and for a while worked at Louis Taveirne's gravel pit— where James himself worked one whole year.

However, by 1980 the marriage was in an open state of crisis. Both James and Darlene were talking about divorce. According to another neighbor, "James went so far as to take dancing lessons to please Darlene." When seen together at Saturday night dances, "Darlene looked very bored at the dances with Jim . . . like she didn't like being there with him."

James, who was considered to be a liar by more than one person who knew him well, was heard frequently to say that his wife was not at home: she was out chasing around. James told one neighbor in whom he frequently confided that he had caught Darlene in bed with one man and that she was spending a lot of time with Louis Taveirne. Reciting gossip or repeating what James himself had said, neighbors reported that Darlene would be away for entire weekends at a time and that James would be left caring for the children and cleaning the house.

One of the neighbors interviewed by Ken Nordin, a private detective retained for Steven's defense, was paraphrased as saying, when asked to describe Darlene, that she had a reputation for chasing men. She would always fix herself up with make-up and dress the best she could. It was not unusual for her to be gone three to four days or even a week at a time. She never really kept up on the wash, as Steven would frequently come over with dirty clothes on. One time his pants were so dirty that the neighbor thought the pants could stand by themselves.

Perhaps there was little or no truth to any of this. Perhaps these were only rumors started by James, who was suspicious and confided his problems quickly and openly to those who would listen, especially women. In any case, Darlene was sick of James and was altogether worn out by his bad deals—which always left the family broke, spending money they didn't have, worrying about debts and bad checks, and, at the end of the cycle, being forced to start life over somewhere else on the promise of another one of James's dreams.

After the children came, James got, in Darlene's opinion, less and less responsible. James was an only child; possibly he couldn't stand the competition of his own children, a family member surmised.

In her first statement to the BCA Darlene said, "Yes, he was my husband for twenty years. . . . I stayed, I led the life of financial troubles. We went through a lot of hard times. . . . When we went to buy things, he had no money. He had no way of paying for it. When I'd ask him how would he pay for something down the line . . . he'd said, 'Oh, I'll have the money,' "

For his small dairy operation to survive, James would have had to obey the laws of economic reality that he persistently defied. As an example of James's poor management, everyone who knew his operation cited his daily trips, taken at night as often as day, to Sleepy Eye, approximately seventy miles away, to obtain free silage—of no special feed value—for his cows. No farmer does that. But James wasn't going to let economics get in the way of his farming. James's inability to handle money unquestionably helped wreck the marriage, as did his constant tendency to go, in his father's opinion, from scheme to scheme.

Claiming Darlene wanted a divorce—and probably convinced there was nothing he could do to keep the marriage together—James sold approximately thirty of his cows in August 1980, having the bank's name put on the check. An equal number of cows disappeared, to the immense anger of Blythe: the disappearance meant the loss of approximately $25,000 in collateral to the young, economically hurting banker. Blythe sought to file fraud charges against James but was persuaded he wouldn't easily succeed in showing that James had purposely defrauded him. What happened to the remaining cattle is unknown. Darlene said Rudy got all the cattle that hadn't died. Others claimed James sold them off.

Blythe found the house—which as much as any place had been home for the Jenkinses, the house they had invested so much money and time remodeling—taken apart. The wall-to-wall beige carpet had been peeled up from the floor, and the new toilet and tub had been pulled out. James's machinery, which included a truck and tractor, was not to be found. James had hidden a piece or two of the machinery at Louis's landfill.

On September 12, James, who had probably returned to the farm for additional things, phoned Lincoln County sheriff Abe Thompson, claiming that someone had broken into the machine shed and stolen his tools as well as eighty gallons of fuel oil.

The family sought to regroup itself in nearby Marshall. They moved into a large trailer court there. Following his established cycle of working with machines and animals, then animals and machines, James found maintenance work at Southwest Coaches. Darlene also worked there for a short time, driving a bus. Steven cleaned buses. The owner and his wife, Marvin and Janet Hey, were pleased with the Jenkinses' work. James had exceptional mechanical ability, and Darlene not only did a good job of driving but was able to pinpoint developing mechanical problems in the buses that she drove.

The family's new arrangement in Marshall did not last for long. James and Darlene could not keep their marriage going. It had split too far apart to be put together again.

As if carried forward by some crazy, irrepressible momentum, James left Marshall to try to start another dairy operation to the north in Hoffman, Minnesota. The operation ended shortly after his barn burned down that fall. Darlene moved in with Louis Taveirne shortly after Louis asked her to be his housekeeper for a few days a week. The Jenkinses' daughter Michele, who graduated from high school in June 1982, worked nights at Schott Corporation, which made electronic equipment. She bought a used Mustang from Louis for $600—half of book value—and spent a lot of time driving around the countryside and dating. Michele got married in January of 1983; she had not wasted any time starting her own family.

In her divorce petition of June 16, 1981, Darlene—then forty-one years old—asked for custody of the children and for modest support for them: $100 a month until Michele and Steven reached legal age. For herself, she asked nothing, claiming she could support herself with her $600-a-month job at Schott Corporation in Marshall. Owning no property and making no reference to bank accounts or any other assets, such as insurance policies or retirement plans, she proposed that she and James divide what little personal property there was between them. There was nothing else, according to the divorce papers, to divide.

Darlene did not fully indicate the pain of living with James. She did not say what it meant to always be broke, constantly forced to move from place to place, uncertain about what James might do next or what would happen to her and the children. She did not describe what it was like to work as hard as she could and still be left without security or a social life—no church, no parties, hardly anything but a stop at a small bar or an occasional visit to relatives. She did not tell the court about the humiliation of living with a man who wrote bad checks, was foreclosed upon several times, and had even exhausted the good will of his own father by borrowing money he never repaid.

Darlene also did not say that, from the very start of her marriage, James had had serious mental problems, which displayed themselves in fits of temper and led him to receive shock therapy at the University of Minnesota in the early 1960s.

Darlene didn't tell the court that she was exhausted from living with James Jenkins—that living with Louis Taveirne, whom she had known and worked for off and on for years, would be a lot better.

In July of that year Darlene and James agreed upon the terms of the dissolution of their marriage. Darlene would have custody of the children. James would pay $200 a month for child support for Michele and Steven until they reached legal age. Darlene would keep the 1974 Torino, and James would keep their 1961 Chevrolet pickup.

On August 14, during a fifteen-minute hearing before Judge Irving Wilrout, the court heard Darlene's reasons for the divorce and granted it to her. James did not appear. When asked by the judge at the divorce hearing if the breakdown of the marriage was "a result of your husband's mistreatment of the children," Darlene replied: "Basically, yes." When asked whether the abuse was physical or verbal, Darlene responded that the abuse, which continued over a substantial period of time, was verbal. When asked if James had assaulted her, Darlene responded, "Just one time."

The judge dissolved the marriage on August 14, 1981. From the judge's point of view, and that of Darlene's lawyer, Gorden Paterson, this divorce was among the least complex of divorces. It was uncontested and there was nothing to divide. (In January 1981, James and Darlene had had attorney DeRycke file a bankruptcy petition for them.) With surprisingly little effort, the law ended a twenty-year marriage.

For James, the divorce meant another failure. This time he had lost more than another job or a farm. This time he had lost the wife who supported him and the family and marriage which gave him a place and a purpose in the countryside. In the face of such a failure, James could only do what he always did: put his head down, work hard, and insist that he could shape the world to his will.

At Hoffman, Minnesota, he started another small dairy farm. It was to Hoffman that his daughter brought the divorce papers for his signature.

JAMES'S WAY: POUNDING AGAINST LIFE

JAMES'S LIFE, however, turned on more than the class into which he had born and the marriage in which he had failed. James's fate was inseparable from his character.

A portrait of the adult James as someone other than simply a good farmer who was wronged came quickly to light after the crime. Many local residents and farmers did not consider him to be a "real" farmer at all. They didn't consider the type of small dairy operation that James had started in Ruthton as having a chance. (In the region, bankers considered 160 acres as the minimum amount of land required for a successful enterprise.) Some people partially blamed Rudolph Blythe for having lent money to James for such an operation in the first place.

Many people had examples of James as a bad farmer. According to Duane DeBettignies, owner of the *Buffalo Ridge Gazette*, "once he never even bothered to pick up a $1,000 worth of hay, leaving it to rot in the field." Almost everyone who knew James had a story about his undertaking an improvement he didn't need, buying a piece of machinery he didn't need, or buying an old and useless piece of machinery and spending days getting it to work. Rather than farm, James seemed to be mired down in junk he couldn't use. A long-time acquaintance remarked, "James was always scouting around . . . trying something he couldn't handle. Anything he did, didn't work."

At his Arco farm—the place he owned before the Ruthton place—James bought an expensive grain bin he didn't need. At the Ruthton farm, he strove to turn his barn into "a palace." People in Tyler mention that he pumped the city's water for his animals for free until complaints caused the city to charge him for the water. When James eventually got his own well drilled, the well driller went unpaid.

Some believed they saw flaws in James's character right from the start. One old neighbor—who knew James when he was a boy and a young man and who had baled hay and threshed with James—described James as "quiet" and "a loner." He wasn't much for conversation and he had "no friends. He didn't even go to town with his dad." James spent his time by himself. He was not much interested in girls. When James was a boy, the neighbor remarked, he resembled his own son Steven: James liked guns and he loved to hunt and trap. Occasionally he poached an animal. "He even wore military fatigues." Even then, according to the neighbor, James had "a bad temper." "He was hard to keep under control. He had to have his own way."

Another neighbor remembered James as a boy who was a loner and an angry, young man. He recalled how "he hunted alone," saying this in such a way as to imply that James was almost wild. James was reckless with equipment. When working for other farmers, he would get mad and throw things and break equipment.

One of James's teachers at Tyler High School also said that James was "by himself and alone." She didn't remember his participating in any activities; he certainly didn't participate in theater or choir, the activities for which she was responsible. Another teacher less generously described James as "a non-entity" whose attitude was "belligerent." He dared the teacher "to teach him something."

Having little common sense, having a sense of his own importance, and having a quick temper were traits that turned up in most portraits of James. One neighbor testified that James bought a lot of machinery he didn't need. On one occasion, when he was unable to fix a baler he had just bought, he flew off the handle, took the baler to town, and sold it on the spot. Another time, seeking to supplement the dairy income from his Ruthton farm, James bought an old road grader from his Louis Taveirne. He paid $1,600. However, there were no roads to grade; a few weeks later, James sold the grader to a dealer for $1,000.

James's sense of self-importance, which usually took the form of enthusiasm for his most recent idea, showed often. Tyler school principal Gary Brosz remembered the one time James came to school to get Steven. (Darlene was the one who in all other cases brought what the children had forgotten or picked them up from school.) James was brusque: as if issuing a command, he said, "I want Steven. I am going to Marshall for parts, and I am going to take him along."

Another time, on a job James had subcontracted from Louis, James sat in the cab of the dragline as Darlene, up to her waist in water, turned the lug nuts on the large culverts they were connecting. If Darlene had known how to run the dragline, she too would have spent time in the cab.

James's temper, however, is what is most remembered about him. A woman who was his classmate in the fourth grade at the rural school in the Tyler area—District 24—remembers very little about him except that "he had thick glasses and a bad temper." She added, "He talked a lot; and when he got mad, he got red in the face."

James never yielded to the world. In a piece in the *Minneapolis Tribune* by Paul Levy—entitled "Woes Were James Jenkins's Companions"—two long-time neighbors described James's temper and his struggle with his father.

"Clayt and Jimmy would argue, and Nina would come between and patch things up," said Lois Johnson. "By the time he was twelve or so, Jimmy seemed a lot closer to his mother." Jimmy and Clayt "were never that close, but later, when Jimmy got into financial trouble, Clayt always bailed him out."

"But they'd argue. I know Clayt and Nina say that the [car] accident Jimmy had [in 1960] changed him, but even back then he had a bad temper."

Carl Johnson said he once received a phone call from Clayton, asking him to come over to the Jenkins home immediately. Upon arrival, Johnson said that he found shattered glass scattered about—the remnants of a glass door Jimmy had apparently broken. An uncle—a fellow called "Big Jim"—was holding Jimmy down when Johnson arrived.

"Another time, Jimmy and Clayton Jenkins were at a neighbor's when Jimmy became frustrated with a tractor that was malfunctioning," said Johnson. "Jimmy began pounding his fist against the tractor. When his father told him to take it easy, Jimmy pounded even harder," Johnson said.

This was not the only instance of James's turning his anger against the machine he was working on, as several farmers would testify. On one occasion, when working for Louis Taveirne, James purposely broke the cable on a dragline and ran the cab into a ditch.

In his original statement to the BCA, made on the day of the crime, James's own father expressed a fear of his son; Clayton left no doubt that he believed his son had a bad temper and was not an easy person to live with. Confessing that he did not trust his own son and implying that he did not believe him either, Clayton said that long ago he had quit lending his son money. "[We] gave them quite a lot of money [during the early days of their marriage] and they still weren't satisfied." Beyond this, Clayton implied that his son was not altogether stable. Clayton suggested that James had had a breakdown twenty years earlier and that "Darlene got him out of Sioux Falls before they treated him."

Paul Levy quoted a neighbor as saying, "James never ran away from a challenge—only from people." Levy quoted another neighbor as saying, "He was to himself. . . . If you pushed his button, he blew his horn. If you wanted to rattle his cage, he would shake you up. Not too many people had too much to do with the man. If they did, they got screwed."

His daughter knew James always to have a temper. She believed he used it to serve his purposes—disguising it when things were going his way and revealing it when he thought he could intimidate someone.

A local insurance agent and the mayor of Tyler, Henry Jacobsen, testified that even by trying to help James, one could elicit his wrath. Trying to help James maintain a favorable status in car insurance, the agent asked James a question about his past driving record. Taking this question to be too personal, James grew terribly angry and threatened to file a complaint against the agent.

Another instance of James's temper was mentioned by Lincoln County attorney Eric DeRycke. (DeRycke worked on a divorce for Louis Taveirne and helped Darlene the first time she attempted to divorce James.) DeRycke said James "could not separate reality from fantasy. He had a temper that was explosive; when his temper exploded, it was of such magnitude that there was no thinking and reasoning function at all." DeRycke believed James "wasn't playing with a full deck. His temper came out of nowhere."

About two years before the murders, DeRycke saw James absolutely beside himself with anger. "He was enraged." James said he was going to kill Michael Carlson for threatening to take him to court. James had written Carlson a bad check; unlike a lot of others, Carlson intended to do something about it. DeRycke tried to quiet James down. He took James's rage seriously enough that he warned the sheriff to keep an eye on James.

One last example can be used to describe James's temper. When in 1980 he discovered that Steven had been injured in a serious bicycle accident along a county road, James roared back at the world. He rushed to the Tyler hospital where his son had been taken. He demanded that his son be taken to Marshall immediately, despite the doctor's advice that moving Steven would be dangerous. James shoved the doctor against the wall and pinned him there, insisting he would not let his son be touched by "any pineapple"—his expression for the Filipino doctor treating Steven.

A violent temper was part of James's character. When Robert Moore, one of James's relatives, first heard of the crime, he "expected a shoot-out," according to a BCA summary. In Moore's opinion, James was a good shot. "While not a gun nut," when "shooting running rats, he never missed." Moore also said to the BCA, "All the family told me: Jimmy was just plain bananas as hell."

Temperament is what is given. James was what he had become. His character was not, as his father believed, the result of a single accident. (In August 1960, on a Sunday morning, James had collided head on with another car. The woman in it was killed. James spent seventeen days in the hospital in Sioux Falls. James never went to see a specialist as the doctor recommended.)

Furthermore, James wasn't coming undone because of little vices or bad habits that over the years can take a person apart. He didn't smoke, gamble, or chase women; he didn't even like parties. He wasn't lazy, and he wasn't much of a drinker. On the job application he filled out for the Brownwood School District in Texas in 1982, he said he had three to four drinks a year. One neighbor, who had seen James drink occasionally during one period in his life, said James could be belligerent when he drank. Others testified that when James lived in Florence he never drank; when he and Darlene went to a bar, she would drink and he wouldn't.

James's vice, if that is what it should be called, was that he was always pounding against life. He didn't respect reality. He insisted he would make the world over his way. His temper tantrums grew instead of subsiding as he grew older. He would buy old machines and repair them for reasons of pride rather than utility. He ran up bills he couldn't pay. He insisted on his dream of owning and running a small dairy farm, regardless of the economic and familial realities involved; when he failed, he grew angry with the world. He tried to live by will alone.

James was a prisoner of his own character, especially of his headstrong will, which across a lifetime had come to animate the short, stocky James—five feet seven inches, 185 pounds. He increasingly challenged truth itself. To his daughter, his wife, his father, his son—to almost everyone—he lied; and his lies were not white lies, but serious distortions of reality. As his marriage came apart, James Jenkins's lying became part of a pervasive paranoia.

Since he had lived in Arco, James had been suspicious of Darlene. He believed she was running around with a well-off neighbor, a cattle rancher there. In Ruthton, he suspected Darlene of running around with anyone he imagined.

In turn, everything that failed, he blamed on somebody else. When asked by the BCA whom James blamed for his financial failures, Darlene replied: "Whoever was around." Asked if he ever took blame himself, she said emphatically, "He never took blame for anything. Nothing has ever been his fault, ever."

James's anger, however, wasn't altogether without focus: there was Darlene, who cost him a farm and family; Blythe, who cost him a farm and family; and Louis, who cost him a wife, a farm, and a family.

There was more to his hatred of Louis than the belief that Louis had cost him everything he had had in his adult life. James had also come to hate Louis for what Louis was.

Louis Taveirne was what James was not: he was successful. Louis, born in 1927, was ten years or so older than James. A hard-working, short, and slightly heavy-set man with blue eyes and a quick intelligence, Louis had accomplished what James could not achieve in his whole life.

Louis was shrewd but not without a temper. He fixed a person or a situation in his mind with a few words. He knew how to put sentences in order to get his point across. He had an eye for detail. He reflected on what makes people work. Louis calculated. He knew what he gave and what he had been given. According to a long-time acquaintance, "Louis is generous. He'll loan any friend money, but he'll make you pay it back too."

Louis was a man of deals. He quickly calculated the direct and indirect costs of things. Louis did not hesitate when telling a story to add a running account of what the expected and real costs of a deal were, even if it had occurred a decade earlier.

James took Louis to be a big man. To James, Louis was rich, powerful, and independent; and he knew about things—machines, costs, prices, bids, and contracts.

Louis had friends in the contracting business. Louis had succeeded, as James had not, at becoming an independent contractor, having started as a foreman of road work in Lincoln County.

Louis had also amassed several businesses. He owned the Lincoln Construction Company, which was involved in building roads and operating a sanitary landfill near Pipestone. He had joint ownership of a car dealership and repair shop in Lynd and was sole owner of the Lynwood Inn, one of the larger bars and supper clubs in southwestern Minnesota. In James's envious mind, Louis—who also owned a nice house and some small farm acreages—must have owned a world of property. Louis turned what he touched to gold. For James, it was the opposite.

There were other reasons for James to hate Louis. Louis supplied him and Darlene with special jobs when they were in need. He also provided Steven and Michele with cars at his cost. In addition, Louis had hired James for a year at his landfill, running "a cat." James's job was to bury refuse for the region. Louis let James go when James's work was not up to standard and when it became evident that James would not accept correction.

In turn, Louis hired Darlene to work at the landfill. Louis liked the hard-working Darlene and, at some point, Darlene saw more of a man and a life in Louis Taveirne than she saw in James Jenkins.

James had a lot of reasons to hate Louis, who had powers to give and take—powers which James could only greedily, angrily, enviously, and revengefully imagine. Louis, James's patron, had accomplished what James could not, and in the end Louis took James's wife. (Louis was himself divorced in 1980. The divorce, which involved a bitter struggle over property, ended Louis's four-year marriage and a thirteen-year relationship with a widow who had three older children.)

Nineteen eighty was another terrible year for James. James's character was tested to the fullest in that forty-fourth year of his life. In 1980, he nearly lost a son in the bike accident. He lost his wife, his farm, a place in southwestern Minnesota, and almost all pride and hope of becoming somebody. In some terrible way, James was at the end of a way of living.

Yet James did not break, surrender, or undergo some sort of conversion—which alone might have changed his character and possibly ended the anger, deceit, envy, hate, and desire for revenge that filled him. Instead, James did what he had always done, what by class and character he alone knew how to do: he put his head down and worked harder.

In 1981, with Darlene living with Louis and the divorce legally under way, James left Marshall to start another dairy operation to the north, near Hoffman, Minnesota. That fall the barn burned down, ending his dairy farm. James blamed Darlene and Louis.

Next, James went to Portsmouth, Ohio, where he worked for a trucking firm. The following summer, in 1982, James went to Texas.

LAST CHANCE IN TEXAS

TEXAS WAS JAMES'S LAST CHANCE. Maybe there he could forget one life and start another. But the odds weren't good. James had spent most of his life in southwestern Minnesota. It was there where he—with the knit stocking cap he usually wore on his head—rammed around the countryside. It was there, back in Minnesota, where he wanted to be somebody.

James's health was going too. At least since 1980, bad health had increasingly nipped at James's heels. He had diabetes, his legs were bad, and he didn't always breathe easily. He was, as he knew, slowly but surely going blind. He suffered not only night blindness, but he had inherited from his mother *retinitis pigmentosa*, a degenerative disease that inevitably leads to blindness.

As if this were not enough, James suffered from hypochondria. He imagined he had cancer, and he told more than one person in Texas about trips—which in fact had never occured—that he had taken to Mexico for a cure. In a BCA interview, Barry DeVine, a friend of Steven, said James frequently spoke to Barry about his health—complaining that he, James, had learned at the hospital that he had leukemia, bone cancer, and diabetes, and that he did not have long to live. Barry said James also informed him that he had problems with his legs hurting and giving out on him and that he couldn't see at night.

In Texas, James first worked for a traveling amusement park. He got the rides up and going, and then he took them down. At Lampasas, Texas, he worked as a packer for a manufacturing company until he went to nearby Brownwood (seventy miles away), a town of 20,000 in the center of Texas. James showed up in Brownwood with nothing but a willingness to work. He found work in maintenance with the Brownwood Independent School District.

As everywhere else, Texas was a place of insult for James. When he was first there, he was without a vehicle and had to hitchhike. On one occasion in 1982, on his way to Texas, he was picked up by and spent a day and a half with Betty Jean Ginhardt of Pocola, Oklahoma. According to the BCA report, James "told her that he was leaving Minnesota and he was having problems with his ex-wife and her husband and that he had to leave the area if he didn't want to get into trouble. . . . There was an insurance policy and he felt that his ex-wife [might] attempt to kill him for money." (Ginhardt and James exchanged letters and calls, and on one occasion he stopped to find work in Pocola.)

When James filled out the job application at Brownwood Independent School in August of 1982, he had no address, so he had to give the address of a friend. Despite his skills in welding, plumbing, carpentry, mechanical work, and general building and contracting, James had to apply for general construction work at or near minimum wage. Aside from service in the National Guard in which he reached E-6 at the time of his honorable discharge, James chose only to list one reference from Minnesota: Tom Rustand at the bank in Russell, Minnesota. Of the many jobs he had held, he only referred to two: the two-month, day-labor position that he held at V. P. Pamco at Lampasas, Texas—which he quit, according to him, because it was "a dead end job"—and an undated period of self-employment as a "farming contractor" in Minnesota—which he claimed he quit for the "personal reason of divorce."

On the application, which checked the "spiritual condition" of the applicant, James answered affirmatively to a question about whether he believed in the existence of a Supreme Being. He affirmed his "loyalty to this nation, its government, its constitution and its flag." He listed boating and camping as his two favorite hobbies and agreed to additional training and assignment outside of school hours "for the good of the school system."

During his first six weeks at the Brownwood school, he slept on a couch in the maintenance shed until he scraped together enough money to buy a trailer measuring eight by fifteen feet. He added a second job as a security guard. James did as well there as he had done anywhere. He began to save money. He again started to nurse his dream: he would return to Minnesota and start a dairy farm.

People treated James well in Brownwood, and they respected him for being a hard and intelligent worker. James Lancaster, the superintendent of the Brownwood Independent School District, appreciated James's mechanical abilities. During his spare time, James made an old, discarded John Deere tractor run. Charles Snow and James Perry, James's foremen, appreciated his ability to work. With nothing else to do and having lost himself, apparently, in his work, James worked hard. He was on the job early and stayed late. He was as likely to skip a rest period as to take advantage of it. James's foremen also appreciated the fact that he worked best by himself. Only when it came to measuring things did they send someone along with James because of his bad eyesight. They also fashioned work to fit James. Finding he was not up to cement work—having neither the legs nor the breathing for it—they assigned James to basic ground work and to repairing their machines and trucks.

Snow took a particular liking to James. Snow found he could use both James and the tractor that James had gotten running on his two-hundred-acre ranch, twenty miles west of town. On more than one occasion, James worked on Snow's ranch for free—in his words, "just to be out in the country." Once he spent a couple days, for no pay, bringing in and stacking 1,500 bales of hay. Another time he built Snow a shed. Snow's ranch became a place in the country for James.

Others in Brownwood were generous to James. Ted Beard, a former farmer and the manager of an appliance repair shop, was one of the first to befriend James. Ted and his wife—who met James through Ted's sister-in-law—fed James regularly; and Ted, without question or guarantee, cosigned a loan for James on the white pickup. Within a few months, the loan was paid off.

Both Beard's sister-in-law, Joyce Mattlock, and recently widowed Brenda Enlow (and perhaps others) did what James needed most: they listened to him talk. He talked about what had gone wrong in Minnesota. He talked about what really and what he only imagined was going wrong with his body—his eyes, teeth, stomach, legs, his actual diabetes, and his fantasized cancer. They listened to him talk angrily about Darlene and Louis and about Steven and his interest in weapons—an interest which worried James.

After James had been in Brownwood for about six months, Steven came to join his father. Joyce and Brenda also listened as James told Steven that one day he would return to Minnesota and have a place of his own.

On the surface, James's days in Brownwood, Texas, looked like good days. More than one person connected with the case couldn't understand why James had ever bothered to leave Texas. There he had work. His son had joined him. Several people had taken an interest in him. He even had a few female friends who cared about him and in whom he confided. What he confided, however, showed that these good days were but weak dikes against twenty years of failure and anger.

James never really took root in Texas. He wasn't on the land there, and he wasn't his own boss. Even when Steven joined him at Brownwood, the most they could call home was the eight-by-fifteen-foot trailer James had purchased and parked without charge at the back of the school lot.

James was worried about Steven. He was not in school, he was preoccupied with weapons; and he had no mother. Late in the spring of 1983, Steven left James and Brownwood for Minnesota.

On July 7, 1983, James resigned. When James left the Brownwood Independent School District, he was making $4.20 an hour. Obviously revealing that he had no intention of returning to work there, James wrote on the district's termination of employment form the following reasons for leaving: "too much suck ass [ass was crossed out but still legible], plus poor pay, Perry [James Perry was his and Steven's foreman]."

James told Snow he was going to Minnesota to start a farm that would work this time. A few days later, James asked Snow for his job back. Snow had hired someone else, and James said it didn't matter anyhow, that he was going back north. James's last chance—if it had ever been a chance at all—was over. On August 5, he worked his last day in Texas.

James was going back to southwestern Minnesota—to home where Nina and Clayton, Steve, and Darlene and Louis were. He would show them; he would show all of them—everyone who had said Jimmy Jenkins wasn't somebody; or, if he couldn't show them, as he always used to say to Darlene, "a guy just as well be dead."

CHAPTER THREE

The Father and the Son

Abused children may become tough soldiers instead of violent criminals, and of the latter, some will confine their violence to intimate settings and others will attack strangers.

—JAMES Q. WILSON AND
RICHARD J. HERRNSTEIN,
Crime & Human Nature

Which of us has looked into his father's heart? . . .
Which of us is not forever a stranger and alone?

—THOMAS WOLFE, *Look Homeward Angel*

Just months before the crime, James did not have the heart to kill an injured horse; and just weeks before the crime, Steven could not kill a stray dog.

ABOUT six months after James went to Texas, Steven joined him. Steven had always sought his father out. He was, in the words of his own family, "his father's boy." His schoolmates in Tyler, where Steven had gone to school when the family lived on the Ruthton farm, remarked that he was hardly ever around. He was usually with his father—and that was, as Darlene knew, Steven's downfall.

Even though the divorce granted custody of Steven to Darlene, Steven acted always as if his place in the world was with his dad. Even though his mother did most of the nurturing and was the one who usually hauled Steven and his sister Michele about, Steven was his father's boy. He looked to his father for praise, even though he rarely received it.

Steven spent much of his time on the road with his dad. During the two and one-half years from the dissolution of the family until the crime, Steven had no place he could really call home. He went from parent to parent, to Nina and Clayton, and back to his parents. He joined his father, to whom he was always drawn, in at least four different places—two in Minnesota, one in Ohio, and one in Texas.

In the spring of 1981, Steven joined his father at his newly started milking operation in Hoffman, Minnesota. Then he lived with his mother in Marshall until he quit school in the winter of 1981. He then joined his father, who had gone to Portsmouth, Ohio, to work for a trucking firm. Steven returned from Ohio in the summer of 1982 to live intermittently with Nina and Clayton and then with Darlene and Louis. (Louis's place was in Lynd, Minnesota, a small village of a couple hundred people, nestled in the valley of the Redwood River.) Then he and his father hitchhiked back and forth to Texas a couple of times in search of work or a farm. Eventually, Steven joined his father at Thanksgiving in Brownwood, Texas, and remained there until May of 1983, when he returned to live primarily with Nina and Clayton but also for a short time with Louis and Darlene.

In August, his father returned from Texas. Both Steven and his father lived with Nina and Clayton for approximately one month while James scoured the region for a place to farm and for the credit required to start a small dairy operation. After considering six or more places—one as far away as Wisconsin—James located a place in the vicinity of Hardwick, Minnesota, a village of 280, located about thirty miles south of Ruthton. It was from Hardwick that James and Steven made their violent return to the Ruthton farm.

"LIKE FATHER, LIKE SON"

IN THE CASE of James and Steven, there is no escaping the old saying, "like father, like son." They were together much of the time; when apart, they sought each other out. Steven took himself to be his father's boy and a Jenkins, not an Abraham. An only son of an only son, his second home was with Nina and

Clayton. According to Clayton, Steven always treated them respectfully, sassing Clayton only once.

In many ways young Steven resembled the young James. They were both rural farm boys of the same social class, brought up in the same "neck of the woods." They knew the same towns, places, families, and people. They knew Nina and Clayton's farm like the backs of their hands. They worked the same fields, hunted the same river valleys, and traveled the same roads. They lived in a world that had remained relatively unchanged from the boyhood of the father to the boyhood of the son.

James and Steven both worked hard at what they did. They liked to be around machines. They knew about guns and hunting. James and Steven lived minimal lives. Sports, music, schooling, fancy cooking, the arts, travel—none of these caught their fancy.

When asked by the BCA whether James had been hunting, Darlene replied, "No. He never went deer hunting. He never went pheasant hunting. He never went nothing."

Unlike his father, Steven did not have a strong gregarious streak in him. When he was young, he was "really shy," according to his family. He would talk to his mother and sister, but he did not talk easily to strangers. His sister remembered his being most talkative when he and she were out on horseback in the countryside, playing cowboys and Indians. Michele remembered that Steven would heatedly explain to her—she usually "got it wrong"—what she was to do next.

Like his father, young Steven was a loner with a will of his own. He spent a lot of time by himself. He was, when younger, a passionate hunter. He spent days alone, out in the countryside, hunting in river valleys and sloughs. Also Steven passed a considerable amount of time watching TV.

Through the years, Steven had only a handful of friends. Steven Shriver, who was by all accounts Steven's best friend during the two years before the murders, knew almost nothing about Steven's feelings. On one occasion, in the late spring or summer of 1983, he saw Steven shoot holes in the yellow Volkswagen that Louis Taverne had given him. Yet Shriver didn't know what emotional state Steven was in. He took

Steven to be in "the same state" as before he shot.

Shriver indicated Steven shot the car on the driver's side through the window and along the edge of the roof above the window. Asked if the shots would have hit a person sitting there, Shriver said, "Pretty much!" Asked whether or not the shots could have been meant for Louis, who gave Steven the car, Shriver replied, "It could be something like that." Did Steven show any change of emotion before or after he shot? "None, that I could see," Shriver commented.

Michele's boyfriend, Reid Jorgensen, knew Steven when the Jenkinses lived at Ruthton and afterwards. He knew nothing about Steven's feelings—or even Michele's feelings—about their parents' failing marriage. Jorgensen didn't consider Steven a close friend.

Jorgensen said that Steven, who was interested in "guns a lot like any farm kid around here," didn't show emotions. "Steven rarely got mad, but once he decided to, he got real mad." Once Steven started to fight Jorgensen for something that he, Jorgensen, had said. Laughing, Jorgensen said he put a quick end to the fight. Jorgensen and Steve would make CO_2 bombs together while watching television and then would go out and light them. "We were just having fun," Jorgensen remarked.

Jorgensen didn't think Steven was jealous of him when he enlisted in the Marines, even though they had rejected Steven because of an injury to his spleen. (Jorgensen, who had dated Michele for four years, also didn't know how Michele felt about his joining the Marines, although he expected she might wait to marry him.)

Steven was a withdrawn boy who rarely showed his emotions. Like his friends, he liked guns. Unlike some of the farm kids and most of the kids in the villages, Steven didn't belong to clubs or groups. He didn't engage in school activities.

Like his father, he had an interest in machines and an ability with tools. At one time, Louis helped Steven with the layout and Steven built a room all by himself in Louis's auto sale and repair shop. But Steven's interest in weapons surpassed everything else. Shooting was his emotional outlet.

Steven had scholastic ability. He passed his classes year after year and showed an IQ of 116, as measured by the Shipley-Hartford Test. He had excellent abstract thinking abilities, according to the measure of the Benjamin Proverbs Technique. Nevertheless, Steven, like his father, quit school. Steven quit in the eleventh grade; his father had quit in the tenth.

Father and son also both suffered serious accidents. A car accident in 1960 severely injured James. In 1980, Steven was in a serious accident on his bicycle; his ruptured spleen kept him from realizing his dream of joining the Marines.

More significantly, both Steven and James suffered profoundly from the dissolution of their family. The end of the family drove James and Steven together. James, the father, tried to build a new home for Steven, his son and favorite child. Steven took his father's side. Needing his father's recognition—which he never got, according to his sister—Steven tried to "care for his father." "Steven," according to members of his family, "felt sorry for his father." "He tried to be his nursemaid." "Somehow they would always get back together."

James and Steven were a lost father and son. They were two emotionally uncentered persons who sought to furnish each other with a family. They were two men who, each in his own way, was trying "to tough out" his homeless condition.

Both James and Steven believed Darlene destroyed the family. As Michele, the daughter, openly sided with Darlene and despised her father, so Steven joined equally strongly with James. They held Darlene and Louis responsible for the destruction of the family and for the loss of the Ruthton farm. They believed Darlene and Louis, not the banker Blythe, had done them in. Also, James and, at least at times, Steven believed Darlene and Louis were responsible for burning down the Hoffman farm.

For three years, James and Steven told each other stories about how unjustly life had treated them. James continually fed Steven bitter stories about the end of the family and the loss of the farm. As Darlene so clearly knew, James excited Steven. In Steven's presence, James told others about Darlene's infidelity. James eventually added the name of Blythe to his list of Darlene's lovers.

Father and son came to share a terrible anger about what had happened to them. At some point, father and son, two different generations, became one angry spirit. Like Siamese twins, they were joined in some kind of terrible madness.

James's anger, while perhaps always just below the surface, was often disguised by a social graciousness which led more than one person to describe him as a kind and sensitive man. Louis Taverne was not alone in believing that James Jenkins would talk a person's leg off if given a chance. A neighbor who had known James a long time ago said, "He was just plain windy."

By contrast, Steven's anger, which could explode on occasions, was not disguised by an exterior sociability. While Steven was at times gentle and possessed a mild sense of humor, people who saw him often—or who had him in their homes often—heard only a handful of words from him.

During the years preceding the crime, Steven clearly advertised his anger. While he was not insolent to adults, the very presence of the reticent and withdrawn Steven spooked many adults. A young person from rural Cottonwood, who saw Steven in the summer of 1982, said, "He was creepy—just walking about—with a big knife, a Bowie knife or some kind of big knife, stuck down his back pocket. He just wandered around in Lynd, back and forth, like he didn't know where he was going."

Not all interviews gave the impression that Steven was dangerously obsessed with his military fantasies. Gary Brosz, the principal at Russell-Tyler High School—where Steven spent his first two years of high school—remembered Steven as "a quiet young man" who was "very polite" and "never a troublemaker or disciplinary problem." Brosz judged Steven to be an average student who did not participate in extracurricular activities or athletics and who had a small circle of friends. Brosz remarked that Steven did not show an inordinate interest in guns during that time. "He went hunting like any other kid in Minnesota."

Neal Nelson, the school's physical education and social studies teacher, agreed with Brosz: Steven was polite and pleasant. "Of quiet behavior." He did not participate in sports, but he was interested in hunting, "which was rather common with boys of his age." Probably neither Brosz nor Nelson knew that Steven never had a hunting license.

Another of Steven's classmates, Dale VanDerostyne, who hunted with Steven, said in his interview with the BCA that Steven was not a party-goer nor a drinker. Shriver, Steven's friend from near Marshall, remarked that Steven never swore or drank. According to Shriver, he kept his own counsel. "He was kind of careful who he talked to. He just wouldn't talk to anyone." "Steven," Shriver offered as a conclusion, was "a quiet, polite person who kept to himself, enjoyed firearms, hunting, and target shooting, and liked to wear military fatigues."

A darker portrait of Steven emerged from other interviews. His grandparents remarked that Steven had been interested in military things since he was very young—maybe even four. On one occasion, they remarked, young Steven turned a small child's wagon—that they used to transport clothes back and forth from the backyard clothesline—into a pretend military vehicle by painting "U.S. Army" on it. Also, they remarked that his father, who had served some time in the National Guard, used to repeat his few tales—which may have been "prolonged and exaggerated"—to his eager son. James apparently "fostered Steven's military leanings and allowed . . . his military fantasies." Weapons and the military became one way for father and son to relate to one another. A family photograph of young Steven at an early birthday party, perhaps his tenth, shows him dressed in full military costume.

As Steven went from childhood to adolescence, military things came to form an unchallenged fantasy life for him. Steven's interest was not in cars or motorcycles. (He did not have the money nor did he get his driving permit until he was seventeen.) It was with weapons that Steven told himself and the world who he was. He and his friends flaunted their weapons in public. He and one friend occasionally trailed other students to amuse themselves. For fun, Steven made bombs—pipe bombs as well as CO$_2$ cartridge bombs. Steven was sixteen years old and still playing with real guns; but he was playing with real guns and, according to Reid Jorgensen, shooting at lifelike dummies.

In retrospect, it appears that Steven had been preparing for a day of violence for years. Weapons became his single emotional and imaginative outlet. He practiced shooting continually. What friends he had shared his interest in weapons. His free time and his extra money, which never amounted to much, were spent on weapons and military things. He frequented stores with guns and military things, like Poor Borch's in Marshall, which had a great black six-shooter sign pointing from the roadway where the sign stood to the front door.

If by any one act Steven externally symbolized his transformation from hunter to soldier, it was when, approximately two years before the crime—in violation of federal firearms law—he sawed off the barrel of his .410 shotgun and affixed a bayonet to it with electrical tape and a water hose clamp. (A .410 is a small-gauge shotgun, useful for shooting gophers, ground squirrels, and pigeons. A .410 or a .22 rifle is often the first gun a father gives his son.)

There is no exact point at which Steven made the transition from hunter to soldier. Fantasy's road is not clearly marked. However, the transition was completed with the loss of the family farm at Ruthton. As Steven spent his many hours alone in the country or up in the loft of the garage at the Ruthton farm, he fantasized about guns and shooting. Guns became inseparable from his manhood, and his revenge to strike back against a world which had hurt him so.

AN M-1 IN TEXAS

THE STEVEN WHO ARRIVED in Texas to join his father was undisguisedly angry. James Lancaster, superintendent of the Brownwood Independent School District in Texas where James and Steven worked, was quoted as saying, "I liked James. But there was something about the boy that bothered me, nothing I could put my finger on, but as my boy says [Steven was] kind of one brick shy of a load."

Most people in Texas who were interviewed judged Steven to be strange and distant—he gave them an eerie feeling. Arvil Gardner, construction superintendent of Stein Construction of Richland Springs, Texas—a company that worked for the Brownwood district—described Steven as "a goofball who was always talking about blowing someone's head off."

Norma Parker, who worked as a secretary for Stein Construction, remarked that Steven was a strange individual with a proclivity for violence. As an example, she pointed out how Steven, while engaged in the demolition of a building, had used a crowbar to smash out windows, despite specific instructions that he was to remove the windows before demolishing the walls. Norma Parker also indicated that Steven frequently made comments like "Kill that son of a bitch!" or "Bash his head in!" She indicated that Steven "was always talking about guns." When he discovered that she had a .38-caliber pistol, Steven wondered what type of hole it would make if it were used to shoot a piece of plywood or a person.

It was there, at the Brownwood Independent School District in Texas, where Steven and James became as close as they could be. Steven worked right alongside his father, often working for no pay at all. They hitchhiked together. They slept and ate together, living in their small trailer at the back of the school lot. They spent their free time together and ate the same meals at the same two restaurants that they almost always frequented. They were, according to more than one person who knew them, "buddies." They had nothing at all like a traditional father-and-son relationship.

James Lancaster remarked to a BCA officer that he didn't believe "James had an undue influence over Steven." His impression was that Steven had a mind of his own and did whatever he pleased. He offered as proof Steven's trips back and forth to Minnesota and his infatuation with military things.

James and Steven shared each other's ups and downs. One revealing instance of this was the mutual and surprisingly manifest pleasure they took in making Lancaster's rusty, old John Deere tractor run. "The Jenkins boys" had shown their ability—had shown what they were made of. They had done something that no ordinary Joe could do.

Machines were important to them. Their lives revolved around machines, garages, car repair shops, and metal and welding shops. At such places, Steven and James were at home. Nevertheless, nothing diminished Steven's mounting interest in weapons. By the time father and son were together in Texas, Steven's obsession with weapons rivaled and began to surpass James's dream about cows and dairy farms. As another teenage boy might continually pluck away at a guitar, practice jumpshots, or lose himself in reading, Steven monomaniacally focused on weapons. When James, knowingly and against his better judgment, gave Steven—then only seventeen—permission to buy an M-1 carbine, he confirmed what had long ago been baptized.

Steven had three other guns—a .22-caliber pistol, a pump 12-gauge shotgun, and his modified .410 shotgun. It was, however, his M-1 that was his love. He kept it with him all the time. He put a strap on it so it would more closely resemble the heavier, authentic army M-1. At one point in his grand jury testimony, Steven revealed just how close he was to his M-1.

State prosecutor Fabel asked: "You usually took the M-1 out [of the pickup] at night?"

Steven replied, "Yes."

Fabel: "Where did you bring the M-1 with you at night usually?"

Steven: "Brought it in the house."

Fabel: "Where did you keep it in the house?"

Steven: "In the corner of the room that I was in . . . that I slept in."

Fabel: "Was that customary practice for you to take that M-1 out and to keep it in the corner of your room?"

Steven: "Yes."

The M-1 became Steven's constant companion. He didn't go anywhere without it. It was his identity, his talisman. Perfecting his shooting of the M-1 became the center of his life.

Several BCA interviews revealed Steven's preoccupation with weapons. Harvey Parker, manager of Bowie Lumber in Brownwood, indicated that his employee sold Steven ten boxes of .30-caliber ammunition. Each box contained twenty .30-caliber shells at an average cost of eleven dollars a box. Norman Cox, an employee of Brownwood Independent School District, indicated that Steven questioned him about various types of military explosives, including hand grenades, and their operation. Barry DeVine, a senior at Brownwood High who also worked in the school's maintenance division, said he spent a considerable amount of time with Steven and most of their conversations centered around military hardware and guns. During the one time they went to a rifle range, the ejector on Steven's carbine did not function properly, so DeVine had no idea whether or not Steven was a good shot.

While Steven and James were in Texas, former first sergeant Charles Snow—who had served three combat tours in Vietnam, ran the maintenance operation for the Brownwood Independent School District, and got along well with James—took Steven under his wing and taught Steven how to shoot his M-1.

Snow was impressed by Steven's knowledge of military things, a knowledge Steven honed by constant questions and avidly reading *Soldier of Fortune* and other survivalist magazines. In turn, Steven was captivated by Snow, who survived today's boring and peaceful world with stories of his role in yesterday's wars. James had told Steven countless times the few stories of his stateside years in the National Guard. Now Snow was telling him fascinating stories about real war—mortars, helicopters, hand-to-hand combat, and all the emotions elicited by being shot at and shooting back. Snow had a flair for talking; he laid it on thick. For Steven, this was the real McCoy. A seasoned soldier, Snow was willing to try to satisfy Steven's endless questions with endless stories.

Snow taught Steven how to shoot his new M-1. Snow showed Steven how to set his sight, plant his legs, fix his elbow, take a slight breath, and then gently squeeze off a shot. Steven was good, according to Snow. Once Snow saw Steven, his lefty sharpshooter, skip a can across a pond with a rapid succession of shots.

Snow allowed Steven to use his isolated ranch as a practice range. Often he would return to his ranch to see Steven dressed in full military gear, with a helmet on his head and a knapsack on his back. Steven would be running, throwing himself on the ground, firing a few shots, and then repeating and varying this pattern. Snow told himself he had made another good soldier— a man out of a boy. When Steven left for Minnesota in the late spring, he did not bother to say goodbye to Snow—nor did he ever write to him.

James could not disregard this transformation of his son. Since getting his M-1, Steven had had his right arm tattooed with a pair of crossed battleaxes, Sylvester the Cat, his first name, and the Special Forces insignia; Steven's left arm had his Social Security number (which the Army now uses for soldiers' ID tags).

James expressed concern about Steven and his infatuation with guns to Brenda Enlow, whom James dated regularly. Enlow stated in a BCA interview that James told her, "It really bothers me that Stevie is so intense about guns." James—who had signed for the M-1—tried, as Enlow quoted him, "to talk Steve out of buying the gun."

James told Enlow that Steven was plotting to get even with his mother and her boyfriend. James said Steven was "buttering up to his mother and her boyfriend so he could get back at her for the divorce." Enlow suggested that Steven blamed his mom for the fire on the farm. Steven—who, in all the time Enlow had known him, had spoken only a handful of words—once told her, when she tried to talk him into staying in Texas rather than returning to Minnesota, "I've got things I have to do."

Most adults in Texas sensed that Steven was dangerous. Ted Beard's sister-in-law Joyce—who dated James—fought with him because she believed Steven's obsession with weapons was corrupting her own son, who was becoming interested in shooting. More than anyone else, James himself knew how dangerous Steven was. When Enlow told him, "Steve's going to get in trouble," James replied, "I know, but there's not a damn thing I can do about it."

James did all he could to please Steven, but apparently Steven had enrolled himself in his own imaginary army. He did pretty much what he felt like doing. Steven, who appeared at times to be James's shadow—chameleon-like in the way he fit in when his father was around—had his own angry mission. It was not to start anew on a farm; it was something quite different. Even when they were together, father and son were apart.

One last Texas witness, Debra Placker—whom Steven had dated, against his father's wishes—described the angry Steven who returned to Minnesota. Placker, whom Steven met at the Kountry Korner Restaurant in Brownwood where James and Steven ate more often than anywhere else, testified that Steven constantly talked about weapons. On one date, he attempted to teach Placker how to shoot a .22-caliber rifle.

According to Placker—in what, retrospectively, seems to have been anything but a random act of sympathetic identity—Steven offered to kill the meddlesome mother of a runaway girl who lived with Placker. Steven, according to Placker, devised a plan to get even with the girl's mother. He made a bomb out of a golf ball and filled it with bleach. He intended to drop the golf ball into the gas tank of the woman's car. The bleach would have mixed with the gasoline and exploded. Steven, Placker indicated, had already made two of these bombs. Steven also confided to Placker that his own mother had been killed by two unnamed Minnesota businessmen (Taveirne and Blythe?). They had wrecked his life, and he was "going back to Minnesota to bomb them."

BACK TO MINNESOTA

ON THE SURFACE, there was a profound difference between the attitudes of Steven and James upon their return to Minnesota. Steven was angrier than ever. By contrast, James appeared, at least to some, to be buoyant with optimism when he left Texas.

According to Brownwood School secretary Peggy Dobbins, James was confident he had enough money to start a farm. She heard James—whom she normally found to be reticent—say enthusiastically when leaving: "Some people walk around with hundreds of dollars in their pocket; I'm walking around with thousands." At least in his best moments, James must have told himself he would reestablish himself on the land, that all he had lost would be restored.

James soon discovered, however, that he had not returned to Eden, the garden of promise. Steven had not changed; weapons were still his singular obsession. Thousands of dollars were, in truth, only hundreds when measured against the money needed to reestablish himself on a farm. James found himself having to live at his parents' home and having to seek out other jobs. James did not discover a new world. Indeed, he had returned to the old world.

In his grand jury testimony, Steven estimated that his father had gone to six places, one of which was as far away as Wisconsin, before he finally found a place to rent near Hardwick, Minnesota. For $250 a month, he got a twenty-acre farm with a small, two-story, old farm house and a few buildings. The farm house was in good condition but was unfurnished. James and Steven had a table and a few chairs. They slept on air mattresses.

Characteristically, James secured his machinery first. He got his old flatbed truck out of storage at his father's place. Then, in order to start his operation, he bought an old tractor, a grinder-mixer, and a baler. As he repaired and put his machinery in place, James still caught glimpses of the good life. But whatever his dreams were, he lacked credit to buy animals and feed.

In his grand jury testimony, Steven recalled his father's unsuccessful bids for credit. At the end of August, he tried "five or six times" to secure a loan from the Production Credit Association in Pipestone. Then he tried to obtain credit from the First National Bank of Pipestone, the First Bank Pipestone, the Edgerton State Bank, the Hardwick Bank, and the Thorp Loan and Thrift Company of Worthington. Sometimes, Steven would go inside, staying off to one side; more often, he would wait in the truck while his father made another unsuccessful bid for money. When asking for credit, James was as ingratiating as he could be. Later, in the truck—having been turned down—he and Steven would rage together against a world that treated them so badly.

Three weeks before the killings, James went to see Louis Tavierne at his landfill. James told Louis he was going to kill Blythe. James openly spoke about Blythe's sleeping with Darlene.

James and Steven found it easier to blame the world than to read the numbers. No matter how he fudged the figures, James could not make a case with anyone—especially not with bankers, who were by now quite wary about farm loans in general. In one confidential financial statement for an agricultural loan, James listed as assets: cash, $1,400; savings, $350; retirement, $680; stocks and bonds $1,130; and—obviously an exaggerated estimate—machinery worth $13,150; for a total of $16,710. He listed those assets against $2,000 still owed for his pickup and $250 a month for rent for his twenty-acre place at Hardwick. Beyond this, James—a forty-six-year-old man who so often thought he was a hot shot—had nothing to write except the lie: "dairy-farmed whole life."

For First Bank Pipestone, there were many reasons to reject James's application. In addition to checking "insufficient credit references," "unable to verify income," "too short a period of residence," and "no credit file"; the bank could also have checked on their form "temporary or irregular employment," "insufficient income," "inadequate collateral," "temporary resident," "delinquent credit obligations," "garnishment foreclosure repossession or suit," and possibly a few others. There was no banker, not even one as generous as Blythe had been several years before, who was going to lend James Jenkins money. It was inevitable that James would receive a string of rejection letters like the one from First Bank Pipestone:

Dear Jim:

We deny your request for $3,000.00 to purchase feed for leased milk cows. The reason for the denial is that we have no record of your past farming experience nor are we interested in making a loan to purchase feed covered by machinery as collateral. If you have any questions regarding this matter please contact me at the bank. Thank you for considering First Bank Pipestone.

Sincerely,

MARK MOSBRUCKER
Ass't Vice President

Refusal by banks and lending agencies drove James to seek credit from the cattle sellers themselves. They too denied him.

On September 28, 1983, the last hope—which in truth had never been much of a hope at all—vanished. No doubt James and Steven waited all week at Nina and Clayton's home for a call from cattle jockey Daryl Mammenga, who was located near Long Prairie and Little Falls. (James and Steven had no telephone of their own at the Hardwick place.) Finally, having run out of patience, they went to Pipestone to use a phone booth to call Mammenga. Mammenga told them no. He said he based his answer on a credit reference supplied to him by the Buffalo Ridge State Bank, which James said he never used on his credit application to Mammenga.

Asked by the grand jury whether his father connected Rudolph Blythe with the Buffalo Ridge State Bank, Steven replied: "Well, he said that he [Blythe] was the one that was behind him [Mammenga] turning it down." (In the October 2 police interview, Mammenga confirmed that he had spoken to Blythe twice—and he was afraid a guy like Jenkins "might just go door to door and shoot the whole works.")

According to Steven, James drew one conclusion: "[it] was because of the bankruptcy and the Ruthton bank turning the loans down." It seemed to James that one thing—credit—stood in his way, and credit meant Rudolph Blythe, the Ruthton banker. From James's point of view, it was Blythe who had destroyed his dream of returning to the land. Now his and Steven's desire for revenge was more alive than ever.

Since his return from Texas, Steven had continued training himself to run and shoot. While staying with Darlene and Louis for a short period, Steven spent most of the time at his grandparents'. There he climbed ropes, ran, experimented with pipe bombs, and constantly practiced shooting.

At the end of July, Steven had James purchase for him a used 12-gauge Weston, a riot-type shotgun that was commonly used in Vietnam. The salesman at Poor Borch's in Marshall, Wayne Shellenberg, remembered how Steven—who appeared so militant to him—had examined the gun a week before. Returning on July 29, Steven approached Shellenberg and asked to purchase the weapon. When Shellenberg asked for identification, Steven called James over, and James purchased the gun. Shellenberg had no doubt that James, who would be killed by this gun, had purchased it—yet another gun—for Steven.

Steven kept to himself most of the time. Occasionly he got together with his friend Steven Shriver. Shriver, who saw Steven once a week at the most, recalled that they camped together for two days at a nearby river-valley state park, Camden Park. They left Louis's in the afternoon and spent their first night near the swimming pool. The second day they hiked ten miles or so from Camden to nearby Russell, where they ate lunch. While Shriver said, "Steven made the first shot count," he did mention that Steven fired at a deer at 250 yards and missed.

The intensity of Steven's anger was only thinly disguised. He told his mother some Mexicans from Texas had shot up his car and, according to Shriver, "Steven almost came to believe the story himself." He proposed to his grandfather that on the way by Ruthton they should stop off and shoot Blythe.

James and Steven fed on each other's anger. His father's failure to get credit stimulated Steven's anger, which became even more open and direct.

In the middle of September, Steven had three practice hand grenades welded shut. On September 24, according to Steven's own testimony to the grand jury, he had a conversation with Richard Hartson, owner of D & M Glass in Pipestone, about

Rudolph Blythe and what kind of projectiles might penetrate bulletproof glass—the kind banks have.

We were talking about there was an incident with the bank foreclosing on some farm where a bull got shot. . . . While we were talking about this, he [Hartson] was cutting a piece of glass. . . . He would start it on fire along where he cut, and I asked him why he was doing that, and there's a piece of plastic in between the layers, the layers of glass, and it's tough plastic. You'd have to burn it to cut the tough plastic. You'd have to burn it to cut the glass. And we just got to talking about that, and I asked him if that was what they used for bulletproof glass . . . and he said yes. And he said about his nephew before he died that he had taken an inch, built up an inch of glass like that and taken and shot it with a 30.06, and the bullet had gone halfway through it, and that was about it. Oh, we talked about the banker, too: Rudy Blythe. Richard said that he was foreclosing on three other farms in that area.

Four days later, on September 28—the day before the crime and the day during which James received Mammenga's denial—Steven had a discussion with Marvin Minett at his friend Shriver's farm. Steven asked Minett how to obtain dynamite and how to "construct a fertilizer bomb."

Steven's anger and his father's had converged. Together they would pursue the banker who stood in their way. Louis Taverne was also a likely target.

According to Steven, after Mammenga's refusal, James took Steven back to the farm at Hardwick and returned around 4:00 P.M. to tell Steven they were going to meet with Rudolph Blythe. Steven gave the grand jury the following description of the conversation about his father's plan: "He just said that he called the bank; he made an appointment to go out to look at the place at 10:00 the next day. . . . He said that he had given them a false name [Ron Anderson]; he was going to meet them out there."

Steven said there was no plan. "The only thing he told me," Steven continued during his testimony, "is that we were going to go there and rob him and scare him, scare the hell out of him."

After the phone call to Blythe and before going to supper, from approximately 4:00 to 7:00 P.M., James took Steven along to Pipestone to visit Vicki Nelsen. Vicki Nelsen was a divorcee whom James had dated in the past and with whom Darlene once worked at Bayliner Boat Company. When asked why they went there, Steven replied, "[My father] just wanted to see her."

No doubt, following his well-established habit, James had to talk to a woman about his situation one last time. This was the second time they had visited Nelson since being back. According to Steven, during the two to three hours they spent together, they did not discuss their plan, nor did they reveal anything else about the following day. James told Vicki his wife was having an affair with attorney DeRycke and "another guy who ran the landfill in Pipestone County." James also talked about bank foreclosures and a banker who was shady, claiming he never got credit for the cattle he sold off. In a phone interview, Vicki Nelsen added that James and Steven told her that the next day they were going up north to buy cattle.

That evening James and Steven had their supper at the Mayfair Cafe, where they regularly ate their meals. They did not, according to Steven, discuss their plan for the next day. The owner of the restaurant remarked that their conversation was unusually animated. After eating, they bought several bags of groceries. Steven made a quick call to his only friend, Steven Shriver. Steven said he called Shriver "just to see if they got his pickup running." Steven claimed, as Shriver later verified to the BCA, that Steven said nothing about any plans nor did he say anything unusual. James and Steven returned home around 10:00 or 10:30 P.M. It was raining. A few groceries, which were to nourish them later during their flight, spilled in the truck.

According to Steven, he and his father discussed nothing before going to bed. To the prosecutor's query before the grand jury, "What did you do after you woke?", Steven replied, "Just . . . turned the TV on for a little bit." To the question, "What caused you to leave the house?", Steven answered "My dad told me we were going." If Steven were to be believed, this was an unplanned crime as far as he was concerned: he only did what his father ordered—no more, no less.

Evidence gathered from their farm confirms that whatever plan Steven or his father had did not involve immediate flight. The household was filled with signs that indicated the crime was not planned at all rationally. The plan called for a return to their place. They left behind the food they had purchased the night before. They also left behind other useful things, such as James's flashlight, which he needed to see at night. Moreover, they did not destroy incriminating evidence, such as Steven's books and drawings on how to make weapons. In addition, they left behind another gun and Rudolph Blythe's Texas phone number. (For a time in 1982, Blythe had tried to sell his bank in Ruthton; during that time, he and his family had moved to Texas.)

James's and Steven's possession of Blythe's Texas phone number indicates that far more than spontaneity underlay the plan. It supports—as does the single bath towel they took to the scene of the crime—the conjecture that their intention was kidnapping.

Also showing the haste in which they left was the fact that the living room space heater was left on. Additionally, they left out jelly and bread, a bottle of orange pop, and a glass of orange pop, half drunk. They never ate well.

"I FIXED RUDY"

ON THE WAY to the Ruthton farm site, according to Steven, there was no conversation. "He didn't say anything [about] what was going to take place." To summarize his line of questioning, the prosecutor asked, "There had been no additional discussion between you and your father about the plan . . . from the time he first mentioned it on the afternoon of September 28 until the time you arrived at the farm sometime about 8:00 A.M. . . . September 29, 1983?" Steven answered, "No."

While Steven and James were changing their Minnesota license plates for Texas plates, they were surprised by the early arrival of Blythe and Thulin. Blythe did not come alone; he brought his first loan officer, Deems Thulin. Blythe had come at least an hour earlier than Steven and James had expected him.

As the banker's car made its way up the long driveway toward the farm house, James and Steven scattered. According to Steven, James grabbed the M-1 from the hood where Steven had placed the weapons and ran off. Steven had no idea where James went. Steven took the shotgun and ran behind the garage. He claimed he stayed there, crouching down, until the shooting was over.

Steven claimed he faced west during the entire time. He saw nothing and was only able to hear indistinct snatches of conversation and the occasional call. "Who is there?" Steven did admit he heard a person moving along the west side of the garage. He also acknowledged that he heard another car arrive, followed by "just more conversation and then somebody said something about going to get the police."

"Were you able to tell," prosecuter Thomas Fabel asked, "whether the person who came in the second car was a man or a woman?" Steven answered, "No."

No sooner had the newly arrived car departed—"it was just a little ways down the road," Steven testified—when shots rang out. Just before or after the shots were fired back by the granary, Steven said someone yelled, "He's got a gun!" Then Steven claimed that, just as he was getting ready to come out—after only "a few seconds had passed"—he heard a second volley of shots in front of the house.

When he emerged from behind the garage, Steven said he saw nothing at first but the empty yard, his father's pickup, and a station wagon; then he saw a body protruding from the station wagon. "Yeah," Steven commented, "he was laying with his feet in and his head out." "Then," Steven continued, "my dad came around the corner of the house, and he hollered for me to get in and start driving."

Steven said that he did drive for a while. Again, according to Steven, there was no conversation. When he finally asked his father what had happened, his father just replied, "I fixed Rudy."

Steven was not clear about which roads they had followed. The prosecution did not ask him to explain, and Steven did not say what happened during the approximately two-hour period from the time of the killings until Steven's and James's reappearance in Luverne, Minnesota. (Luverne is only forty miles away from Ruthton—at most an hour-and-fifteen-minute drive by back roads. James and Steven did not return to Hardwick.)

Steven said he stopped driving after four or five miles, because he couldn't keep the pickup on the road. He added that he dissuaded his father from going after Louis Taveirne because they would have to cross a major highway to hunt him down. (Louis was at a dealer's wholesale car auction south of the Twin Cities that day.)

Steven testified further that they arrived in Luverne, where they purchased more shells at Harvey's Gun and Trading Post and a flashlight at Schutz's OK Hardware Store. Just outside Luverne, they evaded a deputy who had begun to follow them by quickly pulling off on a gravel road and stopping. Then, Steven admitted, he jumped out and fired several shots "at the tires" of the deputy's vehicle until his M-1 jammed. (The deputy, not fully armed and fearing another trap beyond the first knoll of the gravel road, gave up the pursuit.)

Steven and James drove from Luverne twenty-five miles west to the the South Dakota border. In South Dakota, they stopped to change license plates. From there they went south to Texas, traveling by night and sleeping by day.

They were without money. The only food they had with them was "three cans of beans and two cans of sliced pineapple" that had spilled in the pickup after the previous night's shopping. They were hungry; they had no money; they were on the run.

Steven claims he persuaded his father not to commit a number of holdups on their way south. They were returning to Texas, but they had no good reason to go there—nor anywhere else for that matter.

On an abandoned farm a few miles north of Paducah, Texas, James and Steven reached the end of the road. According to Steven, he wanted to turn himself in; but his father said he would rather commit suicide than turn himself in. Then, Steven said, his father helped him push their pickup out of the sand. According to Steven, his father was alive when he left.

"I WISH THINGS COULD BE DIFFERENT"

ON THE BACK of his Minnesota fishing license, Steven wrote the following note, which he asked the police to deliver to his mother:

I love you Mom. Tell Grandma and Grandpa and Mickey that I love them.

I am sorry that this happened. Please forgive me and Daddy.

I love all of you for being there and helping when I needed it. I wish things could be different. If I could change what happened I would. I wish I could be with you.

I love you
STEVE

Steven told the police to tell Louis that Steven and his dad had put ball bearings in the oil of Louis's Caterpillar, which would have destroyed its gears. Steven was quoted as saying he didn't want to cause any more damage.

Steven's grandparents suffered the shame of what their only son and only grandson had done. Michele suffered the shame and the disintegration of her family; her hatred of her father became even more intense. But it was Darlene who perhaps suffered most. James and Steven were her men. Even if she could not have done anything, people would ask and she couldn't help wonder what she, and she alone, might have done differently.

Darlene knew all along that no good would come to Steven as long as he was with his father. She feared how much James could get Steven worked up. On more than one occasion immediately after the crime, she told someone how James could cause Steven to do anything.

Darlene knew James screwed up everything he touched and that he was no good for the children. In her October 4 statement, she responded to a question about possible abuse of the children. "He never, he never really physically abused them, but mentally he did a real number on them." "Mind games?" she was asked. "Yeah," she replied.

One of the games James played, according to Darlene, was to make Steven care for him. Darlene speculated: "Stevie felt that his dad was alone. Maybe he tried to be everything to him, maybe he tried to give him—he knew his dad was weak, he had to know that—the support that nobody else would."

Darlene recognized that she could not keep them apart. Steven kept going to his father. They were magnets constantly attracted to each other.

When BCA officer Dennis A. Sigafoos asked how Steven's Volkswagen had gotten bullet holes in it, Darlene immediately named James as the source of the problem. "Well, as far as I can figure out, his dad as usual got him into some big mess down there . . . with some dope thing. I really don't know what all was involved, but anyway, I came home one night and Stevie was just in a frantic state. . . . He said that somebody shot him. . . . I said, 'what do you mean somebody shot at you, nobody shoots at anybody.' "

Darlene did not doubt Steven's story that someone had shot at him as he drove to his grandparents' or that the shooters may have been "some Mexicans or something [sic] down there, down in Texas." She didn't doubt that he was grazed by a bullet, nor did she challenge his refusal to go to the sheriff because he was afraid.

Darlene did, however, doubt Steven's farfetched story that James was dating some kind of secret service woman who kept a tape recorder in her bra.

Regardless of what Darlene believed of Steven's stories, she knew James was bad for Steven and that Steven had a dangerous attachment to weapons. She also knew the fear she and Louis had felt for their lives—especially for Louis's life—after Blythe and Thulin had been killed.

When asked by Officer Sigafoos whether Steven had ever expressed any dislike of Rudolph Blythe, she replied, "No. He, he's . . . tried to keep him away from his dad, because I knew his dad was hammering on him about things; his dad was sick."

She explained that James was "mentally sick. Mentally sick, and he worked on Stevie so that I think that he twisted his mind and I know Stevie needs to go to a psychiatrist. And I hope to God he can get . . ." Her voice trailed off.

Darlene told Sigafoos she never paid attention to guns—"never cared that much for guns." She never took much interest in Steven's guns "to even know really what he does have." "Except," she interrupted Sigafoos to continue, "that he had one gun that was"—she continued, her voice breaking—"I said, 'My God, Stevie, where did you get that awful thing' . . . that big thing with the strap on it."

However, in her interview with Sigafoos, Darlene resisted the idea that any inference could be drawn from the fact that Steven practiced shooting at human-like targets. Darlene admitted that James made Steven crazy, that Steven had weapons, that James got Steven in one mess after another—all that she conceded; but she refused to acknowledge that Steven was prepared to kill or that he might be the killer.

Darlene struggled against the idea that enough hatred was pent up in her son for him to kill. She could accept the idea that she had left James, that she had not kept Steven and James apart, that James had driven Steven crazy. But she could not acknowledge publicly the final tragedy: James, who had destroyed so much of her life, had in the end led their only son to murder.

The law, however, was not interested in the tragedy Darlene suffered. The law's interest was different. The law was concerned with the murder of two innocent men. Steven would stand trial.

There was evidence to show that Steven was the killer. He could run and shoot; his father could not. The murder weapon was his; he had practiced shooting continually since he purchased it in Texas. James, on the contrary, hadn't shot for years.

Furthermore, Steven had not told a story that would placate the law. Three of four men were dead—and he, the sole survivor, did not tell the grand jury a story worthy of the deaths of two men and his father.

Steven's failure to convince the grand jury of the truth of his story denied what compassion the law and the jurors might have extended to an eighteen-year-old boy caught in the terrible circumstances in which Steven found himself. Given his weak story, plentiful circumstantial evidence of his guilt, and the requirement of the law to serve injured innocence, on October 28, 1983, the grand jury charged Steven Todd Jenkins with the murders of Rudolph Blythe and Deems Thulin.

THE FARM HOUSE where the Jenkinses once lived and the murders occurred is aproximately five miles south of Tyler and two and a half miles south of Ruthton, Minnesota. Courtesy of the *Worthington Daily Globe*.

THE BODY of banker Rudolph Blythe in the ditch where he was slain on the morning of September 29, 1983. Courtesy of the *Marshall Independent*.

A LOCAL TEXAS LAW OFFICER stands near the spot where father and son spent their last day together in the vicinity of Paducah, Texas. Courtesy of the Minnesota Bureau of Criminal Apprehension.

THE SHADY SPOT at the old foundation in rural Texas where James and Steven had their last meal. Courtesy of the Minnesota Bureau of Criminal Apprehension.

AERIAL OVERVIEW of the Jenkinses' farm site, ch shows Blythe's car, the farm house and garage, ell as the grove and other farm buildings. Cour- of the Minnesota Bureau of Criminal Apprehen-

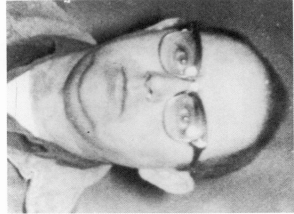

THIS DRIVER'S LICENSE PHOTO of James Jenkins was sent across the country in the aftermath of the shootings. Courtesy of the Minnesota Bureau of Criminal Apprehension.

STEVEN JENKINS, accompanied by two Lincoln County deputies, is returned to Minnesota from Texas where he surrendered. Courtesy of the *Marshall Independent.*

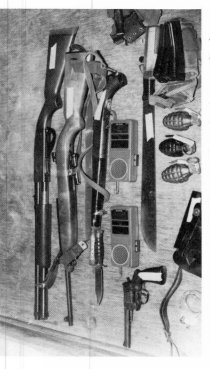

THESE WEAPONS were found in Steven's pickup when he surrendered to police in Paducah, Texas.

STEVEN ARRIVES at the Ivanhoe County Court for the opening day of his trial, April 10, 1984. Courtesy of the *Marshall Independent*.

SWEN ANDERSON, Steven Jenkins's attorney, is followed out of the courthouse by Steven, his mother, and his sister Michelle. Courtesy of the *Marshall Independent*.

STEVEN AND HIS MOTHER Darlene during a court recess. Courtesy of the *Worthington Daily Globe*.

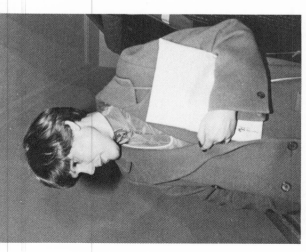

SUSAN BLYTHE, widow of slain banker Rudolph Blythe, leaves the courtroom having just given her lengthy testimony on April 17, 1984. Courtesy of the *Marshall Independent.*

TOM FABEL, prosecuting attorney, leaves the courthouse. Courtesy of the *Marshall Independent.*

CHAPTER FOUR

The Defense

The defense of a man involves only a little
common sense and a good story.

—S. KEVIN

It is a foolish thing to make a long prologue,
and to be short in the story itself.

—2 Maccabees 2:32

THE grand jury's indictment of Steven made the main lines of the prosecution's case predictable. In the death of Rudolph Blythe, the prosecution would first seek to convict Steven of the most serious crime possible in the state of Minnesota: premeditated murder. If not successful in that, the prosecution would seek to convict Steven of a first-degree felony murder (which in this case was a killing that occurred during the course of an armed robbery). If not successful in that, the prosecution would seek a charge of second-degree murder in the case of Rudolph Blythe, to match the charge of second-degree murder it sought in the case of Deems Thulin. (Second-degree murder in Minnesota presumes intentional but not premeditated murder.) As a last option, the prosecution would seek to convict Steven on two charges of conspiracy leading to the deaths of Blythe and Thulin.

Steven had virtually confessed to the two charges of conspiracy—counts five and six—by his admission that he went with his father "to rob and scare" Rudolph Blythe, that he had supplied the murder weapon and other weapons for the crime, and that he himself had taken the weapons and set them on the hood of the truck prior to the arrival of the bankers. If the prosecution were to succeed in convicting Steven of counts two and three ("intentionally causing the death of Blythe while committing or attempting to commit the offense of aggravated robbery"), it would have to show that Steven had been the shooter. This would require a successful orchestration of a range of strong circumstantial evidence, while at the same time discrediting significant portions of Steven's testimony as incomplete, contradictory, and false. The pivotal matter in discrediting Steven's testimony and in giving order to the evidence was demonstrating, or strongly suggesting, that the father could not have done the shooting and that Steven—who by all evidence was capable of doing the shooting—did in fact do so.

Convicting Steven of count one of the murder ("of willfully, wrongfully, intentionally and with premeditation causing the death of Blythe") would be difficult. The prosecution would have to establish premeditation in a crime that was manifestly confused in its planning, motives, and execution, was spontaneous in its unfolding (the banker's car arrived early by surprise and first James and Steven ran and hid), and in which one of the two men killed was absolutely unknown to the father and son.

The prosecution, with good reason, would seek to establish that the premeditation occurred at the scene of the crime itself by stressing that Blythe (the object of the Jenkinses' anger) was killed after Thulin was and that he was chased for over one hundred yards and shot in the back. The prosecution would have to convince the jury that the killing of Blythe arose not merely out of the situation but had its source instead in a wrongful, intentional, and premeditated will. Given the age of the defendant, the absence of eye witnesses, and the amount of effort the prosecution would have to expend in identifying Steven as the shooter, the prosecution could not have reasonably expected success in securing a conviction on the first count of murder.

As the prosecution's case seemed predictable from the outset, so the defense's case seemed predictable at least in its main lines. Searches and interviews by the Bureau of Criminal Apprehension had already established that Steven was a good shot, that he was the owner of the murder weapon, and that he had a violent streak. In addition, the grand jury, whose indictment might be considered a reasonable indicator, was not moved to leniency by Steven's age nor by the fact that he had turned himself in. Nor did the grand jury soften its judgment because Steven's father once threatened to kill Steven.

Steven had responded to a juror by saying his father had not threatened him in Texas when Steven planned to turn himself in. Steven explained his father had made this statement a few years earlier:

He said he was going to sell his car and all the tools and everything and just leave the country. And I asked him what he was going to do, you know, how he was going to make a living and all, and he said he didn't care what happened anymore. And he said about since Mom left him and all and the divorce, and losing the farm, that he didn't have much to live for anyway. And he—he said about that he just as well take me with him.

The grand jury was also not deterred from its findings by Steven's statements about how he dissuaded his father from killing Louis Taveirne immediately after killing Rudolph Blythe and Deems Thulin. Nor were they dissuaded by Steven's testimony that, while en route to Texas, he discouraged his father from committing several holdups of gas stations. (Steven testified that his father proposed "over twenty or so" holdups.) Furthermore, the grand jury was not swayed by Steven's statement that he refused, in spite of his father's anger, to continue their efforts to escape.

Steven's statements to the police, his testimony to the grand jury, the prosecution's evidence, and the findings of the grand jury, all pointed in the direction of a plea-bargained agreement. This seemed logical for three reasons. First, unless Steven pled guilty, he might be convicted of first-degree murder and spend a good portion of his life in jail. Also, unless Steven entirely changed his story of the crime itself—and it was probably already too late—and admitted he was the murderer but that he went beserk (he thought they were going to hurt his dad, or once he started shooting he simply couldn't control himself), there was a chance he would be found guilty of first-degree murder.

Second, an entirely different set of factors pushed the defense's case toward resolution through plea bargaining. There were mitigating factors that—while holding little strength in the courtroom—could, if adroitly used, prove to be powerful at the bargaining table. There was Steven's age: he had turned eighteen only a few months before the crime. Steven came from a bad family situation. He had been virtually homeless for the two years preceding the crime. For many years, he lacked adult direction. His father, to whom he was profoundly attached, was a bad influence. James had an especially bad temper and was unstable.

Third, factors of a different nature encouraged the prosecutor's interest in plea bargaining: the trial would prove to be expensive. Even with considerable free aid from the state district attorney's office, which furnished a prosecutor and the services of the Bureau of Criminal Apprehension, the trial placed a considerable expense on county taxpayers. Ivanhoe, where the trial was scheduled to occur, is two hundred miles from St. Paul, where the attorney general's office is located, and eight hundred miles from Texas, from which a number of witnesses would have to be brought. The expense of the trial might also have encouraged the defense to plea bargain. The trial, so dependent on varied and diverse circumstantial evidence, would involve many witnesses, experts, and considerable investigation. The Bureau had already invested a large effort in gathering evidence, carrying out interviews, and reconstructing the crime; it would take a considerable effort to refute their story and to create one for the defense. Yet all the reasons that pointed in the direction of a plea-bargained case and made plea bargaining seem almost inevitable didn't count after local attorney Allan Swen Anderson became Steven's defense counsel.

Soon after Steven was returned to Minnesota, Swen Anderson proposed to Darlene and Louis, for whom he had once worked, that he would take the case for $10,000 up front. They declined. The following day he returned and said he would take the case for free. They accepted, believing he would do a better job than the appointed public defender.

SWEN ANDERSON

SWEN ANDERSON was the region's most controversial attorney. Born to Swedish parents in the southwestern Minnesota town of

St. James in 1936, Swen didn't start speaking English until he was seven. As a boy he suffered from a severe case of rheumatic fever. He was bedridden with it for two years and as a result of it was left with a weak heart. He didn't graduate from high school until he was twenty.

After attending the University of Minnesota, Anderson worked his way through William Mitchell Law School in St. Paul, graduating *cum laude* in 1965. In the same year, he started his law career as an attorney in Granite Falls, Minnesota, a town of 3,500 located in Yellow Medicine County, forty-five miles northeast of Ivanhoe.

In addition to his private practice, Anderson served as county attorney for twelve years, boasting a "98 percent conviction record." He was not reelected in 1978. He then turned his skills to being a defense attorney. By the time of his death, February 2, 1986, he had become southwestern Minnesota's best-known defense attorney.

By all measures of dress, appearance, speech and manners, Anderson was one of a kind. He was a big man with a large face. He walked and stood as if he were off balance. His head, face, and shoulders were in constant motion, as court artists were heard to complain during the trial. He often—some would say always—talked loudly, very loudly. On occasion he was profane, seeming to be as profane as a man could get.

He had a powerful voice. It boomed and echoed through courthouses, restaurants, bookstores—wherever he was. Words like "fuck" and "cocksucker" sprinkled his often-shouted conversations. Whether women were present or not, Swen wasn't detoured or inhibited. One Marshall merchant believed Swen always increased the volume of his voice and the amount of his profanity when the merchant's female worker appeared. Swen's uninterrupted and often profane monologues embarrassed fellow professionals; more than one person told of groups of men being driven away from him when he started swearing. A fellow lawyer said his profanity was not altogether uncalculated. In fact, it was used directly in relation to its ability to shock: Swen saved his worst words for those most likely to be offended. In any case, Swen was noticed. Wherever he went, he was seen and heard.

Swen was—and in some measure knew himself to be and

enjoyed being—a man of extreme contradictions. He was basic; he was religious; he was earthy; he was flawed. Swen was self-indulgent. He dropped in on friends and fellow professionals whenever he felt like it. More than one of Swen's colleagues pointed out the chair in his office in which Swen sat or the couch on which he slept. "My door to him was always open," said his close friend LuVern Hansen, who remembered Swen Anderson since the day Swen had first unloaded his goods in Granite Falls. More than one of his clients mentioned that Swen's stop at the client's home coincided with the regular 6:00 P.M. meal. A client's case no doubt merited a free supper for the voracious Swen. Swen often dressed in the same, worn clothes day in and day out, and often his body odors were noticeably strong.

He was often self-righteous and—more than a few would add—arrogant. When he was a prosecutor, he was confident that right was on his side; when defending—which he did later in his career—he claimed to represent a surprisingly high number of innocent victims.

Swen was vain. "Swen was not after money, but he wanted notoriety," remarked his friend LuVern Hansen, a father of twelve and a keen observer of human nature (who, by his own account, reads nothing but Louis L'Amour westerns). Swen Anderson was, Hanson explained, an insecure man who needed friends and attention. In law school, he sat in the hall with his legs spread out so other students had to step over him, a fellow student remarked. While he was quick to criticize "the establishment," Swen wanted and cherished its recognition. He made additions to his credentials known to his fellow lawyers and others as quickly as they came.

For Hansen, much of Swen's insecurity could be traced back to the two years when, as a teenager, he had been confined to bed with a severe case of rheumatic fever. It was then that he read so much, fought so much with his mother, lost step with students his own age, and thus in some sense became a maverick.

Swen Anderson was not without virtues. Many praised him. For Hansen, Anderson had a multifaceted personality. He had, Hansen said, "tremendous capacities" and "near perfect recall." Swen was "a deep-feeling person whose very crudity was a mirror off which he could repel the world." He was a generous man, with his time, if not with his money, Hansen noted.

On that point, many joined Hansen in praising Swen Anderson, saying his office was open to the poor. He took—often quickly and energetically—cases few other attorneys would even listen to. (No one said he wasn't interested in making a dollar.) Swen was always willing to attack "the establishment." More than one of his clients said, "I chose him as my attorney because he has enough 'guts and teeth' to win."

Fellow attorneys said under their breath, however, "Steer clear of him. He's trouble." They also feared and respected him. They knew he was clever and dangerous in the courtroom, yet none said he didn't keep his word.

In his private life, contradictions also abounded. Anderson married Elizabeth Christianson, an Augsburg College graduate in sociology and biology. He was the proud father of five children: Clifford, Knute, Kris, Karl, and Naomi. Four of the children were still at home at the time of the trial; the oldest, Clifford, was on duty in the Air Force. In many ways, Swen was dependent upon Elizabeth who, bright and articulate, kept his books and edited and typed many of his legal briefs. She ran their home despite Swen's irregular hours and his tendency, as well as perhaps her own, to spend more than they had.

The Andersons lived in a moderately sized home on a small lot in the west end of Granite Falls. Swen's household, however, was not—as it is for many professionals—a quiet sanctuary that sheltered him from the world. His office, which revealed his interest in hunting and fishing and the outdoors, was filled with oak and was usually in order; his home was less orderly. His furniture was worn and tattered; his house and garage were crammed with things. Dogs were always part of the household. At one period, until neighbors stopped it, his house was filled with hunting dogs and emitted a considerable stench. For another period, a monkey had the run of his house. High weeds often covered his lawn.

Swen Anderson would often leave home early in the morning—7:00 A.M. or so—catch a good-sized breakfast of eggs, toast, and meat, and then make his swing down through Marshall, over to Ivanhoe, and around. If he stopped along the way to eat or visit—which he might—he wouldn't return home until midnight or one in the morning. One place where Anderson frequently stopped—sometimes as often as three and four times a week—was the home of his best friend, Kermit Ness. Swen Anderson had known Kermit for twelve years, and the Ness home had become his "watering hole" as much as any other place.

Kermit Ness was a retired Granite Falls secondary English teacher who, after college, started to farm. (His family farm had been opened up by Ness's ancestors in the 1860s. They were among the original river valley settlers of the region.) Kermit got to know and came to cherish Swen Anderson as the vain and kind, profane and holy, simply contradictory man Swen Anderson was. For Kermit, Swen was a kind of Christ-figure.

It was not uncommon for Kermit to receive a call from Swen at 7:00 A.M.: "Kermit, I am coming out for breakfast, and I would like two eggs up, bacon, and sausage, and juice. I'll take orange juice if you have it." For the last five years, it was usual for Swen to appear at Kermit's as often as three nights a week and to stay late. Sometimes Kermit would return home to find Swen asleep on his davenport. On some occasions, Kermit might hint as many as four or five times before Swen left, and at other times, Kermit himself would simply leave. In the end, Swen came to pretty much have the run of Kermit and his wife Lynn's house. Although Lynn was eventually successful in talking Swen into taking off his muddy boots before coming in, she didn't succeed in protecting her furniture from him on every occasion—like the time he pounded the gun he was repairing down on her table.

Kermit Ness knew Swen Anderson's contradictions. He chuckled when his brother said Swen ate like the Hollywood actor "who in some famous film or other threw bones over his shoulder to his dogs." "It may just have happened that way at Swen's house," Kermit commented. He knew the picture Swen had taken of himself in the Twin Cities, which hung prominently in his office. Swen was dressed in a full Yankee Civil War officer's uniform with shiny buttons. Swen also sported a feathered hat and a sword. Swen identified with the Civil War. Both Kermit and his mother received framed certificates from Swen that certified that Swen Anderson was a recognized national trial lawyer.

When things got bad for Swen, he often called Kermit and told him, "Get your car out—your good one, the Cadillac." They would make the forty-mile drive around Lac Qui Parle, a large lake northwest of Granite Falls. As they drove, Swen talked to himself as much as to Kermit. The idea of "getting back to nature" meant something to Swen Anderson.

When Kermit was asked "What did you get in exchange for your friendship with Swen?" he replied: "Swen's friendship was his reciprocity." When Kermit was in the Marshall hospital with colon cancer that had metastasized, Swen was his constant companion and a source of hope. Thinking he was psychic, Swen Anderson told Kermit, "I see great things in your future." When Kermit was home again, Swen made Kermit go fishing. "I'll launch the boat," Swen good-naturedly encouraged Kermit.

One day, Anderson—who "wasn't one to joke or engage in horseplay with children"—gave Kermit and Lynn's son Chris an hour-long lecture on the history of the Colt .45. (Cowboy stuff was big with Swen. His favorite artist was Charlie Russell, 1864–1926, a cowboy artist and philosopher.) Another time, Swen arrived at seven on Christmas morning. He had with him a King James Bible, and for two hours he read to Chris all the Gospel accounts of the virgin birth, as well as Old Testament prophecy on Christ's birth.

Swen Anderson—a reformed alcoholic who could outcurse a trooper and who was in his own words "a maverick and a Brahma bull rider"—had a philosophical and religious side. Eric DeRycke said Swen was as well read as anyone he knew. According to DeRycke, "He read that medieval stuff like Nietzsche." In his later years, according to Kermit, Swen wanted to know about Hemingway and Melville; before his death, he was reading *Moby Dick*. (He wrote to his son Clifford, who was then in the service in England, that Ishmael escaped the whale because he renounced vengeance.)

Two weeks before his death, Swen lectured Kermit on religion. "Man was stuck with the Ten Commandments," Swen told Kermit, "but he never could keep them. . . .Luther was right," Swen concluded, "grace made all the difference."

Swen Anderson, Kermit said, was "a walking paradox: a libertarian at heart, a conservative fundamentalist to the bone." In Granite Falls, Swen broke with one church of the American

Lutheran Synod when its minister questioned the suitability of Anderson's home for an adopted child. Swen joined the town's other Lutheran church, a member of the Missouri Synod. In any case, Swen wasn't much of a church-goer. In Kermit's words, he was—maybe a bit like Kermit himself—"a fundamentalist who didn't go to church, couldn't stand the phoniness of it."

Swen Anderson's politics were much the same. He took the side of the underdog, yet he had no time for liberal preachments—except when they fit the interests of his cases. While he had a lot of empathy for the scattered remnants of the Dakota Indians who lived at the edge of Granite Falls along the Minnesota River, he chastised the liberal preachers of "affirmative action." He wouldn't be bullied by their official pieties about victims. At one meeting of lawyers, Swen loudly espoused the cause of the American Indian Movement; in the face of opposition, he joined his support to a proposed Indian assault upon Mt. Rushmore.

Swen's favorite president was Richard Nixon, whom he supported unreservedly throughout the Watergate ordeal—to the anger of fellow lawyers. According to attorney Eric De-Rycke, one judge appeared to be on the verge of starting a fight with Swen over his defense of Nixon.

Swen—and this as much as anything was what made him tick, according to Kermit—hated phonies and facades. He was no joiner, no Chamber-of-Commerce type; he was rather one who bucked the system. He rattled cages, twisted tails. "He was," Kermit's asserted, "the conscience of Granite Falls."

Swen Anderson was a big wave in a small pond. He utilized "big-city" methods in a small, rural town. He was quick to sue. For instance, Swen threatened to sue David Putnam, former owner-editor of the *Granite Falls Tribune* and client of Swen's, four times: once for someone who slipped on Putnam's sidewalk, once for the paper's omission of an auction bill, and twice for the paper's handling of a controversial case in which Anderson represented the rights of terminated hospital administrator Bruce Berg. (Berg claimed he could only be dismissed by the city for cause, since he was a veteran. While Berg failed to regain his position or to collect damages, he did continue to collect wages during the four-and-half-year trial and appeal procedure.)

Another of Anderson's favorite techniques was to call a

press conference, as he did in the Hubert case: "the case of the missing tooth and casket." In January of 1982, Anderson called a press conference to announce his intention of starting a fund to exhume the body of Joseph Bradley Hubert. Hubert might have been purposely killed in 1969—according to Anderson—rather than having been struck by a hit-and-run driver. Swen's announced intention was to help a mother, dying of emphysema, and the victim's brothers and sisters to finally know what had happened to him. Following his approach of making all possible arguments, Anderson also made the farfetched claim that a successful inquiry might rid the community of a dangerous killer. On the basis of the exhumation, which proved to be inconclusive about the cause of death, Swen compounded the drama by impugning the work of the local undertaker and by claiming that the cadaver—which had been sliced in two by the accident—was missing a tooth and had been buried in a wooden instead of a metal coffin. Anderson had to promptly offer his public apologies when additional research showed that the unfortunate boy had lost his tooth in a football game and that he was indeed buried properly in a wooden coffin (even though the coffin was called a Silver Austin).

In Swen Anderson's case, notoriety made for notoriety; courtroom work made for courtroom work. "One 'outlaw attorney' keeps another seven attorneys busy," according to the old saw. Many in the region who wanted or had to go to trial with unusual cases chose Swen Anderson. He had a nose for unusual cases. For instance, a young man in Marshall was charged with a particularly brutal killing of a child; Swen Anderson became his counsel.

Another young man who had Swen Anderson as his attorney was convicted of a drug charge and then claimed he had been used, while in police custody, to infiltrate and inform on other drug sellers. Seeming to ignore the young man's free choice and consultation with his attorney, Anderson argued that his client had been put in bondage, had suffered great harm, and had become readdicted to drugs as a consequence of police exploitation. (Anderson appealed this case to the federal district court, which eventually returned it to a state district court. There the case was declared to be frivolous; the court also ruled that the county should be reimbursed for its attorney fees.)

Another young man in Granite Falls was charged in December of 1984 with growing marijuana in his girlfriend's apartment. The young man and his girlfriend emerged from Anderson's office not only with legal counsel but married as well.

In August of 1985, Anderson solicited and received responsibility for the defense of a sixty-two-year-old Lake Wilson man who killed his wife and her ninety-two-year-old acquaintance. (Lake Wilson is only fifteen miles southeast of Ruthton.)

Anderson's best-known and most successful case, prior to that of Steven Jenkins, was that of Luella Thompson, who belongs to the folklore of the region. In November 1980, Luella Thompson, in her early sixties, was charged with the murder of her boyfriend, Raymond Petroff, to whom she had been engaged for three and a half years and with whom she was planning to adopt a child. The prosecution and its witnesses claimed that Luella Thompson burned down Petroff's barn, killed some of his animals, and burned down his new girlfriend's house.

Petroff feared Luella. He often said Luella would kill him. He would break out in a sweat when he spoke about her. One witness said he couldn't hold a cup of coffee when he talked about Luella, and he slept with his clothes on. Because of Luella, he carried a sidearm. Yet he went to Luella Thompson's house—in fact, he went twice—perhaps to recover his gun collection which Luella Thompson had. (She was an excellent shot and had hunted elk and buffalo in Wyoming with her first husband.)

Luella Thompson claimed (in some of the most vivid testimony in the regional court record) that Petroff wouldn't leave and that he demanded she give him oral sex, chased her upstairs, fought her into submission, and raped her. Then, when he had relaxed, she got a pistol from under the bed and pointed it at him. Trying to push it aside, he hit the gun and it discharged, killing him. She called Swen Anderson to her home and, at least an hour later, he and Luella called the police.

The prosecution argued that Luella Thompson was not sexually assaulted, that her knife wounds were self-inflicted, that her clothes were ripped, not torn, and that other things on the scene were not consistent with her story of self-defense. With the use of experts, especially Professor Herbert MacDonell of Corring, New York, whom Anderson later called on to help with Steven's case, Anderson convinced Judge John Lindstrom—who tried the case without a jury at Swen Anderson's request—that Luella Thompson's story was consistent with the evidence from the scene of the crime and was too elaborate to be contrived.

Swen Anderson won this, his most famous case. He and Luella Thompson—two regional legends—had come together in one story. With no modesty, Swen Anderson began then to describe himself to fellow lawyers and to judges as one of the nation's great defense lawyers.

It was almost inevitable that Swen Anderson would make a strong effort to get the Jenkins case. It was also inevitable that once he got it, the case would be tried in the most grandiose style. For those who knew Swen Anderson—who had come into his own during the Luella Thompson case—it was no surprise that Steven's case did not take the subdued and quiet route of plea bargaining. Those who knew Swen Anderson correctly expected that the trial would be filled with surprise. One local attorney who knew and worked with Swen Anderson for several years said with considerable respect that Swen was "a master of confusion. He led many juries into left field."

Anderson saw the Jenkins case as a once-in-a-lifetime chance. No similar case had presented itself in southwestern Minnesota in recent memory. It was a great opportunity for Anderson to test and consolidate his reputation in a case that had already received national attention. Anderson wanted fame; Steven needed a lawyer. After negotiating with Darlene and Louis—Louis having been a client of his in the past—Anderson took the case for free.

From the beginning of his defense, Swen Anderson tried "to make every stick into an arrow." In his first written act addressing the court, he sought in a memorandum for bail reduction to remind the court that excessive bail is unconstitutional—in that it denies due process and the right to equal protection under the law—and that it amounts to cruel and unusual punishment.

In the bail request itself—in contradistinction to the high-blown grounds of constitutional rights embodied in the earlier memorandum—Anderson joined an unusual personal promise to the $150,000 in collateral that Louis Taveirne provided by putting up his supper club and home: Swen Anderson offered his house as a home to Steven. According to Anderson, Steven would "eat my food and sleep in my home." Apparently assured of Steven's innocence on the basis of a polygraph test he had the boy take, Anderson assured the court that Steven would pose no threat to him or his family. (To a set of questions, Steven replied that he was telling the truth and had not shot the bankers. To the specific question, "Did your father ask you to kill him?" Steven replied, "Yes." Swen Anderson did not ask the question, "Did you shoot your father?") Anderson's effort to get Steven released on bail was rewarded: Steven was released to him on the proposed terms and the condition that Steven, except when at school, would always be in the presence of Swen Anderson and the members of his family. Anderson's client had become—in some sense—a foster child. Steven had a new father.

Swen Anderson prepared to go to trial, disregarding the grand jury's findings. The grand jury had believed the prosecution's story and not Steven's. Anderson did not, to the surprise of many, ask for a change of venue. He was quoted as saying he would trust the good sense and basic fairness of the people of the region. (Matters of cost and inconvenience were not mentioned.) Also, according to attorney DeRycke, Anderson believed the farm crisis assured him a sympathetic jury in Lincoln County.

Swen Anderson attacked on all fronts. In a number of separate actions, he tried to destroy the state's case by denying their evidence, on the one hand, and by challenging the very law which convicts, on the other. On November 1, he filed a motion challenging the constitutionality of the accomplice statute of the Minnesota statutes on the grounds that it contradicted the First, Fourth, Fifth, Sixth, Eighth, and Fourteenth Amendments to the United States Constitution. Also, on November 1, he called for an omnibus hearing, as required by Rule II of Minnesota Rules of Criminal Procedure, to examine all probable cause, the constitutionality of all Steven's written and oral statements, and the constitutionality of the accomplice statute. He argued at length in a January 10, 1984, memorandum that the accomplice statute was unconstitutional because of its vagueness.

In a December 29 motion, Swen Anderson argued that Officers O'Gorman and Berg had used "Gestapo-like" interrogation methods with "the boy." Furthermore, he contended that the belated request of Steven and his mother for a lawyer should invalidate the six statements that Steven gave prior to having a lawyer. In a January 10 motion, Anderson argued that the police lacked sufficient probable cause for the search of the Hardwick house. In addition, he argued that the police illegally extended the search from the house to include the whole farm grounds. If all of Anderson's shots had found their target, the state would have been denied all the evidence it had attained by confession and search and seizure and would have had no statute under which to convict Steven as even an accomplice. The prosecution would have been *ipso facto* without a case at all.

THE DURESS DEFENSE

THE CONSTITUTIONAL MOTIONS, however, seemed secondary for Swen Anderson. His main attraction was a duress defense, which he had announced right in the beginning in an October 13 "Notice of Affirmative Defense." The duress defense was Swen's bid for a total victory; it was an all-or-nothing defense. In the words of one of Swen's fellow attorneys, "the duress defense was the basket in which Swen put all his eggs." If it worked, Steven would go scot-free: Steven would not be considered responsible for anything he had done; he had only obeyed his father. Anderson, in effect, would argue as if duress were identical to criminal insanity. He would, if he could, rewrite the law, transforming duress from an immediate and life-threatening hold of one person upon another into an abiding state of mind that freed one of all responsibility and thus from criminal culpability.

Swen Anderson's duress defense, which was the version of the crime he chose to tell, had serious problems inherent in it. Steven's own statements did not offer any evidence that his father had coerced him into committing the crime: there had been no gun held to his head; no threat to his life had been issued if he didn't come along. Steven never once indicated there was anything wrong with the idea of luring Rudolph Blythe out to the farm and "robbing and scaring him." Nowhere did Steven testify to offering any resistance to the crime itself. Apparently, Steven went along of his own free will. He willingly furnished the weapons for the crime. By his own admission, he drove as they fled from the crime, and he fired the murder weapon at the vehicle of the deputy who pursued them.

If Swen Anderson's story was to hold, he would have to show that Steven was totally under his father's control. Was this possible? Steven came to and went from Texas on his own. By his own claim, Steven showed enough will power to dissuade his father from additional crimes. Yet Anderson was going to have to show that somehow, in going to the crime, Steven was absolutely under his father's sway.

There was an additional and serious catch in Anderson's strategy. Anderson would have to tell the story that the son, though fully under the control of the father, did nothing more than go to and flee from the scene of the crime. Anderson thus engaged in postulating the darkest coercive powers of father over son, while, at the same time, paradoxically limiting those powers from having compelled Steven to shoot.

Perhaps all along, at least in his lucid moments, Swen Anderson knew that his duress defense was a sham legal defense. His strategies often involved throwing and keeping the other side off balance. Perhaps he wanted to use his duress defense to do two other things: to carry the trial to the public and so to try Steven's dead father. In the realm of public imagination, he could tell of an abused child, who suffered the ravages of a broken family and an insane father. There he could conjure up the image of a father so evil that he not only killed two men, but compelled his son to help commit the crime. With regional sympathy and without a change of venue, Swen Anderson could exonerate Steven of every count of murder: Steven was not the murderer; his father was. Steven did not come to the crime as a willing accomplice; he was not an active partner but the passive shadow of his mad father. Swen Anderson would try the dead father and free the living son—whom Swen Anderson believed to be innocent.

As in his successful Luella Thompson case, Swen Anderson sought to use experts. Foremost among the experts Swen Anderson relied upon was psychiatrist Carl Schwartz of Lakeville, Minnesota. (Anderson had used Schwartz before.) Based on a host of standard psychological examinations and several hours of interviews with Steven's mother, sister, and grandparents, Carl Schwartz offered the following portrait of Steven, his father, and their relationship.

A PSYCHIATRIST'S REPORT

THE SCHWARTZ REPORT was divided into two parts: a psychiatric profile of Steven and a psychiatric profile of James. Both parts served the single conclusion that Steven was a relatively normal and average young man who lived under the influence of his maniacal father.

Schwartz's profile of Steven made no case for mental or moral incompetence. Steven's senses of time, person, and place were judged to be normal. His mathematical abilities were judged to be average or above, with a particular strength in abstract reasoning. His memory, recent and remote, was judged to be good.

Steven, Schwartz remarked, "appeared to have an exceptionally good moral code, expecially when it came to any questions of what he felt were his social and moral obligations toward people."

In interpreting the Minnesota Multiphasic Personality Inventory (MMPI), Schwartz chose to discount what could have been extremes in Steven's test results. Instead, Schwartz suggested that Steven had "a valid profile which is almost totally within usual limits for people who are not mentally ill, except for a slightly elevated psychasthenia [Scale 7], [which] clinically may be represented as intense internalized anxiety." Schwartz also noted an elevation [Scale 0] of "internalized discomfort in his relationship with people," while vaguely judging "some peaking" in Scales 4, 5, and 6 as "a clinical complex of an individual who is usually concerned in a comparative fashion about how he rates as an adult male, and," Schwartz vaguely adds, "who also might have concern in interpersonal relationships when it comes to the point of being aggressive."

Roger Greene's standard interpretive manual of the Minnesota Multiphasic Personality Inventory (*The MMPI: Interpretive Manual*, New York, 1980) depicts clients with 4-5/5-4 high-point pairs in the following manner: They are almost always males, with the exception of women who are murderers. These males "are passively unconventional, usually in both their appearance and behavior. They are rebelling against social conventions and delight in defying and challenging any form of rule or convention. Although they [clients with 4-5/5-4 high-point pairs] have strong needs for dependency, they fear domination by significant others." (Also, they "may be concerned about homoerotic impulses.")

Clients with 4-6/6-4 high-point pairs, according to the interpretive manual, are "angry, resentful, argumentative individuals who are difficult to interact with personally or socially because of these characteristics. They are usually able to control the acting out of their hostility but do exhibit violent outbursts on occasion. They will externalize blame for their anger. They are suspicious of the motives of other people . . . and these clients have a long history of social maladjustment."

Schwartz remarked that Steven appeared to be well controlled, even overcontrolled. He observed a monotony in Steven's replies. However, there was one important exception. "The only affective responses . . . were frequent episodes of crying when we were discussing his deep feelings toward his father." "He became," Schwartz noted, "very irritated when I challenged him on his lack of overt anger toward his father, and when I expressed disbelief that he did not have deep-seated feelings of hatred and a desire to retaliate toward his father."

Schwartz paid far less attention to Steven's relationship to his mother. Although Schwartz was perhaps unaware of this, Steven had also expressed fantasies about his mother's death. Schwartz, however, did note that Steven had some problems with "sexual identification." On card 7 of the Rorschach Ink Blot Test—which is usually considered the mother card—"he saw a couple of independent women who were changing directions."

Schwartz perceptively asked Steven to interpret the tattoos he had given himself. Predictably enough, one set of tattoos represented the military and masculine side of himself, which he affirmed. "The important tattoo on his right arm," Schwartz wrote, "is a skull with a beret which is an emblem, according to Steve, of a special services combat unit in the United States Army. He readily identified the right arm tattoos as representing

[his] father." Other tattoos represented his mother and the sexual woman. "On his left arm is a picture of Sylvester the Cat who . . . [is] chasing the little Tweety-Bird. He identified this tattoo as a partial representation of his feelings toward his mother— perhaps the mother and the woman neither he nor his father could find. "There is another tattoo of a somewhat voluptuous nude female in his breastbone area. He identifies this tattoo with [his] mother."

More interested in accounting for Steven's interest in military matters than explaining what appear to be suppressed feelings about his relationship with his mother and his sexuality, Schwartz directed considerable attention to Steven's military identity and his uninterrupted fantasy of playing soldier. He noted that Grandmother and Grandfather Jenkins had remarked that Steven had been interested in military things since he was very young—maybe even four.

They also remarked that Steven's father, who had served some time in the National Guard, used to repeat his few tales— which may have been "exaggerated"—to his eager son. Apparently, James "fostered Steven's military leanings and allowed . . . his military fantasies." What is clear, although the report does not make it explicit, is that at an early age weapons and the military became one way for the father and son to relate to each other.

If correctly paraphrased by Schwartz, Grandfather Jenkins may have revealed more about being a man in the Jenkins family than he wished. "Although Steve by intensive practice may have become a sharpshooter, Grandpa Jenkins indicated to me that James was not a bad shot in his own right. Grandpa Jenkins's comment to me in regard to ability to shoot [was] . . . that Steve would not have wasted three or four bullets in shooting a man, but that he could have brought any man down in reasonable range with just one shot."

Schwartz resisted the obvious interpretation that Steven, finally given the chance to shoot, had shot. Schwartz chose a more abstract explanation. For him, Steven's fantasies and behavior were not expressions of severe innate hostility. "It is more probable," Schwartz concluded, "that they represent a sublimation of his conflict in being inferior as a male." Attempting to clarify his meaning, Schwartz added that Steven was displaying "in essence, a reaction formation in which he could be a soldier-hero."

Schwartz downplayed Steven's capacity for violence. He offered this explanation for the one time Steven acted violently in order to secure his mother's attention. Caught in the turmoil of his parent's divorce, Steven was buffeted about. His father demanded that Steven come and live with him, threatening to "come after Steven and kill him and then kill himself if Steve left him to live with his mother." Steven conceived it to be "his mission to attempt to reunite his father and mother and, therefore, to reunite the entire family." Steven alternated between them and hoped that by staying close to both of them, he could rejoin them. "He recalls the breakup and his mother's growing relationship with Louis Taverine which angered him. On one occasion he fired a shot into an empty family vehicle because he felt a desparate need for attention from his mother."

Without corroborating Steven's story with other evidence, Schwartz uncritically reported Steven's story as Steven had told it to him. He even went so far as to accept Steven's account of shooting at the deputy: Steven aimed at the deputy's tire; he closed his eyes because "he was afraid to visualize what could have happened." "It was an easy shot," Schwartz, the psychologist, commented—in the same vein as had Grandfather Jenkins on Steven's marksmanship—"and if Steven had so desired, he could have killed the deputy without any difficulty whatsoever."

Schwartz had sympathy for Steven. Steven was a troubled but innocent young man—according to Schwartz—who paid the price of his parents' divorce and his father's madness.

Schwartz's judgments of James were devoid of sympathy. For Schwartz, James was pathologically paranoid. The origin of James's mental disease, Schwartz suggested, may have been a car accident or it may have resulted from another trauma several years earlier when James observed the death of a child and carried the child in his arms from a field.

Whatever the turning point in the development of his illness, Schwartz argued, James's life manifested a growing deterioration of mind. He had been unable to develop an independent life and career. His sense of inferiority and his economic and vocational failure went hand in hand. He was unable to leave home. He was especially tied to his mother and needed the supervision of his authoritarian father, with whom he had a highly ambivalent relationship. According to Schwartz, James's own father "saw his son James as a nasty person and 'a deadbeat' [father's word]."

By the time of the crime, according to Schwartz, James had become "a homicidal, a paranoidally psychotic maniac." In Schwartz's interpretation, almost every element of his personality was an expression of his madness: his stubbornness, his lack of reality, his anger.

James had been brutal to animals. Schwartz offered a few hideous examples: James enmeshed the family dog, Lassie, in a piece of farm machinery, and he laughed as "the dog screamed in pain." James cut off the tails of his cows because one swished her tail in his face. James drowned a calf because it had left the yard.

In his marriage, said Schwartz, summarizing Darlene's statement, James was an increasingly difficult husband. While their marriage had its beginnings in "a pleasant courtship of two people in love and a few happy years following the marriage," it began to go downhill as James "manifested his increased irritability, hostility, and violence." He was unable to keep a job, support the family, or establish himself or the family on a stable course. Already in the early 1970s—Steven would have only been five, six, or seven years old—Darlene was considering a divorce. James paid almost no attention to their two children, and Darlene played the roles of both mother and father. "Over and over again," Schwartz said, "Jim had promised her that he would mend his ways. . . . Darlene would forgive him and accept him and start all over again. She describes Jim as being demanding, dependent, crying and begging and needing someone to take care of him. To her, Jim was a third child."

In Schwartz's opinion, Darlene was the strong person in the family. Whereas James was "emotionally flamboyant and vicious," Darlene was "cool and controlled." Where James was "impulsive," Darlene was "cautious, planning. . . ." Drawing one last contrast, Schwartz contended that James did not care at all about people's feelings, "while Darlene was very highly moral, well behaved, and very sensitive about hurting others."

Darlene—upon whom Steven modeled himself, according to Schwartz—was "the family peacekeeper," which meant she was the manager of James.

Reaching what was the central part of his story, Schwartz contended that James was unable to focus his anger on the women in his family. His anger was, therefore, focused on Steven; this helped explain "the 'sick' relationship he had with his father." "Darlene," Schwartz noted, "would not let James be physically violent toward her. . . . She confronted him . . . [and] threatened separation and Jim would back down and apologize and promise to reform." Michele, the daughter, also successfully used the same tactic: "[She] would confront him and ignore him and walk away. Michele stood her ground and became a very strong-willed woman who later was dominant in her own marriage." Ultimately, according to Schwartz, women were safe from James's anger because he "was basically an overdependent child in his emotional operation with women," whereas "Steven's maleness," Schwartz generalized, "placed him in danger because his father's fury was directed toward men exclusively." Schwartz stressed that James's anger focused on Steven and noted that James "repeatedly castigated Steven when things went wrong or Steven made an error." On one occasion, James purportedly threatened to hit Steven with a lead pipe.

Steven, according to Schwartz, never learned to defy his father. Fearing for "the physical safety of her son," Darlene taught "Steve to be obedient." She taught him that his "father was sick," and "not to upset Dad, and to run for his life when [he] became severely violent." Bearing the awful burden of nursing his parents' marriage, Steven shouldered—if Schwartz is correct—the equally terrible burden of nursing his father's personality.

Steven was like many children caught in a divorce; on this Schwartz couldn't have been more correct. Steven was trapped in an awful situation. He had a mother who was profoundly dissatisfied and wanted to leave the marriage. She had not allied with Steven in confronting the father. After filing for the divorce, she began to live with another man; when she did leave the marriage, she gave Steven the choice of whether to live with her or with his father.

Steven had a father who loved him, terrorized him, and filled him with pity. To have affection, Steven needed a mother; to have respect and to become a man, Steven needed a father.

His father both attracted and repelled him. Schwartz commented: "Steve's love needs toward his father were tremendous and never really satisfied. His father alternately seduced Steve by having him with him and teaching him mechanical skills and then scared him to death with his violence."

Steven, according to Schwartz, could not free himself from his father. "Steve's relationship with his father was a psychiatrically ill relationship. Steven had become embroiled in his conflicts of his great love needs from his father, his neurotic mission to be a caretaker for his father, and a very real and deeply developed fear of what his father would do if Steve had demanded a separation."

Steven, to use language other than Schwartz's, was simultaneously the son, the father, and the friend of his own father. Disregarding or subordinating evidence that suggested that father and son acted like equals and that Steven frequently spent lengthy periods of time away from his father, Schwartz argued that Steven was bound to his father. His father held him in an abiding state of psychological bondage. This was Swen Anderson's duress defense.

Schwartz served Swen Anderson's case. He accepted Darlene's, the grandparents', and Steven's statements without significant reservation. Schwartz told the family's story.

At the same time, he did not seek interviews with other witnesses (already on record in interviews with the Bureau of Criminal Apprehension) who could have testified about Steven's expressions and outbursts of violence, as well as about what appeared to be the noncoercive nature of the father and son relationship. More significantly, Schwartz—at least it could be argued—fled from all the evidence according to which Steven could be considered the shooter, evidence such as the fact that he was a skilled shooter, that he practiced shooting at humanlike figures, and so forth. In an identical fashion, Schwartz seemed to ignore evidence—some of which he offered himself—that suggested Steven was confused and filled with anger and rage, ready to explode at the adult world that had so wronged him. While observing Steven's military fantasies about himself, Schwartz never connected them to Steven's attachment to his M-1 nor to his potential to become a killer.

Schwartz offered this portrait of Steven: "[He] is a courteous, clean, perfectionistic, moral, emotionally overcontrolled individual. Externally he appeared to be a military man," whose rolled up sleeves revealed "his tattoos of which he seemed very proud." "Steve indicated to me"—apparently Schwartz accepted what Steven said *prima facie*—"no particular difficulties in growing up except in his relationship with his father and its tragic ending. He portrayed a deep moral conviction that he must always respect his parents and never hurt anyone. He indicated to me that he never assaulted anyone."

The matter of Steven's duress was never left in doubt by Schwartz, but just what that duress was and what it accounted for was not altogether clear: "Steve felt quite guilty in that he believed that none of the recent tragedies would have occurred had he been totally obedient and never done anything to anger his father."

Schwartz's report was written as if James were on trial. Inside James—the paranoid psychotic who tried to rule all by fear—there was, according to Schwartz,

a fearful, inferior, and inadequate person. . . . At [his] deepest level, Jim's feelings were those of a fearful lonely little child. In his final act of suicide, James . . . left an emotional trauma with his son, Steven, that will be eternally remembered. When Steven talks about his father's death and his loneliness and his love for his father . . . he sobs. . . . It is only Steven who will shed a tear. . . . The horrific duress projected upon the young Steven has been concluded by [his] father's suicide but will last forever.

THE DURESS DEFENSE EXPLAINED

SWEN ANDERSON spent a lot of money on the Schwartz report. Anderson expected to make it central to his case. In an unusual move, he joined the Schwartz report to the memorandum for bail reduction (December 15, 1983), making the report—in its entirety—public. He would defend Steven and try his father in public.

Anderson requested an additional report from Schwartz. In the second report (January 5, 1984), Schwartz was even more explicit about how Steven lived under the inescapable compulsion of his father. From additional interviews with Steven, Schwartz discovered—in conformity with Anderson's contention—more reasons to believe that Steven's father was the killer and that Steven acted under his duress. "Steven was able to recall James's threats on a number of occasions, over a period of several years, to dynamite Louis Taverire's car while Louis was in it." Schwartz reiterated how James told Steven that if Steven left him, he would kill Steven and himself. "Steven indicated," Schwartz added, "that when he finally discussed giving himself up to the authorities . . . James indicated in no uncertain terms that if Steven did he would commit suicide."

Schwartz parenthetically added—as if his intention were to convince his readers of the veracity of his psychological autopsy of James—that when Steven left, he left from a place where "there would have been a minimal chance for Jim to shoot him." Hence, James could not carry out the threat he had long made.

Lending Swen Anderson the most specific aid, Schwartz mitigated Steven's role as accomplice. "At the time of the shooting . . . [Steven] wasn't at all clear that his father was going to carry out the robbery as planned. . . . Apparently [Steven] did not know what was in his father's mind and there is a strong logical suggestion that whatever Jim's plan was, [it] might well have been modified by the appearance of the second car and the banker's wife and her being instructed to go for the sheriff." Schwartz concluded that, indeed, "there looms the very definite possibility that if she had not appeared the shootings might not have occurred because they were never planned."

Schwartz did not proceed to explore what was planned between the father and son, and how—if they were capable at all of planning—they did plan. Likewise, Schwartz did not entertain the possibility that Steven confused himself with his father. Had his father's anger become Steven's own anger? Wasn't it Steven who talked about bombing Louis and even confusedly talked about two businessmen who supposedly had killed his mother? Did Steven act out his father's frustration? Had he become not only his father's nurse, as Schwartz suggested in his first letter, but also his father's avenger? Had Steven truly confused himself with his dead father? (One of the detectives close to the case suggested this when he offered the hypothesis that Steven was a reverse liar; that is, that much of what he claimed his father did during the crime, he himself did.)

The closest Schwartz approached this kind of speculation was when he noted that he "continued to be impressed about [Steven's] confused relation with his father. . . . His continuing to stay with his father is something which he really doesn't understand. We talked at length about his ambivalence toward his father. These mixed feelings of love, anger, and need in regard to his father are still somewhat jumbled in his mind."

Schwartz then backed away from this sort of speculation. He simply said that Steven was "a mentally ill individual," who "has begun to question his military fantasies and his preoccupation with guns and ammunition." Schwartz concluded his second letter by saying that Steven's mental illness was neurotic instead of psychotic, however, in no way did Schwartz consider Steven "to be dangerous to any human being."

In his classic defense of Leopold and Loeb, Clarence Darrow argued that their crime was determined like all other occurrences in nature. So Swen Anderson contended that the internal laws that commanded Steven were as ironclad as anything else in the world. (Anderson, however, never escaped the contradiction of arguing, on the one hand, that Steven was most maliciously determined by his father; yet, on the other hand, that Steven was absolutely innocent of the killings.)

In his April 9, 1984, motion against the state's motion to suppress the psychiatric report and the duress defense, Swen Anderson added new information to his defense. According to him, Steven's paternal grandparents, Clayton and Nina Jenkins, would "testify that their son James one time, when angry, stated in front of them that he would kill Rudy Blythe" and that Clayton alone would "testify that his son one time, when angry, said that you have to blow a few heads off to get anywhere." Moreover, Anderson claimed that Steven's maternal grandparents, Laura and Reuben Abraham, would testify that James put the family dog through the corn picker and cut tails off his cattle. Darlene, Anderson noted, would testify that when Steven was a boy, James attacked him with a pitchfork and later with a pipe wrench. The daughter Michele, according to Anderson, would testify that her father once choked Steven. Anderson also had testimony from the family that James ran over a calf he considered to be naughty and that once he choked a horse in the stable. From these instances, Anderson concluded in his memorandum that James "had an intense hate and wanted to kill many people." He was "vicious and nuts and the very presence of this insane maniac created absolute duress with the need of nothing more."

Swen Anderson went beyond the family in his effort to develop his duress defense. He gathered other testimonies. Anderson told the court that a local lawyer, Eric DeRycke, would testify to James's terrible temper. In a February 22 letter to Anderson, DeRycke told how James threatened to kill a Mr. Carlson, who was considering pressing a bad check charge against him. Anderson also noted that another local person would cite that James often "blew up and flew off the handle." Yet another person would, according to Anderson, testify that twenty years earlier, James had pointed a gun at him and two other youths having a beer party on a nearby farm. Another local man would suggest that James had a reverse touch of Midas: "Anything he touched turned to crap; . . . he wasn't much of a manager."

Anderson also gathered several witnesses to James's outrageous behavior in the Tyler hospital at the time when Steven had had his serious bicycle accident. Swen used these witnesses and others to offer to the court a cumulative portrait of a highly irrational and angry man.

A BELATED SUICIDE NOTE

SWEN ANDERSON'S SECOND POTENTIAL EXPERT was graphologist Jane Green. She came on the scene due to a most unusual occurrence. In early January, Louis Taveirne and his friend James Dwire returned to the scene of the alleged suicide and supposedly found a note, written in pencil, in a fuse box attached to a telephone post near the place where James committed suicide. The note was, supposedly, a suicide note from James Jenkins. Unpunctuated, it read in irregularly printed and spaced capital letters: "I KILLED RUDY BLYTHE / THE S O B / STEVE

LEAVING / WONT LISTEN ANYMORE / A GUY JUST AS WELL BE DEAD." It was signed James L. Jenkins.

The revelation of the note was as stunning as it was scandalous. The note was found three months after the alleged suicide occurred. It was actually found by Louis's friend James Dwire, a well-known local businessman who at one time had seriously considered purchasing the Ruthton bank from Rudolph Blythe and who had recently been indicted for his role as an organizer and chief officer in the multimillion dollar Jerusalem artichoke scam. (Dwire's company invited farmers throughout the region to invest their money and fields in Jerusalem artichokes. Despite the company's predictions and efforts, the Jerusalem artichoke remained only a useless weed. Farmers throughout the region lost millions of dollars, which they never recovered. They felt they had been swindled. Not only was there no demand for Jerusalem artichoke seeds—the pyramid had collapsed—but they had also filled their fields with what proved to be a pernicious weed. Furthermore—and this was the basis of the indictments—the three officers of the rapidly expanding, Marshall-based company allegedly used investors' funds for personal gain. Dwire and his colleagues rented their fields to the company at high rates and developed their own property, which they rented to the artichoke company with investors' money. The connection of several of the company's strongest boosters to a local fundamentalist church made one local person remark, "If you only have the faith of the seed of a Jerusalem artichoke, you will surely go broke.")

When contacted by the officers of the Bureau of Criminal Apprehension regarding his discovery of the suicide note, James Dwire declined to be interviewed without having his lawyer present. He simply said he had flown his friend Louis to Texas to do him a favor.

Louis claimed Dwire came along only by accident when the woman who had been giving Louis flying lessons couldn't go at the last moment. Louis further told the BCA interviewer, "I always thought there was a possibility of a note . . . [but] I never took it too serious until I got Stevie out on bail. I discussed it with him . . . [Going to look for the note] might have been a shot in the dark, but I thought it was a possibility. . . James was always writing notes. He always had . . . a pen or pencil with him." Louis said he discussed his idea with Swen Anderson and Luigi DiFonzo, neither of whom encouraged Louis to leave when he did. However, the weather was so favorable for flying in January that Louis chose to leave "on the spur of the moment."

According to Anderson's friend LuVern Hansen, Swen never lent any credence to the suicide note and saw it simply as another device to keep the prosecution off guard. Possibly Anderson feigned interest to please Louis and Darlene.

The prosecution had reasons to distrust the authenticity of the note. The writing itself could be challenged, despite the fact that Anderson had found an expert who authenticated the note. Furthermore, Anderson's expert, Ann Hooten, could easily be challenged. (She was openly challenged in the Twin Cities by Leonard Richards, who sponsored a contest in 1983 in which Hooten's name was the right answer to a set of questions which included the query: "Who testified that Howard Hughes' 'Mormon will' was genuine?")

Materially aiding the prosecution was the fact that the suicide note did not show any signs of weathering even though it had, supposedly, been in a leaky fuse box for three months.

Last, and most substantial, the prosecution had a witness, a local farmer, who would testify that he found no note in the box when he had cleaned it out after the death of James and prior to Louis Taveirne's trip to Texas. At the time when Louis Taveirne and James Dwire claimed to find the note, the farmer—who was on the scene—challenged the note and questioned what Taveirne and Dwire were trying to pull off. Louis counterchallenged. He had made plans the previous day for the police to be with him when he searched for the note he intuitively thought would be there. If indeed the note hadn't been there for three months, his question was: Who planted it, and why? In a February BCA interview with Robert Berg, Louis—who did not think the local farmer or sheriff were lying—said that if the note was not authentic, "there was a lot of people under suspicion as far as me and Jim [Dwire] were concerned. . . . Now, if it wasn't authentic, we suspicion Swen Anderson. We suspicion Luigi Di-Fonzo. We suspicion [Ken] Nordin, his [Swen's] investigator." Yet Louis insisted the note itself was authentic "because," Louis claimed to Berg, "it has been analyzed by three different experts." Ann Hooten was the only one whom Louis knew by name.

Perhaps pressured to use the note as evidence, Swen Anderson found another expert in addition to Ann Hooten—this time a graphologist—to substantiate the note for his duress defense. Assuming the note's authenticity, graphologist Jane Green rendered a judgment on the note's writer that squared with Anderson's and Schwartz's view of James Jenkins as a monster who killed two bankers and who perversely dominated those around him.

Green said about the author of the surprise suicide note: "He relates to himself rather than the world. [He] lacks a stable self-concept," manifesting "a generalized defensiveness and abiding fear of being dominated," and a "rebelliousness, stubbornness and a compelling need to control and mask underlying feelings of inadequacy."

Green then proceeded to say: "The writer will at times make awkward intrusions into others' lives with a desire for love and attention, but inner resentments set himself up for failure and make his efforts self-destructive." In her final two paragraphs, she concluded that the writer felt a sadness and a despair about his son, although "the signature betrays rage, violence, and depression incorporating total self-destruction. In my opinion, the writer is capable of committing any crimes which he decided were necessary and would use any possible method to control those who opposed him at the time of writing." She found Swen Anderson's whole story in that small note.

In the end, however, Swen Anderson chose not to introduce the note as evidence. The decision to withdraw the note marked the beginning of a split between Anderson and Louis Taveirne, whose concern for Steven's defense had been exceptionally active up to that point.

Swen Anderson also sought the help of other experts. Locally, he retained detective Ken Nordin of Marshall, who by his own admission brought forth in the course of the trial no significant evidence.

With fanfare, Anderson announced that he would also use well-known New Jersey criminal investigator, Professor Herbert MacDonnell. MacDonnell had worked on the murder of Doctor Herman Tarnower by Jean Harris in the nationally prominent

"Scarsdale Diet" case, and his testimony had proven to be important to Anderson's victory in the Luella Thompson case. The state sent MacDonnell some of the evidence, including Rudolph Blythe's clothing. Apparently, he was unable to supply anything of use, since the defense never mentioned him again.

Anderson also tried, unsuccessfully, to introduce a polygraph test administered to Steven as evidence. The polygraph test, legally inadmissible, recorded Steven saying that he didn't do the shooting nor did he plan it.

Swen's story was complete. It was erected upon a highly speculative distortion of the duress defense. Perhaps Swen started the defense believing it had potential in the courtroom. Certainly it seemed consistent with his concern about freeing his client by appealing to the most recent interpretations of the Constitution. The duress defense was also consistent with Anderson's style of advocacy by publicity. The duress defense became a way to conduct "the real trial" by paper. This would square with other materials that Anderson sought—against almost all precedent—to introduce as evidence.

Having forsaken the obvious path of having Steven plead guilty to two counts of second-degree murder and seeking to mitigate Steven's sentence by pleading for a reduced sentence because of Steven's age, family background, and so forth, Anderson was forced to prepare a more elaborate defense to tell a more enthralling and compelling story. In Anderson's story, Steven was depicted as a quiet, obedient boy, whose only defects were an obsession with weapons and military things and the fact that he loved his family and father too much. Steven did what his father wanted. Furthermore, Anderson had to be careful: if he went too far in stressing Steven's obedience to and imitation of his father, it could be concluded that the father's dark influence had made his son a murderer. The duress story cut both ways; it was a dangerous story to tell.

Anderson was telling a story from which others, like the jury, might draw conclusions different from Anderson's. The more they thought about the father and the son, the more they might think it was the father who was the talker—he had been talking his whole life—and the son who was the doer. The jury might think the father—who by all counts was more social than the son—was a bluff, while the son was for real. It would not be difficult to suppose, as prosecutor Thomas Fabel implied, that the father threatened and the son acted. They might conclude that the father was bad; the son—maybe because of the father and the family—evil. Just maybe, some might speculate, the son exploited the old man's desire to rough Rudy up. The jury might conclude that the son took advantage of the situation by trying out his M-1.

Questions circled the crime. Steven's story was incomplete; it raised more questions than it answered. Swen Anderson's defense raised as many questions as it put to rest. Nevertheless, Anderson led his client onto the high road of a full courtroom defense. He did this despite the grand jury's conclusions and at the risk of a trial that could convict Steven of first-degree murder. If Steven's and Anderson's stories were not believed, or if the prosecution's case could not be taken apart, Anderson could lose the biggest case of his life and Steven could spend an extra five or ten years in prison.

WITHOUT A STORY TO TELL

SWEN ANDERSON'S DURESS DEFENSE tried to split apart what two lifetimes had put together. It sought to separate James and Steven who, as much as any father and son could be, were one. Anderson as much as conceded this when he argued that James had an all-powerful and all-present hold on Steven.

Anderson's story—the duress defense—failed from the outset. It almost came undone as fast as Anderson had created it. Legally, the duress defense simply was not what he wanted it to be. The duress defense, which represented his best effort, did not survive long enough to go to court.

In a struggle of motions and countermotions, Swen Anderson was vanquished. He was defeated on every significant point raised. In a written order (filed March 14, 1984), the result of an omnibus hearing called on various motions by the defense and the motion of the prosecution to suppress the psychiatric opinion of Carl Schwartz, District Judge Walter A. Mann set forth the following rulings, each of which turned against Swen Anderson's case.

1) Judge Mann ruled that the Minnesota accomplice statute was constitutional. "The defendant has not cited a single authority which holds that an accomplice statute such as the one contained in the Minnesota Statute is unconstitutional."

2) The judge ruled that the searches of the pickup truck and of the Hardwick homestead were constitutional. The application for the warrants and the supporting affidavits were based on probable cause and issued under appropriate circumstances.

3) Judge Mann allowed the statements made by the defendant to stand, since they "were made voluntarily and under circumstances whereby the defendant waived his right against self-incrimination." The defense's attempt to substitute the mother's request for counsel for the defendant's request contradicts all authorities, none of which suggest that "a third person's desire in some manner affects the voluntariness of a statement by a defendant."

4) The judge allowed the testimony of Susan Blythe, the widow of decedent Rudolph Blythe, to stand, since her knowledge of parts of the crime was based upon legally obtained information and not that of illegal search and seizure as the defense claimed.

5) Agreeing with the prosecution, the judge declared the expert opinion of Carl Schwartz to be inadmissible.

Judge Mann found Schwartz's report "extremely disturbing to the court." "It appeared that for Dr. Schwartz to express an opinion concerning the nature of the duress imposed on the defendant by the defendant's father, it was necessary for Schwartz to accept as true the statements of third persons which had been related to him concerning the defendant's father. It is the conclusion of the court that opinions so based are so unreliable and based on such speculation and conjecture as to be incompetent." Judge Mann declared that while expert opinion can be used to speak to the competence of the defendant, it cannot be permitted to decide the matter of criminal intent, which belongs to the grand jury and to the jury. "It is the position of the court that persons of common knowledge are fully capable of evaluating whether or not threats such as may be evidenced by relevant testimony constituted 'reasonable apprehension' in the mind of the defendant, that if he refused to participate in the offense he would have been 'liable to instant death.'"

Judge Mann offered the opinion that the Minnesota duress statute did not intend "to encompass those infinite psychological factors to which every human being is constantly subject, which may be analyzed as the totality of past environmental circumstances which may explain a person's behavior or reaction at any given moment."

On the eve of the trial, Swen Anderson's defense suffered yet another serious setback. In a bold motion, on April 6, the prosecution called for an evidentiary hearing. The prosecution argued that this would avoid frequent objections and lengthy arguments during the trial, thereby "maximizing the jury's ability to comprehend the evidence . . . while diminishing the possibility of a mistrial." Specifically, the state asked Judge Mann to prohibit the defense from introducing all evidence that fell into the following categories:

1) evidence that sought to prove the character of a person in order to show that a later act conformed to that character; 2) testimony by graphologist Jane Green which was speculative and improper; and 3) all testimony by defense witnesses that stated that James intended to kill someone other than the victims or the defendant.

All three types of evidence, the prosecution maintained, were not only invalid but aimed at making a single argument: James Jenkins had "a violent, explosive personality," and therefore "the murders were a result of that trait. . . . The conclusion, quite simply, is that the defendant cannot corroborate his claim that his father did the killing by attacking his father's character."

The prosecution sought to exclude all instances and statements pertaining to James's character—such as the fact that James pointed a gun at someone twenty years before or had said he would kill someone. Such evidence was not directly related to the shooting nor to the father's or son's role in the shooting. The prosecution, above all else, wanted to prevent Swen Anderson from freeing Steven Jenkins by successfully trying James Jenkins.

In the introductory paragraph of his opposing motion, filed April 10, Anderson revealed how deeply the prosecution's motion cut into his already injured defense: "The defendant through his counsel Allan Swen Anderson opposes all of the State's motions . . . and states if all of this evidence is excluded, he probably won't have any witnesses to call for any purpose."

In the end, Anderson really didn't have any witnesses to call. He argued that the Minnesota Supreme Court had not outlawed the testimony of graphologists. He tried again to put James on trial. "Our fine psychiatrist Carl Schwartz [showed that] James was vicious and nuts and the very presence of this insane maniac created absolute duress with the need of nothing more." He mentioned many witnesses who could testify to James's violence and irrationality. He recited several of the worst instances of James's cruelty: how James put a family dog through the corn picker and "bragged about cutting the tails off of twenty cows who were seen still bleeding, because James Lee Jenkins . . . would not be swatted anymore while milking or his glasses knocked off in the cow dung." He repeated the claim—which would not surface in the trial—that Clayton and Nina Jenkins heard their son say he would kill Rudolph Blythe.

Anderson's examples, as well as his extended arguments as to what constituted admissible evidence, were not effective. At the opening of the trial, Judge Mann ruled that testimony from the graphologist would not be admitted. In essential agreement with the prosecution, Judge Mann further ruled that all evidence about James's character and acts in general would be excluded, unless it was relevant to the motives for and the act of killing the two bankers.

The tables had been turned on Swen Anderson. He who had sought to deny the prosecution its evidence, statements, and witnesses now found himself without a story to tell. His duress defense had vanished. His motions had produced smoke without fire. He was heading to trial without a defense, and now it was too late for plea bargaining (which he did try to initiate in earnest less than two weeks before the trial's announced opening). Anderson had tried every trick he could. He sought to make his case in the press. The prosecution was in no mood to let Anderson and his client escape through plea bargaining.

According to one of Swen's closest acquaintances, it was Steven who didn't want to take the stand. Steven was afraid. Another friend believed Darlene did not want Steven to take the stand. More than likely, Anderson desired to go to trial even though he had lost much of his case before the beginning of the trial. Even when he forced the duress defense beyond legal recognition, his gaze was focused on the jury. Duress was his chosen way to tell the jury that this son had suffered a terrible father.

In his most optimistic moments, Anderson thought of the duress story as a no-loss idea. If the defense succeeded, Steven would go scot-free; if it failed, it would still provide a publicity vehicle for blaming the crime on James. Perhaps Anderson calculated that the duress defense offered two more possible means to obtain victory: first, complexity can lead an adversary into error and error can free; and second, juries don't demand good law but good stories.

For those who were rooting for Swen Anderson against the state—and there were plenty of them, especially in western Lincoln County—there were reasons for gloom. Anderson had a reputation for being the best; it was common to hear the opinion, "Swen Anderson has the case: Steven Jenkins will go free." However, Anderson's invincibility was being strongly tested. Clear signs of his weakness were accumulating at the clerk of court's office. The prosecution's motions were well-written and cogent, whereas Anderson's appeared to be hastily written and unevenly argued. Exaggeration and spelling errors went hand in hand with arguments that, in places, lacked discipline. On pretrial motions, Judge Mann consistently ruled for the prosecution. Other negative signs for the defense's case came in the form of a steady stream of information that made it clear that Steven could run and shoot, while James could probably do neither. Even Anderson's most hopeful supporters had good reason to expect the worst when the state did not buckle before "the blinding revelation" of the suicide note but stood ready to bring forth its own experts to dispute its authenticity.

The defense appeared in great disarray when Swen Anderson announced that the exclusive rights to the defense's story had been sold to an Eastern writer, Luigi DiFonzo. What exactly was sold and for how much was not made public, but one source close to the case estimated the initial amount Anderson was given at approximately $17,000. The agreement did mean that Steven, his family (Darlene, Michele, and Nina and Clayton Jenkins), and Swen Anderson would only tell their story to Luigi DiFonzo, a young Sicilian-American author who had written a well-publicized book titled St. Peter's Bankers.

The agreement to sell the exclusive rights resonated with irony. There was the obvious and contradictory state in which the agreement left Anderson: he who had lived by the press had now decided to avoid the press. There was the additional irony of author DiFonzo's buying a story whose most intimate side had already been made public in the Schwartz report, which essentially gave Darlene's, Michele's, and the grandparents' view of things. Were Steven and his family going to tell DiFonzo something different than they had told Schwartz? If they did, to whom would they have told the true story? How would Di-Fonzo, or anyone else for that matter, corroborate the truth?

Beyond these ironies, the agreement led the defense into a morally ambiguous and suspect position. There is, it could be argued, something intrinsically wrong with a writer trying to buy, and thereby control, the sources of a story. Stories are not—or at least they should not be—property. It would seem that a writer, above all others, would believe that a story belongs to everyone. There should not be commerce in human meanings. The buying and selling of stories is bad business.

Other things felt wrong about the sale of the Jenkinses' story. It was a local story, yet even before it had been completed, it—like the region's corn and soybeans—was being harvested and prepared for shipment to the nation. Before a jury had been chosen, had deliberated, and had rendered a judgment, an outsider had come and taken the story. (Later Susan Blythe's story would be obtained by Andrew Malcolm and sold as a tale of the farm crisis that, in this instance, had brought into deadly collision a poor, uprooted farmer and an ambitious, rural banker. Malcolm and Susan Blythe collaborated closely on the story.)

Steven Jenkins, Swen Anderson, Darlene Jenkins, Louis Taveirne, and others were being written up for the nation even as they experienced the trial. They might be in a book and then—with a little success—in a movie or on television. In some way, it seemed that local people and their words, ways, and stories—like their crops—were being purchased at one price and sold in the city at another. Potential conflicts of interest flowed in several directions here.

Most of these conflicts had to do with money. Steven didn't have any. Darlene apparently didn't have much, and Anderson didn't have enough. They sold their story for money. In one sense, they effected an important circle of commerce. Steven and his family gave their stories to Anderson, who in turn sold them to DiFonzo. Aside from the noneconomic matter of fame, Anderson used the money he received to pay the costs incurred in defending Steven. One way to conceive of the transaction is this: Anderson sold one story to DiFonzo at the cost of purchasing another from Carl Schwartz. With the help of Louis Taveirne, Swen Anderson sold a "literary" story and bought a "scientific" one.

In April of 1984, DiFonzo, Anderson, Darlene Jenkins, and Nina and Clayton Jenkins were notified by the State of Minnesota's Crime Victims Reparation Board that, under its "Son of Sam Law," all proceeds gained from the sale of Steven's story would be taken from them and assigned to the board to pay benefits to the victims of crime.

The whole business of selling a story to an outsider did not put the best face on Swen Anderson's interest in the case. To the cynical, it looked as if he were out for a buck and for fame instead of acting in the interests of his client and justice. Of course, Swen's believers enjoyed the surprise of the story's sale and took it as proof that Anderson indeed was a wizard—some kind of magician who could pull a rabbit out of any hat.

Still, for Swen's fans, who were hoping for the victory of the "country lawyer" over the "big city-slicker lawyer," the scoreboard read "Visitors 10, Home 0." Swen was going to trial without a story. He was going on wits, luck, and bravado alone.

CHAPTER FIVE

The Prosecution

Revenge is a kind of wild justice, which the more man's nature runs to, the more ought law to weed it out.

—FRANCIS BACON

COUNT 1: On or about September 29, 1983, in the County of Lincoln, State of Minnesota, Steven Todd Jenkins did willfully, wrongfully, intentionally and with premeditation cause the death of a person, to-wit: Rudolph H. Blythe, Jr.

T HE trial featured a traditional confrontation. In one corner was the "old country lawyer" Swen Anderson—eccentric yet shrewd, tenacious, and possessed of an ability to win. In the other corner sat state prosecutor Thomas Fabel—a bright, young attorney from the Twin Cities, congenial and ingratiating. Folklore required that the country lawyer, Swen Anderson, be superior to the state prosecutor, Tom Fabel.

Tom Fabel came to the case with a reputation as one of the best prosecutors in the state. He had won a number of tough cases, cases he wasn't expected to win. Anyone who read his briefs knew he was analytical and concise. What he wrote was well crafted. He took an obvious pleasure in being lucid as well as in using the dramatic modes of satire and irony.

Fabel was a tall man, at least six feet four inches. He wore a hearing aid. He appeared to be at home with people. He had a nose for small ethnic restaurants and was at home with the wide range of ethnic groups that flavor St. Paul and Minnesota Democratic party politics. In any given conversation, Fabel moved easily from discussions of Mark Twain and Abraham Lincoln, to the Swedes and Germans who settled a given part of St. Paul, to bills pending in the legislature, to the question of which groups vote for which candidates.

While quick witted and humorous, there was a melancholy tinge to him. Of the criminals he had tried, he once remarked, "We are all made of the same clay." (Perhaps all prosecutors, given enough time, become melancholy in some way—worn down by what they have seen of their fellow humans and by the clumsy justice of the courts.)

Fabel remembered some of his cases vividly, not just his wins and losses in the courtroom but the defendants he prosecuted. He realized, especially in violent criminal cases, that the lives and tragedies of defendants were larger than the single act for which they were tried. With a moving pathos, Fabel told of a mother who had scalded her own infant to death. Her husband and their two friends abandoned her. Not insane, yet in no way in full possession of her mind, she was sent to prison. In Fabel's opinion, she was never quite clear in her own mind about what she had done or why she had been forsaken.

At times, Fabel expressed compassion for Steven Jenkins and his father. Yet there was no chance that compassion would deflect the energetic, young prosecutor from his duty. He took pride in doing well. He visibly enjoyed being clever and insightful, and he knew how "to play hardball," to use his phrase. In one case of white-collar crime—a type of crime for which Fabel had a particular aversion—he threatened to put the defendants' children on the stand in order to successfully try a whole network of businessmen who were bilking nursing homes.

Reasons other than the luck of the draw put Steven Jenkins and Swen Anderson in confrontation with Tom Fabel. The case was important; it had received national attention. It attracted Fabel because it was a double homicide, and it seemed to Fabel at first blush to be associated with the growing farm protest.

In contrast to Anderson, Fabel might be caricatured as the all-American boy. Thirty-eight years old, he was married and had three daughters. (A son was born during the trial itself.) Fabel lived in the Twin Cities suburb of Arden Hills. On his father's side, he could trace his family back to a time in St. Paul before Minnesota became a state. (His great-great-grandfather, a

German immigrant from Hesse, ended up in St. Paul as the territorial governor's bootmaker. In 1856, he founded Fabel's Orthopedic Shoes, a small neighborhood shoe store that continued in existence until 1981.)

Tom Fabel had been an eagle scout. He was married to his ninth-grade sweetheart, regularly went to church, and had received a fine education. He received his A.B. degree with honor in 1968 from Carleton College, where he played football. He received his J.D. degree in 1971 from the University of Chicago Law School.

Fabel arrived at the University of Chicago in the fall of 1968 as an idealist who—while critical of youth who, in his words, "spoke to hear themselves talk"—believed America should be socially transformed from the center out and from the bottom up. Chicago, Fabel believed, was where the action was. Particularly interested in urban reform, he believed with youthful fervor that "the world was salvageable." (One night during the tumultuous Chicago Democratic convention, Tom Fabel walked in downtown Chicago. In his words, he "knew the world had changed" as he saw guns on top of the Chicago Museum of Natural History, jeeps with rolls of wire on their fronts, line after line of police with armed weapons, and groups of protesters shouting in the faces of the police. Fabel described himself as "stunned and awed." Fabel's candidate had been Robert Kennedy.)

Married just before going to Chicago, Fabel had worked in the steel mills before beginning law school. Toward the end of law school, Fabel was tempted by the allure of a legal career on the Alaskan frontier. With his wife's first pregnancy came other thoughts, however, and the young family returned home to Minnesota.

Fabel took a position with the Minnesota Attorney General's office, where he served under Warren Spannaus and Hubert (Skip) H. Humphrey III—first as a special assistant attorney general and later as an anti-trust group leader (1972–1973). He then served as a deputy attorney general for the welfare division, in which post he supervised five other attorneys and engaged in extensive state and federal litigation from 1973 to 1977. Next Fabel was deputy attorney general and division director for criminal investigation (1977–1980). In this position—supervising seven attorneys and five investigators—he advised and represented the Department of Corrections and the State Crime Bureau in civil litigation while managing a substantial caseload, which included several homocides and major white-collar offenses.

At the time of the Jenkins case, Fabel had been serving since 1980 as deputy attorney general in the Office of Public Protection, where he supervised four other divisions in addition to Criminal and Public Safety. With continuing emphasis on trial work, he supervised the work of twenty-three lawyers and fifteen investigators. In addition, Fabel taught a variety of seminars and served as an adjunct instructor of advanced trial advocacy courses at William Mitchell College. Fabel preferred "to be out on the road and doing trials," according to him, rather than working with the range of administrative details that was also part of his job.

Fabel was more than a two-dimensional character whose life was simply a success story at home and at work. When he was sixteen and at summer camp Fabel took a terrible fall from a cliff and landed on his head. His skull was smashed. His heart stopped twice while he was being operated on. With his skull pieced together and his jaw wired shut for a year, he found himself hurting in all sorts of ways. He discovered that he was mortal. His budding sports career seemed wrecked. When he looked in the mirror (as only a teenager can), what he saw was ugly. He said he was "humiliated."

This accident partially explained Fabel's compassion, his buoyancy, and much of his belief that every day is one more than was expected. The accident could not, however, account for one distinguishing mixture of elements in his personality. On the one hand, he had a boyish vivacity and spontaneity, which sent him, when in conversation, rushing enthusiastically down almost any path. Ideas and stories elicited his passions. Stories of human adventures and misadventures excited his frequent laughter. On the other hand, his innocence and spontaneity were counterbalanced by a nose for wrong and by a sense that the correction of things is never easy. Fabel seemed simultaneously young and old. He was aware that much of life in general and of the courtroom in particular involved no more and no less than carrying out roles. He denied that he had a background in speech, acting, and literature, yet his easy manner, his facility with words, and his occasional use of a line from Shakespeare might have caused some to doubt him.

In any case, it was clear from the start that in Tom Fabel Swen Anderson would have his hands full. The state had sent one of its best attorneys to try Steven Jenkins.

Fabel's first briefs, in contrast to those of Swen Anderson, were confident and incisive. In a reply memorandum supporting the state's motion to suppress psychiatric opinion testimony (filed January 12, 1984), Fabel underlined the misguided attempts of the defense to confuse the issues of criminal intent and mental capacity, and thus to have expert opinion speak about intent, a task that belonged to the jury alone. He wrote that the Schwartz report, "while masquerading as a psychiatric analysis, is first, last, and throughout an argumentative essay supporting the defendant's account of the killings." In Fabel's opinion, the report lacked even the pretense of objectivity: "Dr. Schwartz, the scientist, gave no heed to the plethora of information suggesting that his sources may have been less than truthful." Fabel left no doubt about his opinion that Anderson's desire to use Schwartz as a witness constituted merely "a wish to have his final argument cloaked in the legitimacy of psychiatric opinion."

Fabel did not treat Anderson's high-flung constitutional claims with any more respect. In the state's memorandum in response to the defendant's omnibus motion (filed February 3, 1984)—after lengthy and careful argument—Fabel summarized his opinions regarding the defense's objection to the searches: "Defendant's professed outrage over these searches must be recognized for what it is—another diatribe which is oblivious to the facts and unrelated to the governing principles of law."

At points Fabel satirized and mocked Anderson's style. To Anderson's charge that in their interrogation of Steven Officers Berg and O'Gorman displayed "all the qualities of a fascist government," Fabel responded that this was another example of his opponent's "characteristic restraint." Fabel then proceeded to show that in one case (*Brown v. Mississippi*, 297 U.S. 278, 56 S. Ct. 461, 1936) that Anderson cited as applicable, "a confession was obtained after a suspect was twice hanged from a tree and subsequently whipped until he confessed to a crime." In another case (*Lyons v. Oklahoma*, 322 U.S. 596, 64 S. Ct. 1208, 1944) that Anderson considered relevant, "a confession was obtained after a second interrogation, lasting nine hours during which physical abuse and the bones of the dead victim were used to override the suspect's assertions of innocence."

Fabel's strategy revealed his confidence. He was patient. He let Anderson make his claims before he replied.

Aside from the motion to suppress the Schwartz report and his response to the defendant's omnibus motions, Fabel's second memorandum called for an unusual pretrial hearing. In this piece Fabel sought to prevent "confusion" in the forthcoming trial that might work to Anderson's advantage. In this unusual move, Fabel objected to Anderson's attempt to put James Jenkins on trial instead of Steven. Fabel argued at length—and won the point—that Steven Jenkins, not his father, was on trial in this case and that the only information that would be relevant regarding James would be that which showed how he committed the crime or how he coerced Steven to commit it. Likewise, Fabel successfully showed that statements by James did not qualify for consideration under the catchall exceptions to the state's hearsay rule. Fabel pointed out that not only were many of James's threats irrelevant because they were made against people other than the victims, but they were made before Steven was born or were made when Steven was not present. Additionally, he noted that James never carried out his threats and that this might even suggest he lacked the power to coerce Steven.

Fabel concluded his memorandum by arguing that if Steven were telling the truth, then by his own admission there was no possible connection between James's temper and the crime itself. From the time the father announced his intention to commit the crime until the next morning when James and Steven arrived at the scene of the crime, there was no display of temper. "According to the defendant," Fabel said, "the evening [before] and the morning of the murders were otherwise occupied by normal events: dinner at a restaurant, visit to friends, shopping, and a normal night's sleep." Also, if Steven were telling the truth, there was no evidence of explosive anger at the murder scene. James and Steven "methodically prepared for the arrival of Blythe." "They went into hiding until the moment the shooting began. . . . There was no confrontation, no argument, no conduct of any kind reflecting impulsive, emotional anger—just shooting."

By the defendant's own testimony, James's temper neither produced the killings, nor compelled Steven to the scene of the crime, nor forced him to play a part in the crime. If Steven were telling the truth, he and his father went dispassionately to commit a crime that would set most hearts trembling.

The strength of the prosecution's case was not due to Fabel alone. The prosecution had resources that far exceeded those of Anderson. It had the full use of Officers Robert Berg and Michael O'Gorman, as well as several other officers from the Bureau of Criminal Apprehension (BCA). This meant that prior to and during the trial, at any given moment, Fabel could pursue the evidence he needed. For instance, one morning during the trial, to the surprise of those in the courtroom, Anderson announced he would offer on the following day as a witness Highway Patrolman Eugene Abraham—Darlene's brother—who would testify what a good shot James was with a pistol. By that very evening, officers of the Bureau of Criminal Apprehension had driven almost two hundred miles north to Brainard and interviewed Officer Abraham. As it happened, he declined to testify as Anderson had said he would, and the following day Anderson had to apologize to the court.

Beyond the state's resources, Fabel had the full cooperation of Lincoln County, its sheriff's office, headed by Abe Thompson, and its young county attorney, Michael Cable.

Cable, born in 1950, received his B.A. in marketing in 1972 and his J.D. from the University of Indiana in 1975. He paid much of his way through school by working for seven years in the steel mills of Gary, Indiana. Just out of law school and in search of life in a rural area, Cable came to Minnesota, where he eventually found employment in Ivanhoe with a regional law firm. With the job came the post of assistant county attorney. In 1978 he ran for and was elected county attorney.

Fabel and Cable—whose rhyming names seemed to suggest any kind of partnership other than one dedicated to the prosecution of one of the most serious murder cases in southwestern Minnesota's history—worked well together. Cable started the case by issuing the first successful search and arrest warrants and by directing the investigation. Cable had the case well under way when Fabel joined him as co-counsel. Fabel did almost all the writing and all the speaking. Cable made sure things were not forgotten. Always at Fabel's side in the courtroom, Cable frequently whispered to Fabel. He brought to the case a quick intelligence, a solid knowledge of the local area (thanks especially to his marriage to a local woman, whose parents were close friends of Nina and Clayton Jenkins), and a tenacious determination to carry the case properly through to its end. He did not like Anderson, especially his braggadocio and his tendency to practice the law as he wished. What especially angered Cable was Anderson's attempt to try the crime by means of publicity.

The grand jury, accepting the prosecution's story, had found reason to try Steven both for being an accomplice and for the intentional murder of two men. Furthermore, the grand jury charged Steven with the premeditated murder of Rudolph Blythe. Judge Walter Mann, in preliminary rulings, had substantiated the state's evidence gained from search and interrogation, had denied Anderson his experts and his fundamental attempt to try James Jenkins, and had made the decisions that eliminated the duress story Anderson wished to tell. When the trial began, the prosecution started from as good a position as could be imagined. Thus far, everything had gone its way.

THE TRIAL BEGAN

AT ONE TABLE SAT FABEL,; next to him was Cable. At the other table was Anderson, his wife Elizabeth, and Steven Jenkins.

Steven's military appearance was gone. His hair had grown longer and he wore a long-sleeved white sweater. He kept his eyes to himself and spent considerable time writing and sketching on a pad of paper. It was not yet fully apparent how much he had become a passive bystander in one of the most complex of all adult activities, a trial. (Ironically, James Jenkins had been chosen at random as a prospective juror—a fact known by only a few courthouse regulars.)

The small oak courtroom, built just after the First World War and repainted for the trial, was not filled to its capacity of one hundred spectators on the first day. There were approximately twenty people from the press (most of them local or from the Twin Cities, plus one *New York Times* writer) and an equal number of onlookers, including Darlene Jenkins and Susan Blythe, both of whom attended the trial regularly. As each day passed, the number of visitors grew, including people who came from considerable distances and a few teenage girls who were attracted to Steven. Eventually, more visitors were refused admittance than were allowed to enter. One day near the conclusion of the trial, the courtroom door was ripped from its hinges as visitors pushed, shoved, and jammed their way into the small courtroom. Thereafter, passes were issued to visitors.

At the start of the trial, there were things Fabel and Cable didn't know. Most importantly they did not know whether Steven would take the stand. This caused them concern, since in their opinion Steven had done well in previous interrogations. They were not sure how their own witnesses would do—especially Susan Blythe, who was quick to take offense and thus could easily be provoked by Anderson, whom she detested. Also, they had to wonder what sort of defense Anderson would present. They especially feared a line of argument that would suggest that the state made Steven its scapegoat because it had to have someone to blame for the two dead men. There was also the chance that Anderson might challenge counts five and six—those accusing Steven of conspiracy in the deaths of Blythe and Thulin—arguing that the crime was not, to use the language of Minnesota's criminal code, "reasonably foreseeable by him as a probable consequence of committing or attempting to commit the crime intended." An attack on the grounds of the crime's foreseeability might not only challenge the specific charges involved but—yet more dangerously from the state's point of view—might prove to be a way for Anderson to bring before the court a full examination of the character of James Jenkins. On this basis, Swen might air everything that was erratic about James Jenkins and irrational about the crime. All this would help the defense of Steven.

Fabel prepared his case as thoroughly and resourcefully as he could. While not encumbering his presentation with redundant evidence and testimony, he added piece to piece, joining witness to witness, to tell a long, thorough, and analytical story. Fabel's approach fit his need to prove his case with various types of circumstantial evidence. With the introduction of Steven's grand jury testimony, Fabel sought to demonstrate that Steven went willfully to the crime, that he and James went to the crime believing they were going "to rob and scare Rudolph Blythe," that Steven furnished the weapons, and that the murder weapon itself was Steven's. (The controversial interrogation by Officers Berg and O'Gorman, which on videotape showed a large Texas ranger sitting behind and looming over Steven, was not—for obvious reasons—entered into evidence.)

More difficult to prove was the theory that Steven did the shooting intentionally and with premeditation. To do this, Fabel needed to show that Steven could have done the killing and that James could not. At the same time, in order to eliminate all remaining doubt, Fabel had to convince the jurors that Steven's account of the crime was false. Fabel claimed at the outset of the trial that he would show that Steven's story was implausible, that there was ample evidence to show that planning preceded the crime, that Steven was thinking of violence before the crime, and that evidence from the shooting showed that an expert marksman—which Steven was and James was not—did the shooting.

Fabel used investigators and experts to establish the evidence that not only made Steven's story implausible but demonstrated that the killings required a good runner and an expert shooter. Experts established where the victims were shot and from where the shots were fired. Fabel also used a ballistics expert and a pathologist to testify about the nature and quality of the shots. Fabel used a gunsmith and a firearms expert to testify to the defectiveness of the M-1, which made it effectively useable only by someone familiar with it. In addition, Fabel used an ophthalmologist and his medical records to establish James's poor eyesight.

Fabel provided the court with a model of the farmstead. It was important to show that the shooter ran 268 feet from the back of the farm yard—where the first shots, which killed Thulin, were fired—to the front of the farm house—where the second group of shots, which killed Rudolph Blythe, were fired. To cover 268 feet took an unusual ability to run and shoot. It meant killing Thulin; then running and chasing Blythe, whom Fabel depicted as athletic; and finally stopping and shooting an additional volley of well-aimed shots.

Using supplementary expert testimony, Fabel sought to demonstrate that the killer was a marksman. He argued that the first three shots—taken from eighty-six feet away, over weeds three and four feet tall—were good shots. The first shot killed the fleeing Thulin instantly by severing Thulin's neck and spine as he entered the car. The following two shots would have—it was conjectured—hit Thulin had he not fallen as a result of the first shot.

One of the two shots that passed through the windshield penetrated the small of Blythe's back. (However, an expert testified that the wound would not necessarily have impaired Blythe's ability to run.) Furthermore, the prosecution argued that the second volley of four shots, taken from ninety-eight feet—which killed the running Blythe—also was the work of a marksman. Two of the four bullets—one of which inflicted a mortal wound—entered the body of the fleeing Blythe less than an inch apart. Only fine marksmanship or the most unusual luck could have made these shots so accurate. The other two bullets of the second volley were also characterized as examples of good shooting; one hit Blythe's arm and the other passed through the hood of his jacket as he fell.

By themselves, the arguments over the quality of the shooting were not overwhelming—or at least not universally convincing. More than one person following the trial remarked that it did not take an expert to shoot at such close distances—which are considered almost point blank with an M-1. Any deer hunter could do as well. However, the prosecution's story was not complete at this point.

Fabel pointed out that the M-1, the murder weapon that Steven took everywhere, was defective. Al Weathers, a gunsmith in Brownwood, Texas, testified that in the process of repairing the M-1, he discovered an ill-fitting extractor and an improperly fitting magazine catch. He advised Steven to return the rifle to the manufacturer. His later examination found additional flaws—an ammunition feeding problem and a crack in the gas chamber—that in his judgment had the cumulative effect of rendering the gun "totally inoperative." A second expert, James

Lansing of the Bureau of Criminal Apprehension's firearms division explained that the rifle became "totally inoperative" during laboratory examinations that showed—in his opinion—that only somebody highly familiar with the weapon could have fired two or three shots in succession without it jamming. In effect, Fabel argued that the M-1 was an effective weapon only in Steven's hands.

Fabel also added the following corollary: if Steven, and Steven alone, could have done the shooting, James could not have done the shooting. Fabel used a variety of means to establish this. James, said Fabel, was not acquainted with the defective weapon; it probably would have jammed in his hands. If its sights had not been readjusted, he would have shot either high or low. (If not adjusted for an individual shooter, an expert weapon could miss from one inch below to ten inches above a target at the range of thirty-five to forty feet.)

Fabel also reiterated Darlene Jenkins's earlier statements to Bureau officers that James had not hunted or target-practiced for a long time nor did he show any real interest in guns or weapons.

Another witness, Ted Beard, a friend of James in Brownwood, testified that James was unable—during a two- to three-minute period to focus his rifle—which was equipped with a scope that magnified from two to seven times—on a nearby house. "He handed the gun back and said, 'I can't see it.'" The same witness testified that when he asked James to go deer hunting, "he said, 'I'd just be in your way. I can't see well enough to deer hunt.'" More poignantly, Beard testified that James never went anywhere at night without carrying a flashlight directed on the toes of his shoes and that James walked at all times in a peculiar way. "James walked," according to Beard, "like he was feeling his way with his feet."

Fabel pushed further. Witness Al Weathers, whose corrective lenses gave him 20/20 vision (which was far superior to James's), acknowledged that he could not have shot the weapon unless it had been equipped with a scope he could adjust for his bifocals.

Another expert Fabel called to the stand was Marshall ophthalmologist Dr. Theodore Fritsche. Dr. Fritsche had examined

James Jenkins's eyes two and one-half years before the crime. Fritsche indicated that Jenkins suffered from night blindness, tunnel vision, and retinitis pigmentosa (a degenerative eye disease which would eventually blind him). Dr. Fritsche elaborated on his diagnosis: James could hardly see at all at night. He looked out at the world as if he were peering through a periscope or a cannister with a diameter of six to eight inches. (His field of vision was forty degrees in the right eye, thirty degrees in the left.)

Dr. Fritsche commented additionally that—during the day, without his glasses—James Jenkins's sight was 20/400 in both eyes, which meant that at twenty feet he could not read an eight-inch-high letter. If he had been wearing the single-lens glasses found on his body at the suicide site and if his eyesight had not significantly deteriorated since Fritsche had examined him, James's sight—at its best—was 20/200 in his right eye and 20/70 in his left eye. (Supportive materials from the state's autopsy were not introduced in order to avoid redundancy.) Dr. Fritsche further conjectured that James only wore his prescription bifocals (which would have corrected his sight to 20/70 in the right eye and to 20/50 in the left) for a short period, since Jenkins returned to Dr. Fritsche shortly after getting his new bifocals and complained about them.

Fabel also used Dr. Fritsche, who was a qualified navy marksman, to testify that given the type of sight the M-1 had, James would have had a great deal of difficulty shooting it accurately. Only an experienced marksman—which James was not—could have made sufficient compensation for his distorted sight.

Fabel used an additional dozen witnesses to provide Steven with a motive, to show that Steven had not told the truth, and to prove Steven had the ability to kill. One witness, Jeffrey Ray Schroder, directly and with considerable impact contradicted Steven's grand jury testimony when he said the shorter of the two men, the one with a stocking cap—James—was driving when Steven and James left the farm yard.

Fabel used Barbara Jean Ihnen, a Buffalo State Bank official, to sketch James Jenkins's financial relations with the bank. The bank loaned $42,000 to Jenkins in 1979 to expand and refinance his Farmers Home Administration loan. At the time, he was milking twenty-five to twenty-eight cows. The $42,000 was his total indebtedness; he offered as collateral his livestock and machinery. Repayment was made from his milk money. "He secured a second loan in October 1979, for an additional $18,000 by giving the bank an assignment of contract for deed on the farm place, taking his equity in the real estate as additional collateral."

According to Ihnen, "James Jenkins made regular payments until August of 1980, when the bank received a call that he was selling off his cattle." He sold thirty-two of the seventy-two or seventy-three for slaughter, for which he received approximately $400 to $500 apiece (instead of $800 as milk cows). On August 6, Jenkins brought the check for the cows and a milk check to the bank and, according to Ihnen, "explained that his wife had left him and that he wanted to quit farming, sell everything, and pay the bank off."

On the same day, Ihnen continued, Jenkins called bank president Rudolph Blythe and said of the thirteen cows he had left: "You might as well come and get them. I'm not going to milk." According to Ihnen, Blythe went out and got the cows. Blythe had no idea where the remaining forty cows were. On August 25, James filed for bankruptcy. In September, Blythe discovered that the place was abandoned; he therefore obtained custody from a judge to protect the bank's collateral.

Insofar as Steven was his father's son, Fabel argued, he too could have been angry at the bank, which was associated with the family's loss of the farm and with the subsequent dissolution of the family itself.

Fabel used Mayfair Cafe owner Nancy Smith, who saw James and Steven once a day and sometimes more often, to testify that on the evening preceding the crime—and on that occasion only—the Jenkinses behaved differently. "Usually," she indicated, "they sat with their backs up against the wall and would just relax. That night when I came in, they were talking to each other, you know, hovered like over the table." Nancy Smith's testimony implied, but did not prove, that Steven discussed and therefore helped plan the crime with his father.

Fabel, in turn, called Richard Hartson of D & M Glass in Pipestone to testify about Steven's interest in what kind of weapon would penetrate the windows in bank teller cages. Hartson also revealed that Darlene had told him that

James's bad eyesight had put the family pickup in the ditch and that James had told him just three days before the crime that "his wife was fooling around with the banker."

Local well driller Marvin Minett took the stand to testify that on the day before the crime Steven had asked him if dynamite was available. Steven's friend Steven Shriver, from the Marshall vicinity, vouched that Steven was a good shot, that he could do a lot of sit-ups and push-ups, and that he could run and shoot. Swen Borresen, a Tyler blacksmith, described how three weeks before the crime Steven had requested, "for ornamental reasons," to have the bottoms of three grenades welded shut; a week before the crime, Steven picked them up and paid for them with cash. With these witnesses, Fabel showed that violent ideas simmered in Steven throughout September.

With his last witnesses, Fabel retold his story. Ted Beard from Brownwood, Texas, whose sister-in-law James had dated and who testified to James's poor eye sight, also believed that father and son got along well. "James seemed to think the world and all of the boy."

James Lee Perry, building and ground supervisor of the Brownwood Independent School District, testified about how well the two got along—"No arguments. No dominance." He added to Fabel's story by describing the limits of James's health. When James was at work, Perry observed, he had an "abnormal shortness of breath." Perry also witnessed an occasional swelling in James's legs that prevented him from carrying out his duties and an inability to do lifting and pushing that sixty-year-old Perry himself could do.

Fabel's last witness was Charles Snow, a maintenance supervisor at the school, who had been an officer in the army for thirty-one years. He had trained Steven to shoot, and he testified about how well Steven could shoot. Fabel chose Snow because he was extremely sympathetic to both James and Steven. Snow first made a place for James to sleep in the maintenance shop. Later Snow allowed James to park his trailer next to the shop at night and to use its electricity. Snow later hired Steven for nineteen hours a week at a minimum wage of $3.35 an hour, but Steven would work forty hours a week. Both father and son liked to work. Snow offered an example of how the two often went to his small ranch twenty miles away and just enjoyed working. Out of scrap lumber, they built Snow a shed.

Contradicting any argument that there was a coercive relationship between father and son, Snow praised the relationship of James and Steven as ideal. "They were extremely compatible with one another. There was never a harsh word. . . . Steven respected his father extremely much: he had done everything that his father asked him to do. It was—I would almost say—probably more of a brother-to-brother relation than a father-to-son, you know, if that makes sense."

Yet, as Fabel knew, Snow's testimony was as devastating as it was sympathetic. He obviously bore Steven no grudge, yet—perhaps more than Snow knew—he painted a portrait of a dangerous Steven whom everyone in the courtroom could fear. Of his many conversations with Steven, Snow said that "almost all the time [they talked of] military subjects or subjects about weapons." Steven was exceptionally interested in Snow's military experience, and Snow—who had taught military marksmanship in the army—trained Steven to fire his newly purchased M-1. (James had signed for the weapon in January or February of 1983.) Snow taught Steven the four basic military positions from which to shoot, especially "the prone position and how to go into it from running." Snow also trained Steven in the proper breathing techniques required for expert shooting. To Fabel's questions about how good a shot Steven was, Snow's replies were unequivocal: Steven was "an excellent student" of the M-1, which was always with Steven and James in the pickup. Steven was "superb," an "excellent shot."

By concluding with Snow, Fabel described a type of unofficial soldier who was ready and able to kill. Fabel brought back into the jurors' minds those first images of the Steven who had surrendered to the police in Texas: the Steven who looked like a captured soldier. That Steven was again alive and present in the courtroom—there for judgment.

SUSAN BLYTHE'S STORY

IF THE PROSECUTION was going to tell a convincing story, it had to give voice to the suffering caused by the defendant. Susan

Blythe, whom the prosecutor called early in the trial, was that voice.

Until Susan came to the stand, it was as if the crime were hidden, as if it had occurred behind a great opaque glass that revealed only the movement of shadows and the muffled sounds of voices. Until Susan appeared upon the stand, the prosecution's story—regardless of how cogently Fabel developed it—pivoted on evidence alone. When Susan Blythe came to the stand, the state's story found a personal voice.

Susan had not suffered alone. Lynette Thulin had suffered too. She would now be alone with three daughters: Linda, fourteen; Deanna, thirteen; and Kara, eight. She had believed that a process of reconciliation was under way between her and her estranged husband, Deems, when he was shot.

If Lynette Thulin had told her story fully on the witness stand, she would have added irony to the trial. She could have told how her husband, Deems "Toby" Thulin, was a Vietnam-era veteran, an active member of an Army Reserve unit, and a former police officer. Yet he was gunned down. She could have told the court how the position at Ruthton had come in the fall of 1982, as, in her words, "an answer to a prayer for our family." After leaving the service in 1969, Toby had had three children and a series of jobs: first in construction with his father in the family's hometown of Litchfield, Minnesota; then in banking in Litchfield at a loan operation (Thorpe Loan); next in banking in Ada, Minnesota, where he did part-time police work; then in banking in Sibley, Iowa; and finally in construction work in Sibley.

Also, if Lynette Thulin had told her full story, she would have explained how Toby, who so often had to play the tough guy for Rudy with the bank's delinquent farmers, was nearly always in debt. (According to one farmer who was interviewed by Ken Nordin for the defense, Toby was the bank's "hatchetman.") In fact, Thulin—who was telling other people to get their houses in order—had not had his own in order since he left the United States Air Force in 1969. Toby was not steady at work; he was not home a lot; and he lied.

Then there were his Vietnam stories. He never went to Vietnam; he served safely behind the lines as an Air Force sergeant in Thailand. Nevertheless, Toby told his stories. He woke up from nightmares, remembering how he had been held captive in Vietnam, and how women and children had been attacked with knives. His stories went on and on. Toby loved to hunt. He drank. He served in the National Guard. He read *Soldier of Fortune*. He was not, however, a Vietnam hero. He was another man getting through everyday life with tall stories.

Lynette also could have testified—perhaps confusedly, but definitely not to the prosecution's advantage—how Rudy had told her and Toby that one time when "he had gone back to check this particular farm, he had been met with a shotgun by someone". (Lynette was not sure who; maybe it was Jenkins.) "Rudy said," according to Lynette, "'I wasn't gonna argue with any shotgun. . . . There is no piece of land that was worth anybody's life.'"

Not without irony, Lynette Thulin could have recounted how she and Toby had considered purchasing the Jenkinses' place. According to Rudy, the man who left the house was "quite bitter" because "his wife had left him." "Rudy showed us the bathroom. The stool was ripped out. The tub was ripped out. There was a hole in the floor and he [Rudy] kept saying, 'Lynette, be careful, don't fall through there.'"

Finally, Lynette Thulin—not to the advantage of the prosecution—could have told how the woman with whom Toby spent so much time in Lynd was just a friend: "Toby always told me that they were just friends. . . . She had a psychiatry background and, at the time, he didn't have money to hire a counselor. . . . He just felt it was somebody to talk to. . . . And I said that even if something did go on, I said the Lord allowed us the last five weeks together. And I said, in that time, there was total forgiveness."

As touching as this was, most of Lynette Thulin's personal story was legally irrelevant. Her story was not important to the prosecution's case. The Jenkinses didn't know—nor did they expect to meet—Deems Thulin at the scene of the crime. He was an innocent bystander. They were only waiting for one man: Susan's husband, Rudolph Blythe.

Further elevating the testimony of Susan Blythe beyond Lynette Thulin's was the fact that Susan had been on the scene of the crime seconds before it occurred and she returned minutes after it had taken place. Among the living, only Steven was closer to the crime than Susan. Just moments before the shooting, her husband had sent her to nearby Tyler to call the sheriff in Ivanhoe. While on the phone at the Tyler city hall, she heard the sheriff say on the short wave radio: "The Jenkinses' place. Yes, I have her on the phone." She put down the phone and, filled with fear, she returned to the farm to find her husband dead.

Susan, as Fabel fully realized, was both a voice of suffering and a voice of evidence. She could be used to help locate the victims just prior to the shooting, and her trip from the farm to Tyler and back gave a close measure of time to the crime.

If Susan did well on the stand, the jury could be moved to convict Steven—only a youth—of first-degree murder. If Susan's story held in fact and tone, she, her husband, and their son Rudolph III (Rolph), would be nothing but innocent and wronged victims.

No matter how sympathetic members of the jury might be to the plight of the countryside's farmers and debtors, if Susan's story succeeded, Rudolph Blythe would not remain in anyone's mind a compassionless banker. He would not be merely a rich son of a well-known Philadelphia pharmaceutical researcher whom life had always treated more than fairly.

Rudolph Blythe had been brought up in one of Philadelphia's most prestigious areas, along the Main Line. He attended one of the city's most prestigious private high schools, from which he graduated in 1959; he then attended Franklin and Marshall College, a men's college in Lancaster, Pennsylvania, for a few years. There was money behind him.

In the courtroom, when Susan spoke, it would be in large part forgotten that Rudolph Blythe was a loud and ambitious outsider who, only a short time after coming to Ruthton from a banking position in Des Moines, Iowa, ambitiously started a Lions Club, ran a close election for school board, and made his opinions known on many things. As testified to by people who attended meetings with him, Rudolph Blythe had opinions—he was heard from.

As Susan told her story, the jury would forget that times turned bad and Blythe himself felt the pinch severely, he became an aggressive banker. He counted debt-to-asset ratios closely and, with Thulin's help, came down hard on farmers whose numbers looked bad. Blythe and Thulin pressed for their payments; when their customers sought new loans or the renegotiation of old loans, they did the very unneighborly thing of pushing them to look elsewhere for money. To many farmers and country people, Rudy had become an obnoxious banker who was easier and easier to wish dead. "He deserved it. If the Jenkinses hadn't done it, someone else should have." In one way or another, this was said a lot where farmers congregated.

Susan's testimony was convincing, Rudolph Blythe would not be the banker who foolishly lent money to James Jenkins for a farming operation of questionable promise. If Susan's testimony found its mark, Rudolph Blythe and Deems Thulin would not appear to the jury to be arrogant men who—having gotten in the habit of bullying farmers—chose to confront the trespassers on the bank's land that fateful day.

Susan's story would not succeed if her story became a contrast of two families—one rich and successful, the other poor and broken. James and Steven went to Texas, to rural Texas, with nothing; and because there was nowhere else to go, they wanted nothing more than to return to southwestern Minnesota. Susan and Rudolph, along with their son Rolph, by contrast, went to Texas at Thanksgiving 1981 because they wanted to leave southwestern Minnesota. Susan and Rudolph both found good work in banking in the Dallas area; Rudolph held the position of vice president of Commerce Southwest Management, Incorporation Division. The only thing that kept them from moving away from Minnesota was the Buffalo Ridge State Bank, its small insurance agency, and a home. The three were priced for sale for $825,000 in January 1983. A floating credit note on Blythe's property that reached 20 percent led Blythe's father to put up a considerable amount of his own stock to secure his son's Ruthton bank with its Minneapolis creditor bank.

Obviously, Susan couldn't tell her whole story. Some of it had no place in the courtoom. She could not blurt out all the truth and all the pain associated with her husband's death. She could not tell the court that it was not she who, in 1978, wanted to buy a small bank in a village in southwestern Minnesota. She never had liked Ruthton nor its people. They were too far out of the mainstream for her. She did not find a lot of difference between Rudy's desire to return to Ethiopia, where he had served in the army, and his idea of owning a small bank in such an out-of-the way place as Ruthton.

Susan could not tell the court how pleased she was to leave Ruthton for Texas at Thanksgiving in 1981. She could not say how awful her four years in Ruthton had been. She could not tell the court she had not wanted to return to Ruthton from Texas when Rudolph found he could not sell the bank and when one officer resigned at the Ruthton bank and another resigned at the Holland branch. She could not tell the court how hard it had been for them to live apart until July of 1983, when she and her son returned to Ruthton, and how painful it had been for her to think through their fourteen-year marriage during the period when she remained in Texas.

A friend from the period noted that "They had to work out a personal thing. . . . She didn't want to be there [in Ruthton]; he did." While Rudy, the same friend noted, didn't have any deep personal friends among the natives of the town, he liked the area, basically got along well with its people, and more or less fit in, whereas Susan did not. For almost a year, only daily phone calls and her husband's monthly visits connected them. She could not tell the jury it was Rudy who took her to Ruthton and, once she had escaped from Ruthton, it was he who had returned her and their son to Ruthton. She had thought about divorce, even mentioned suicide. She could not scream out, "That damn Ruthton and its damn bank has cost us every-thing!"

This was not the time for her to vent her spleen, as she had in her statement to Bureau of Criminal Apprehension officers on the day of her husband's death. There was nothing to be gained by repeating her description to the BCA of the person who drove in front of her as she tried to speed to call the sheriff. "He's . . . kind of putzin' along . . . like all these goddamn farmers around here."

It would not do the prosecution's case any good for Susan to say she was the one who was "always scared out of [her] mind around here." Susan could not say that Rudy had told her, "Susan, don't be so paranoid" —to which she had replied, "But I have always been afraid . . . of people because . . when you foreclose on somebody, they do terrible things. They do horrible things to my son." (In her statement, Susan offered only examples of obscene and harassing phone calls received about their barking dog.) Nor could Susan tell the court what she had said: "The people next door have a crazy daughter . . . and she . . . she made . . . she told me my son was going to die. And . . . my husband."

The law was not interested in hearing just how small and stifling Susan, an educated and energetic woman, found that small village to be. According to one of her friends, she was "enthusiastic and bubbly, a real go-getter." She was not satisfied by simply caring for her child and her home nor occasionally substituting locally as a teacher of English, which had been her college major at Allegheny College in Meadville, Pennsylvania. In the words of another friend, Susan found herself in a small town with "people who were likable, even lovable, traditional, narrow in scope, with a few jerks thrown in." New in town, she ran for the most sacrosanct position in a small town—that of school board. She was defeated. She offered her talents, ideas, enthusiasm, and style to the town—but too quickly and in too much abundance for the inhabitants of Ruthton. Both she and Rudy had forgotten, a friend noted, "that they had moved into a small, conservative town."

Susan also had "the trappings of class," which invariably provoked resentment in some. Her days in the Kappa Alpha sorority and in country clubs showed through. She and Rudolph bought the newest and best house in Ruthton—which was, in truth, neither luxurious nor even pretty. She dressed well—too well for everyday Ruthton. She thought stereotypically about the people of the town, and a considerable number of them reciprocated. On the one hand, she wanted acceptance; on the other hand, she offered a constant supply of criticisms and suggestions about improving the school, building a swimming pool, and improving "the quality of life" in Ruthton.

Much of her "pushiness" seemed related to her son Rolph. She doted on her only son, as a story repeated in Ruthton demonstrated. The other children who appeared at the first practice of Little League came in Levis, tee shirts, tennis shoes, and with gloves. Rolph came fully equipped and outfitted in a new uniform. When he did not get to play often enough, Susan did not talk to the coach; she wrote him a letter.

One of Susan's friends said Susan could not accomodate herself to Ruthton any better than Ruthton could accommodate itself to her. Susan remained a conspicuous outsider in town. She persisted in discovering a Ruthton community that was not really there. Those who wanted change had gone; those who expected things to remain the same had stayed behind.

The law, however, was not particularly interested in either the sociology of Ruthton or the psychology of Susan Blythe. The courtroom was not the place where Susan could tell the world that Rudolph was no ordinary banker—nor could she tell it what a terrible price he had paid for his idealism in wanting to work constructively in an underdeveloped country. While the ambition to own a bank of his own brought Rudolph Blythe out to the prairie, he had been moved by more than wanting to make a profit, to advance a career, and to settle a family. In the small, declining village of Ruthton, Rudolph Blythe did more than buy a bank. He chose to concentrate his still youthful energies and idealism on a small, rural town.

Rudolph Blythe had given a personal form to a career that had been long in the making. The choice of buying a bank in Ruthton followed naturally from Blythe's career up to that point. In the military service in Ethiopia, which he coupled with travel throughout Africa after his discharge in 1965, matters of poverty and rural development occupied him. When he came back to the United States, Blythe returned to the University of Iowa, where he completed his B.A. Later he did graduate work in economics at Temple University. His speciality was the economics of underdeveloped countries. Married in 1969 to Susan, Rudolph came as an economist to serve a three-year bank apprenticeship at Northwestern Bank in Minneapolis. While in Minneapolis, Rudolph Blythe again tried his hand at politics: he served as campaign manager for the Minneapolis progressive Republican Alderman Gladys Brooks. He then spent four years at the Hawkeye Bank Corporation in Des Moines, Iowa.

In Ruthton, where pessimism about the future prevailed, Rudolph Blythe directed his energies to its improvement. He saw himself as a reformer: Ruthton was his Ethiopia. In the words of one of Blythe's Ruthton friends, "He believed that something could be done. He was a real positive thinker. . . . In the spirit of Dale Carnegie and Norman Vincent Peale, he believed that reality is what you will to make it." Indeed, he was, in the opinion of the same friend, "a Don Quixote attacking the windmills of this region." Blythe thought he could improve the region faster than it was deteriorating. In a town "where the trains don't stop anymore" and the majority joke that "the duty of the last one out is to turn off the lights," Rudolph Blythe concentrated his idealism, and he was murdered.

Susan could not tell the jury how terribly unfair it was that her Rudy had been murdered. She could not point out that during the spring of the year in which the murder occurred, her husband had joined a task force on economic stress sponsored by the Countryside Council, a group dedicated to the understanding and improvement of the counties of southwestern Minnesota. On his sheet of proposed interests, Rudy indicated of primary importance was "the relationship of the business community and farmers." It could not make any difference for Susan to tell the court that, when a group of regional bankers had been assembled by the Department of Agriculture on the topic of the emerging farm crisis, her husband alone had been outspoken. Some remembered Rudolph Blythe at that meeting as being both loud and bold; others remember that of the assembled bankers he alone was willing to acknowledge that the bankers themselves were implicated in the crisis by their lending practices. There was a lot about Rudy, Susan's feelings, and their fate that Susan could not tell the court. There were, however, things she could say that would help the prosecution convict Steven Jenkins.

If Susan told her story well, she would essentially strip away the matter of farm foreclosure from this case. Rudolph Blythe, aggressive outsider and banker, would become, above all else, a man like any other man. Susan would no longer be the snob from the East who took her boy out of the Ruthton School District and put him in the larger Pipestone School District. Instead, she would be a young widow with one child who bore the brunt of the deed of James and Steven Jenkins.

Susan Blythe was the natural accuser of Steven Jenkins. A

certain solemnity filled the courtroom when this thirty-nine-year-old widow of Rudolph Blythe took the stand. Her hair was closely cropped yet covered most of her forehead and circled her face. This—in addition to her plain brown dress—made her look like a monk. She wore a single strand of pearls.

Her husband, Susan told Fabel, was in good health. He was forty-one. He jogged and played racquetball. Until fairly recently, he fervently played rugby. Rudy was a big man. He was six feet three inches and weighed 245 pounds. "I could always see him in a crowd," Susan remarked.

Susan Blythe told the court that Rudy was trying to sell the bank. In fact, at one point the whole family had left Ruthton for Texas. However, Rudy returned with Rolph in 1982 when his managing loan officer resigned. Susan stayed in Texas, preparing to return to Ruthton when she finished up her work and sold the house (which they were having a hard time doing). She commuted back and forth, speaking to Rudy almost every night on the phone.

She knew Deems "Toby" Thulin, a thirty-seven-year-old Vietnam-era veteran who had worked previously as a police chief at Shelly, Minnesota. He also worked as a special deputy for Norman County, where in 1978 he ran unsuccessfully for sheriff. Susan had screened Thulin for the position of loan officer. He had lived at the Blythe home, first with his family and then when separated.

Susan did not know defendant Steven Jenkins, and she had only met his father James once: "I bumped into him once between the doors at the bank. . . . [We] met in the dead air space where people stomp their feet and we stored snow shovels." She was well acquainted with the farm where the murder occurred since the Blythes, on occasion, had let their dog run there.

"RUNNING LATE"

SUSAN BLYTHE GOT UP on the morning of the murder, September 29, 1983, running late. She had been running late all week long. A broken air conditioner in their Texas home had stopped her from making it home to Ruthton for her birthday on the twenty-seventh. Her voice broke a little—as it did from time to time, making her sound like a young girl—when she said: "Birthdays are a big deal at our house."

On the morning of September 29, Susan was behind in her schedule. She had to get her son Rolph to school in Pipestone, twenty miles away, and then get the bank car back to her husband. Realizing she was late and afraid her husband would be angry because she was late, Susan decided to exchange the bank car for the station wagon before going to exercise class. Not finding her husband at the bank, Susan then drove the car out to the Jenkinses' place, where Rudy had told her he was to meet a prospective buyer that morning.

When she arrived at the back of the house, she saw in front of the garage the station wagon butted up nose to nose against a white pickup. Her husband and Thulin emerged from the house and told her to roll down her window. They indicated that they had trespassers and that the owners of the white pickup with Texas plates were the Jenkinses. She got out of the car and put on sweat pants over her exercise shorts. While chatting with Toby about her trip from Texas, Susan saw her husband go along the side of the house, the west side of the garage, and then a few steps into the grove. "He got smaller and smaller," Susan remarked. As he returned, she heard a sharp, metallic sound. Rudy returned casually, apparently not at all concerned, and instructed Susan to go to Tyler and phone the sheriff. "He didn't seem afraid. . . . The men weren't afraid, but I was," her voice quavered again.

When Susan left the farm, Deems Thulin—showing no fear of the trespassers—was down at the far end of the farm yard by the granary and the barn. As Susan sped off, she peered back into the grove to see if she could spy the trespassers but a pickup blocked her view.

Susan Blythe drove the six miles to Tyler at seventy miles an hour. She told Sheriff Abe Thompson by phone, "My husband told me to tell you that there are trespassers on our farm." Susan heard on Thompson's end a CB radio report mentioning James Jenkins's place, and she heard the sheriff say to someone else he had her on the phone.

With apprehension, she returned to the farm. She found the driveway to the farm blocked by a vehicle, and she found part-time Tyler police officer Paul Bartz, who was the first and only person on the scene of the crime at the moment.

Susan struggled to get to her husband. She swung at Officer Bartz. "I tried to run up to where Rudy was, but he held me and pinned me to the car. I got really scared then because I thought something was wrong. I pretended I was okay. I said that I had to get to my husband. He's in trouble." Officer Bartz told Susan, "Your husband is dead in the ditch."

Susan did not tell the court she stood vigil over her husband's body in the ditch, arranging it as best she could until the ambulance crew arrived. When they asked to have a look at him, she shouted, "No. Get away! Haven't you all done enough? Leave him alone. Leave us alone. He's dead, can't you see that? They've killed him. That goddamned Jenkins."

Susan Blythe had told her story. Aside from giving heart to the prosecution's story, she provided Fabel important evidence with which to contradict Steven's grand jury testimony. She provided the crime with a clock. By using the speed and the distance she traveled and the point at which Bartz passed her as he was traveling from north to south, Officer O'Gorman estimated that the crime occurred within approximately a three-minute period.

Susan also identified the point from which Thulin came scurrying back to the car where—just as he entered it—he was shot in the neck. Thulin's position and the fact that he had run argued against Steven's story of a silent crime: Thulin no doubt saw something. It is likely he shouted something that brought Blythe back to the car. (Steven claimed to have not heard anything before the first volley of shots.)

With the aid of a police reconstruction, Susan identified the sharp metallic sound she heard as her husband returned along the garage toward her. The sound came from a stack of gut-tering—which lay in low piles, covered with weeds—between the garage (where Steven claimed he was) and the chicken coop, from the far corner of which the first volley of shots was fired. This was another sound Steven claimed he did not hear. If James made the sound and Steven heard it, then Steven knew at least approximately where his father was, which would be in direct contradiction to his claim that he had no idea where his father was during the crime.

Even more significant was Susan's testimony that her husband had gone along the garage and a few steps down into the grove. If he had, he would have seen Steven, who claimed to have been hidden behind the garage. (With videotape and Susan's help, BCA officers reconstructed Rudolph Blythe's walk and what he would have seen looking to the north and the east. The person whom Bureau officers sought to conceal in the weeds at the northeast corner of the garage was easily seen.) Susan's testimony and Steven's could not mutually stand.

If Susan told the truth, Steven Jenkins had lied. If Steven had lied, this was another reason to believe he was the murderer. As the prosecution suggested, Steven had everything to gain if the court believed his father did the killing.

CHAPTER SIX

The Lawyer and the Boy:
Last Days Together

The power of punishment is to silence, not to
confute.

—SAMUEL JOHNSON, *Sermons*

O NLY a major error, which Tom Fabel did not make, or
a great story, which Swen Anderson did not tell,
could have deflected the jury from a judgment of
guilty.

One of the strongest encounters of the trial occurred during
Swen Anderson's cross-examination of Susan Blythe. As Anderson—least fashionable of dressers and most "country" of lawyers—approached Susan, she took a deep breath and raised her
shoulders. Her voice became more strident; her eyes flashed
more. She looked ready for war and hence capable of squan-
dering the sympathy she had won.

Swen Anderson challenged Susan Blythe's testimony. He
believed she had changed her testimony to the BCA. He inferred
that her story about the sharp metallic sound she claimed to
have heard was an addition to her original testimony. He also
cast doubt on her testimony that she had seen her husband
descend a small slope along the garage, saying that if he had he
would have seen Steven. Swen Anderson suggested that Susan
Blythe's husband was bigger and heavier—and thus slower—
than the prosecution described him. To his disadvantage, Swen
Anderson quibbled with Susan's testimony about her husband's
weight. (Between her first and second testimonies, she explained, she had found her husband's daily weight chart. He was
ten pounds lighter than she had originally estimated; he weighed
245 rather than 255 pounds.)

In what proved to be the most sensitive and decisive part of his cross-examination, Anderson approached Susan and took her husband's pants from a brown paper sack. Anderson was trying to show that if Rudolph Blythe had gone along and behind the garage where she said he had, his now clean pant cuffs, as well as his missing shoelaces, would have been covered with weeds. He asked Susan whether she could identify the pants that he handed her as her husband's. She replied, "Yes," and gratuitously added that she had bought the pants for her husband from L. L. Bean, the fashionably rustic Maine clothing cataloguer. Anderson won her agreement that weeds could possibly have clung to a fabric like that of her husband's pants.

As if he had never folded a thing in his life, Anderson then clumsily tried to fold the pants that Susan Blythe had handed back to him. Susan politely offered to help him. She folded the pants of her dead husband reverently, yet as if she had done this a thousand times before, as if she were turning over the communion cloth at the altar.

Anderson cross-examined the other prosecution witnesses no more successfully. He caused no dramatic reversal. He cast no serious doubt on any of the opposing witnesses' main testimonies. Perhaps his case had been demolished when he lost the use of psychiatric testimony, as he himself had been quoted as saying before the trial began. Perhaps he simply did not have much to go on.

As the trial wore on, Anderson appeared tired, especially at the end of the trial. He was sick. Since his decision to not use the suicide note—to which Anderson had never lent any credence—relations between Anderson and Louis Taveirne had broken down. Darlene did not appear to be entirely under Anderson's control, and to compound matters author DiFonzo, who was exceptionally close to Swen, was extremely angry at Louis Taveirne. (An acquaintance of Louis Taveirne had rented DiFonzo a four-wheel drive vehicle. When the rented vehicle was returned with broken gears, the renter threatened to press charges against DiFonzo for recovery of the damages, which amounted to thousands of dollars. Swen delivered DiFonzo's check to the renter, and DiFonzo held Taveirne responsible for the action of the truck's owner. Taveirne believed he was simply caught in the middle of an unfortunate situation.)

In one instance, Anderson apparently had not done his homework. Tom Fabel called Lynette Thulin to the stand with the precise intention of defusing her statement to investigators that she had heard somewhere—she was not sure where—that James Jenkins had once pointed a gun at Rudolph Blythe. Anderson objected to Fabel's line of questioning, consequently having his own sustained objection keep out precisely the part of Lynette Thulin's testimony that the prosecution most feared.

In some instances, Anderson's cross-examination went awry. On more than one occasion, he received an answer that was the opposite of what he expected. He led the owner of the Mayfair Cafe to state emphatically that James and Steven had never before spoken together in such an intense and uninterruped manner as they did on the evening before the murders.

Hoping to confirm that James was a good shot, Anderson asked another witness whether National Guardsmen were good shots. The witness replied that in his opinion National Guardsmen were, indeed, very poor marksmen.

More damaging to his case, in his cross-examination of Marshall opthamologist Theodore Fritsche, Anderson asked whether James Jenkins could have easily seen the bright flourescent yellow of Blythe's rain slicker. Almost as if he had stumbled into a classic "interesting-that-you-should-ask-that," Fritsche replied that he had tested James on that very color and James could hardly see it at all.

Swen Anderson's cross-examination had done no damage to Tom Fabel's story. The court now awaited Anderson's story.

SWEN ANDERSON'S TURN

ON THE DAY SWEN ANDERSON began his defense, the door to the small courtroom was ripped off its hinges as people pushed and shoved their way in. Now it was Anderson's turn. All those who were rooting for Steven and those who were simply hankering for excitement expected that at last Swen Anderson would take command. At last the surprises would begin.

To Anderson's fans, it appeared all along that he was conjuring something. He was constantly taking off and putting on his glasses, swinging his head about, jotting a note, never allowing one look to appear on his face without rapidly replacing it with another.

To the hopeful, another sign of his cleverness was the fact that he mispronounced words, as clever people often do. For instance, he continued throughout his examination of Dr. Fritsche—originally from the distinctly German-American town of New Ulm, Minnesota—to call him "Fritzie." At one point, with Inspector Clouseau–like pronunciation, he asked one witness whether James could shoot well enough to shoot a "renning root." Despite his repetition of the phrase "rrenning root," the witness remained entirely baffled until Anderson translated himself by saying "a big mouse" and thus explaining to the witness and to the court that he had meant "a running rat."

The most noticeable and criticized thing about Anderson's defense was that Steven Jenkins was never called to the stand. One of Swen Anderson's friends and fellow attorneys remarked: "The failure to call Steven was fatal—not calling him was Swen's superfailure." Another friend and fellow attorney, Eric DeRycke, asked, "Do you know what a defendant is who doesn't take the stand?" and then replied to his own question, "A prisoner." DeRycke added: "You don't have your witness go before the grand jury and then not appear at the trial itself."

The prosecution suspected that Steven did not take the stand because on the eve of the trial Steven had confessed the crime to Swen. That accounted for what the prosecution saw as Swen's very belated effort to engage in serious plea-bargaining. Eric DeRycke speculated that Steven was afraid to get on the stand. Another party who was exceptionally close to Swen argued that Swen did not put Steven on the stand because Steven did not seem to catch on: as much as he was prompted, he would not accept the notion that his father was insane and no good. Steven wanted to get on the stand, but Swen believed that Steven would hurt his own case and prejudice any and all chance of appeal. (Possibilities for appeal always played strongly in Swen's trial strategy.) Yet another party who was very close to Swen and Steven claimed that Swen kept Steven off the stand "because he was afraid Fabel would cut him to pieces on the stand. And Swen thought that Steven had already suffered enough."

In any case, Steven sat silently throughout the trial. Most

often his head was down, and he was busy drawing and doodling. It was as if he were a spectator at an elaborate game in which adults argued and guessed what he did or did not do.

Steven's appearance had changed. Throughout the trial, Steven dressed in light-colored, long-sleeved shirts that covered his tattoos. He looked "preppy," like a member of a stylish high school crowd. Nevertheless, his dress did not conceal the fact that Steven, the only one in the courtroom who knew what happened on the farm that day, did not speak.

His silence—from which the jury was instructed not to draw any conclusion—did speak. No one in the courtroom heard Steven say, "I am sorry." No one in the courtroom heard Steven tell what life was like with his father. No one heard what some believed: that Steven was filled with fear, wound up tighter than a spring, and that once he shot the first man he could not stop.

It was as if he were hiding. In the courtroom Steven did not scream, he did not cry, he did not give anyone a chance to sympathize with him. No one saw him react in court, nor could anyone explain why, as one person reported, Steven went home and was sick the day the photographs of the Blythe's and Thulin's bodies were introduced in court.

Anderson did what he could with a handful of weak witnesses. Eric DeRycke testified that several years before he had seen James walk without difficulty on ice. Local mechanic James Lenz testified to James's ability to see and move well approximately ten years before the crime. Hence, Anderson proved he lacked witnesses to say that James had good sight and agility during the last ten years. Anderson also called local investigator and firearms expert Ken Nordin, whose testimony was inconclusive on all points, as Nordin himself later concurred.

On his original list of prospective witnesses, Anderson had included attorney Gorden Paterson of Marshall, who handled Darlene's divorce. The divorce was quick (done in three months, the least possible time), uncontested (James had no attorney), and showed no exterior sign of acrimony over the division of property (there were apparently no assets to divide). There was no question about custody of the children, who went to Darlene. In answer to specific questions about abuse, Darlene had replied that she had been assaulted "just one time." While the mistreatment of the children over a prolonged period was the main reason for the divorce, James's abuse was verbal, not physical. These characteristics of the divorce, as well as the fact that Darlene made no effort—not even in the immediate aftermath of the divorce—to keep Steven from his father, were probably all good reasons why in the end Swen Anderson chose not to call Darlene's attorney, Gorden Paterson, to the stand.

Darlene turned out to be Anderson's major witness. Every day she faithfully attended the trial, often with a friend and once in a while with Steven's sister. During recesses outside the courtroom in the large antechamber at the second floor landing where crowds gathered during recesses, Darlene sat with Steven. Sometimes they held hands on the bench outside the courtroom or as they left the courtroom together.

Darlene and Louis played an active role in the defense. Before the trial in October 1983, Darlene and Swen returned to the Ruthton farm. There they attempted to reconstruct the crime and the time involved in Susan's drive to Tyler. They filed their typed report on Louis's stationery. In January 1984, Louis Taveirne and James Dwire, Louis's friend and neighbor, returned to the scene of James's suicide, where they claimed they discovered a suicide note from James. Even after the trial, Darlene remained active in trying to help prepare the defense's appeal. She took photographs at the scene of the crime. She reported a possible instance of the jury mingling with the public.

Both Susan Blythe and Darlene Jenkins suffered as a result of the crime. Susan's suffering was the suffering of wronged innocence, but Darlene had suffered too. She was innocent of the crime; she made no plan, pulled no trigger. Yet she could not escape the consequences of James's and Steven's deed. She could not help but blame James for what he had done to their son.

Darlene must have carried an awesome burden during the trial. Her face, worn and showing strain, was a difficult face to read. Her eyes were set in a distant gaze. Her face did not shape itself to a certain emotion or mood. What she thought as she sat in the second-floor courtroom—into which filtered, especially on the warmest days, voices from the adjacent high school she had once attended—one could only guess. (A former classmate described Darlene as "a very quiet person." Below her senior class picture were words chosen by a classmate: "I never say much but who knows what I am thinking.")

To a degree, Darlene must have felt that she was on trial. It was not the accusations she saw in the eyes of others that put her on trial. Perhaps long ago she had learned to live with the judgments of others. But what could not be escaped was the fact that her son and her husband had killed. In some sense, she must have felt this trial was about her failed marriage: what kind of wife and mother she had been, what she could have done to save her two men from themselves, why Steven had preferred being with James rather than with her.

Defensively she could have asked herself how she could have guessed the horrible consequences of leaving her two men alone. No doubt, long before the trial, she had resigned herself to the fact that there was simply nothing she could do for James and Steven. But questions still must have chewed at her. Why had she ever married James in the first place? He had never finished high school, he did not come from wealth, nor did he show prospects of it. Even when she had first met him, she must have had glimpses of his willfulness and bad temper. Why hadn't she divorced him earlier? He was such a loser: he had caused so much pain!

Darlene must have mulled these wearying and painful questions over as the trial approached. But now the time had come for her to take the stand. What else could she say except, "Damn my husband and save my son!"

With a flat, emotionless voice, Darlene began. She told the story she wanted to tell—despite her earlier statements to the BCA. She said she knew about weapons. She herself had fired several types of guns—a .38, a .22, and even Steven's M-1. (In earlier testimony she had said, "I don't know anything about [Steven's] guns—his awful gun—that [one] with a strap on it." To Officer Sigafoos she had said that Steven had a lot of guns that she didn't know about except for the "God-awful gun.")

Darlene now gave a different portrait of James also. She transformed him into a marksman. On the farm he averaged shooting once a week. With his .22, he could ping the tail of the old windmill. Darlene remembered how he once hit a running rat in their garbage pit. According to Darlene, James even shot after he got his bifocals. He was capable of hitting beer cans at a hundred feet. Darlene went on to describe how—when living in Marshall—she, James, and Steven ended a family picnic by shooting at targets.

However, this testimony did not square with her earlier statement to the BCA in which she had said: "James never went hunting." Darlene had said that James didn't own guns, except for an old one. "I think he sold [it] off." His eyes were "very poor," according to Darlene. When asked about target practicing, Darlene had responded, "He wasn't into that stuff at all."

Fabel made certain that Darlene's testimony crumbled into contradiction. Darlene had failed to tell a story that could be believed: either she told the truth now or she had before. Either James shot or did not shoot. Either the whole family shot a lot and loved guns or only Steven did. Darlene Jenkins did not tell a convincing story. Swen Anderson's whole case in the end came to rest on Darlene, yet her testimony appeared to surprise Anderson as much as it surprised others in the courtroom.

Darlene was Swen Anderson's most important witness. When she left the stand, his defense was over. Only closing statements remained.

FABEL'S CLOSING STATEMENT

TOM FABEL'S CLOSING STATEMENT conformed to the spirit of the case he had so far conducted. It was logical and thorough.

Explaining the six counts of murder and the elements necessary to establish guilt, Fabel argued that if Steven's grand jury testimony alone were true, Steven was guilty of the fifth and sixth counts. The second-degree charge of the murders of Rudolph Blythe and Deems A. Thulin, which accused Steven of "aiding and conspiring with another," was a felony offense, "where death was reasonably foreseeable as a probable consequence of the attempted felony." However, if, in contradiction to his grand jury testimony, Steven had done the shooting, then he was guilty of the third and fourth counts of murder, both of second degree, for "willfully, wrongfully, and intentionally causing the deaths of Rudolph Blythe and Deems A. Thulin." Furthermore, if the murder of Blythe was premeditated, then

Steven was guilty of the first count of murder in the first degree. If not premeditated, yet willfully, wrongfully, and intentionally caused while committing or attempting to commit the offense of aggravated robbery, Steven was still guilty of the second count of murder, which like the first count called for the charge of first-degree murder.

Fabel reviewed Steven's grand jury testimony. He then told the members of the jury that if they believed Steven and his father had only one brief conversation before the crime in which they decided to rob and scare Rudolph Blythe and if they believed the father did the shooting, then they must find Steven guilty of only counts five and six. On these counts, Fabel argued, there could be no doubt: Steven furnished the guns; he went along willingly; and he drove to and from the scene of the crime, where by the defendant's own testimony he and his father planned assault or robbery. He knew what those weapons did. "Toys of a child?" Fabel queried. He slammed down the gun on the desk and answered his own question: "Some toys! Some child!"

Then Fabel argued against the truthfulness of Steven's testimony. He asked the members of the jury if they believed that while preparing to commit their first crime together, a crime of such proportions, there was only one short conversation between them. Fabel asked how likely it was that the father, without good eyesight, would take the son's favorite gun—the gun the son slept with—and leave the shotgun—a far better weapon for a man who cannot see and who plans to rob—for his son. Fabel asked the jurors to consider how likely it was that the father, who couldn't run well, would grab the gun and run fifty yards. Fabel asked the members of the jury if they believed that Steven heard so little. Didn't the jurors believe there would have been some sound from Thulin or Blythe as they came running for their lives back to their car. Wasn't Steven's story, Fabel asked with all his questions, a highly improbable story.

Fabel then proceeded to a yet more central question: Did the jurors believe it was likely that James, not Steven, did the shooting? Fabel argued that it was extremely doubtful. Steven was the marksman; he could run and shoot. Of the four shots fired at Blythe, Fabel reminded the jurors, two hit within two centimeters of each other, the third passed near the head, and the fourth caught Blythe in the arm. Those were the shots of a marksman; they were not, Fabel stressed, random shots sprayed all over the universe. Steven knew the weapon. He alone could make the jamming gun shoot. His father, Fabel argued, could not have done the shooting. He did not know the gun; he did not have the capacity to run and shoot.

The only explanation that made any sense, Fabel told the jurors, was that Steven did the shooting. He told the jurors that insofar as they were reasonably sure about this, they could find Steven guilty of the third and fourth counts of intentionally killing Rudolph Blythe and Deems Thulin.

Fabel next proposed to the jury that it should consider convicting Steven of either the first or second count of murder, both of which charged Steven with the first-degree murder of Rudolph Blythe. Fabel might have suggested that Steven premeditated a crime of violence before going to the farm, that Steven did this when he had his grenades reactivated, when he and his father lured Rudolph Blythe to the farm, or during the time they lay in wait at the farm. Fabel, however, made a different argument. He argued that the premeditation—which demands no specific length of time—occurred during the course of the crime itself. It took place between the killing of Deems Thulin and Rudolph Blythe.

As the trail through the high weeds showed, according to Fabel, Steven went first to the dead body of Deems Thulin before pursuing and shooting Rudolph Blythe. It was then, Fabel argued with passion, that Steven engaged in the act of premeditation. Steven did not settle for just shooting Thulin, whom he did not know, but he persisted in pursuing a fleeing and injured man. He did not stop. He continued his chase until he brought down Rudolph Blythe with a shot in the back. Each step of his pursuit, Fabel insisted, not only confirmed his intention, but revealed his singularly premeditated desire to kill the intended victim, Rudolph Blythe.

"If you, the jury, do not agree with the first count of first-degree murder," Fabel relentlessly argued, "you must still recognize that Steven killed Rudolph Blythe while committing or attempting to commit aggravated robbery. This, too, constitutes murder in the first degree."

Fabel concluded by telling the jurors that they needed common sense certainty, not absolute certainty. Courts do not deal with mathematical certainty, he instructed them. With his parting words, he commiserated with the jurors: "Not too long from now, you people will be retiring to your jury room to perform one of the most difficult duties that you have been called upon to perform in your entire lives. It is a hard duty . . . a hard duty of citizenship. Your duty is to apply the law to the facts."

ANDERSON'S CLOSING STATEMENT

SWEN ANDERSON'S CASE so far had been totally disappointing. It lacked cohesiveness. It was missing the element of surprise. Anderson appeared to be prepared neither for his nor the state's witnesses. This was his last chance.

Without much eloquence, Anderson addressed the jury. He hoped to convince them of two things. First, the father did the shooting or at least there existed reasonable doubt whether Steven did. Second, even though he might never be able to refute Steven's role as an accomplice, Anderson asserted that from the beginning it was the father who planned the crime and carried it out.

One major problem crippled Anderson's defense. He was in an all-or-nothing situation. He had no story to counter the charges of first-degree murder. He lacked a story to tell of Steven doing the killing but doing it without premeditation. He had put his client in a do-or-die situation. If the jury decided Steven was the murderer, that would be tantamount to deciding Steven was a hardened liar; then there would be nothing to stop the jury from going on to convict Steven of the first-degree murder charges. Steven's silence would be held against him.

Swen Anderson's closing statement was not as long as the prosecution's. Anderson sought to show that only James had a motive for killing Rudolph Blythe. Steven "was only fourteen when the farm was lost." He tried to show that it was the father who was filled with hatred for Rudolph Blythe and was cruel enough to commit such a wanton crime. Once after the divorce, the father had threatened "to kill himself and take Steven with him." He bragged, according to Steven, that he had "fixed Rudy" and that he wanted to kill Louis Taveirne. James, in Swen

Anderson's depiction, was a desperate man in whom hate "festered and festered."

By contrast, Anderson argued, Steven was not filled with hate. Steven shut his eyes when he shot at a sheriff, whom he could have killed. The boy did not shoot in evidence of the crime. He showed his respect for the law by turning himself in. He dissuaded his father from "taking as many as he could with him."

Anderson also tried to show the unpremeditated character of the crime. James and Steven did not take ammunition for their guns to the scene of the crime. They had purchased groceries the night before the crime, but they did not take them along for the flight.

Anderson tried to raise as many doubts as he could. He argued that James was not blind. The murders involved easy shots. The father knew the M-1; he had shot it with the son, and he even had a receipt for it. Anderson postulated that they only took one bath towel because possibly the father alone intended to do the robbing. Perhaps, Anderson suggested, the father was behind the small pump house in front of the granary all along; or, he hypothesized, perhaps it was the father who tripped over the guttering. Anderson suggested that if Steven had been the shooter, the shots would have been better. The irrationality of the crime itself prohibited Steven from being a conspirator in it.

Anderson concluded: "He's eighteen—and his destiny is in your hands."

VERDICT, ADOPTION, AND SENTENCING

THE JURY BEGAN DELIBERATION on the afternoon of Wednesday, April 26. It took a recess late in the evening. (It was not sequestered.) It returned its verdict Thursday morning before noon.

Steven spent much of Wednesday evening wandering around the building, occasionally sitting with his girlfriend from Granite Falls and a few other teenagers on the courthouse steps. Swen Anderson is reported to have spent the night "in agony."

The next day, reporters and a handful of others who had conducted a long vigil the night before appeared, looking bleary. It was obvious from the appearance of Fabel and Cable that they had stayed up late. The clerk of court was glad it was over, and this was the ruling sentiment of a small courthouse grown tired of a murder and of the intricate and lengthy processes of a trial.

The jury found Steven Jenkins guilty of the first-degree premeditated killing of Rudolph Blythe and the second-degree intentional killing of Deems Thulin.

According to jury foreman David Koster, an articulate pharmacist from Tyler, the jury endorsed the main points of the prosecution's case. Steven's story was not believable. He probably had not taken the stand out of fear of being contradicted. His mother's statements were not believable. Two witnesses saw Steven driving when he said he was not. The murders were a result of good shooting. James could not have made the shots nor done the running that the shooting required. James did not like guns. Above all else, Koster stressed, Steven would have "sensed, wondered, known where his father went 'at the scene of the crime.' "

Susan Blythe, who gritted her teeth, made no comment to the press. Lynette Thulin, Deems Thulin's widow, was reported to have said, "I wanted to see justice done. . . . He had a choice and now he is going to have to pay for that choice. We all have to realize the consequences of our choices."

Darlene Jenkins, according to her daughter Michele, was too upset to comment.

Tom Fabel remarked that he thought the first-degree conviction was merited, but he went on to say he was not "exultant" over the outcome, for "it's a culmination of the tragedy of September 29, 1983. The fact he is eighteen makes it more difficult." In the same spirit, Michael Cable praised the Bureau of Criminal Apprehension's investigation, saying, "I am proud to be connected with this one, but saddened at the result."

Swen Anderson met the verdict with a claim about the certainty of appeal and his affection for Steven. "To me, he's like my own son. I love him greatly and thoroughly. I am very grateful he got confirmed before the trial."

"The cameras swung away from Swen," to quote *Marshall Independent* reporter Steve Olson, "as Jenkins, in handcuffs, was spotted being led down the steps by his mother Darlene. 'Steve?' called Anderson. 'Will you wait for me, Steve?' Jenkins, tears on his face, didn't reply but worked his way through the crowd of cameramen at the front door and then around the courthouse to a squad car for transport to Marshall, where he will be held until sentencing."

Swen Anderson kept his promise. Defeat did not chasten him. Within two weeks of the verdict, he filed a "Memorandum and Argument for Motions and Notice of Motions for a New Trial or in the Alternative Motions to Vacate Judgment."

Anderson challenged the validity of the trial on all points: "the irregularity of its proceedings," "the incorrect admission of evidence," "misconduct of the prosecution," "surprise of new evidence," and "a verdict not by law and contrary to law." "The state," Anderson contended, "failed utterly to prove guilt beyond reasonable doubt." "All evidence showed that the Father not the Son, pulled the trigger." Susan Blythe's testimony was "highly and totally unreliable." Furthermore, Anderson contended that Susan had purposely altered her testimony about where her husband went on the farmstead in order to contradict Steven's testimony. He noted that the guttering, which made the sound Susan heard, was not found by Darlene Jenkins after the trial where the prosecution located it. In addition, Swen declared: "The shooting was sloppy, angry, and distorted," which proved to him it was done by the father who was "cruel, sadistic, and crazy."

Replowing the same ground, Anderson argued that by being denied the duress defense—which in fact he had not been—his defendant was *de facto* denied a case. Steven, he reasserted (not in the best English), "was brainwashed by his father in the same manner a U.S. soldier could be brainwashed in Viet Niem [sic] by the Viet Cong. That the father's brain was substituted in the boy's brain. That the father had a suicide pact with his son two years before that he would kill his son and then kill himself and the boy said, 'I will get the gun and the shells.'"

Anderson fired in all directions. He claimed that the prosecutor "indirectly said" that Steven lied and that the prosecutor deceitfully entered the M-1 rifle as evidence without mentioning how the prosecution's own testing had made the gun defective. The prosecutor purposefully pointed, "waved," and poked the M-1 at jurors, the press, and the people of the court in order "to inflame, intimidate, and mentally persuade the jury into a guilty verdict."

Swen Anderson attacked the first-degree findings: no rationally planned robbery occurred; therefore, he argued, there should be no felony murder charge. Attacking the second and more serious charge of first-degree murder, Swen argued that the killing of Rudolph Blythe was "a continuation of the killing of Thulin," hence the charge of the killing of Blythe should be identical to that of the killing of Thulin. How could the state, Swen Anderson asked, request first degree for the killing of Blythe if it did not ask first degree for Thulin? (Anderson overlooked the fact that the grand jury had only asked for a first-degree murder charge in the Blythe killing, that the defendant and his father went to the scene of the crime looking for Rudolph Blythe, not Deems Thulin, and—what the state took most seriously in its argument—that the killer had gone first to Thulin's body before pursuing Blythe.)

Anderson argued that Lincoln County denied the defendant his constitutional rights and his rights under criminal procedures by not "providing facilities to conduct a proper trial on something this publicized and this important." (Most likely referring to the opinions of Luigi DiFonzo and Andrew Malcolm, Anderson noted that "newspapers from New York, Massachusetts, and other places were shocked at the lack of facilities and the lack of sequestering.") He complained about the "insufferable lack of fresh air," and he concluded that "one juror had a heart attack, obviously from breathing foul air." He generalized by saying say that the county's failure to prepare for the trial amounted to a denial of due process and equal protection under the Fourteenth Amendment and the right to fair trial under the Sixth Amendment.

Anderson also claimed a mistrial because a sheriff sat behind Steven throughout the trial, thereby prejudicing the jury. He also reported that he had heard that one juror was pressured to decide against his defendant.

Anderson also complained about the failure to keep the jury separated from the public. He mentioned that Darlene, in one instance, witnessed jurors using the same bathrooms as the general public. He noted another instance in which a reporter consulted the jury foreman, a druggist, about medicine for a bad back.

More significantly, Anderson complained that the members of the jury were not sequestered on the night of their deliberation but were instead allowed to return home to sleep. (Of course, he did not mention that he had not objected at the time nor that sequestration is not a common practice in rural south-western Minnesota.) None of the above arguments—of which only the sequestration argument had any strength—convinced Judge Mann to vacate the jury's judgment and order a new trial.

Swen Anderson appealed on the basis of all these arguments to the Minnesota Supreme Court, asserting that the trial had been a travesty of justice. He claimed: "The state's evidence was, in some areas, totally false." "The defendant is legally, totally innocent. . . . The trial was theatre, not truth—and poor theatre at best. . . . This is one of the most total miscarriages of all time, without truth and with incredible theatre."

Before the sentencing, Swen Anderson added one more twist to the case. To the horror of those who preach the need for objectivity in lawyer-client relations, Swen adopted Steven Jenkins. Swen claimed to love Steven, but his reasons for the adoption were strategic, according to a close friend and others close to the case. In all likelihood Anderson—who often reused what had succeeded in the past—reasoned that if the willingness to have Steven live at his house had gotten Steven released on bail, so adoption might soften Steven's sentence and improve the strength of their appeal. Some local lawyers said cynically that Swen adopted Steven to insulate himself from a malpractice suit.

Darlene thought the adoption was a good thing. According to her, it gave Steven the sense that he belonged somewhere and that someone cared about him. She and Michele did not question Swen's affection for Steven.

In the sentence hearing, Anderson expressed his feelings about Steven. He did not refer to any guilt he might have over the trial's outcome, yet Swen had reason to feel guilty, and some close to him believed he did. He had promised that Steven would go free. He probably made this promise to Steven repeatedly; he surely made it once in the presence of DeRycke and DiFonzo. Yet Anderson had lost this case on all counts.

In adopting Steven, Swen referred not to his guilt, but to his love for Steven. "I was very much in love with and have a very solid bond with the defendant." Steven has "a lot of feeling, tremendous feeling." He is "one of the brightest people I have ever known. He is capable of straight-A college work."

Even though Swen Anderson had told his friend LuVern Hansen that Steven never really opened up to him, Anderson asserted that he, Anderson, was "one of the few people that has every card in the deck in this case." As he consistently did in private and public conversation, Anderson affirmed that Steven is "a victim of, I think, the most severe child abuse I have ever witnessed in my life." Steven's environment, according to Anderson, had made him "an absolute loser." Anderson had paid for and believed in the Schwartz report.

According to Anderson, Steven was the victim of the evil that God has let exist among us. "Steven is a life here that I am bound to. There is a life here that has to be saved. Some way he has to be rehabilitated."

Speaking with an eloquence he had not employed during the trial, Swen Anderson told the court why he adopted Steven:

When this young man lived with me he had the equivalent of age twelve in communication. . . . That is how stunted he was. And I would do certain things with him and express to him certain things, like love, and he felt that he was unworthy. . . . He was ungood because he had been raised in an environment where he was taught he was unworthy. And I don't know what will happen. I wanted to adopt him. I wanted to do that after the decision so they couldn't say I was trying, by people who are cynical, to get some kind of advantage or something. . . . But I wanted to let him know that I would stand by that kid as long as I was alive. I will stand by him. And I want him to succeed. I want him to be a winner. I have compassion for that kid that I have never had for very many others. And I am not bitter or upset with anything. . . . And that bothers me that I can't do more than just simply say you have got something good here and I love that boy. Thank you.

Tom Fabel recommended no specific penalty, leaving it for the court to decide:

The court has heard of evidence of two lives of responsible men—fathers, husbands—lives which were senselessly and immediately snuffed out in their prime. The court has heard of two devastated lives, families with children, widows. The court has heard evidence that all this happened in cold blood for no reason. The human price that is involved on the victim's side of the crime is enormous. . . .

Yet the prosecution pointed to the counterbalancing fact that Steven was young and that he no doubt was the product of a broken family: "The defendant himself could be seen as a further extension and final extension of the tragedy that surrounded several families and has touched many lives."

Fabel claimed that it was originally the prosecution's desire to join in the recommendation of the presentence investigation, which was that "the second-degree murder conviction of Thulin be served concurrently with the first-degree murder of Blythe conviction, which is, as required by the law, life." However, the prosecution argued that the presentence investigation report forbade them from advocating this leniency. The report made it evident that the defendant "expressed no remorse for crimes of which he has been convicted, and has expressed no sorrow or remorse of feeling for the victims . . . and the families whom he has devastated." More importantly, the prosecution claimed that the report says,

Steven is seen to have no insight into his own behavior. He has expressed no willingness to assume the mantle of guilt and deal with that guilt in a way that would be constructive in his life. . . . The failure of the defendant to express remorse, the failure of the defendant to express insight, the failure of the defendant to express any desire to alter his behavior is what deeply, deeply concerns us as we stand before the Court today.

On this basis, the prosecution concluded that it had no opinion regarding the concurrence of sentencing and would leave it to Judge Mann to balance the suffering of the victims and their families against Steven's youth and his own suffering. The prosecution, however, did suggest that "an ongoing concern for public safety should be paramount."

Judge Mann elected to have Steven's first- and second-degree sentences run concurrently. He sentenced Steven to life in prison for killing Rudolph Blythe. He sentenced him to one hundred months for the second-degree murder of Deems Thulin. Judge Mann also incorporated into the sentencing the Rock County assault charge for firing at an officer, giving Steven thirty months to also run concurrently with the life sentence. At the earliest, Steven could be released for parole in seventeen years—in the year 2001.

Justifying his choice of allowing Steven to serve his terms concurrently instead of consecutively, Judge Mann argued that the defendant before him was different from the defendant on the day of the crime. On the day of the crime, the defendant was obsessed with weapons and he was prepared for that horrible violence especially because "a retired, high-ranking military officer [Judge Mann was referring to Charles Snow], without any apparent concern for the consequences . . . saw fit to teach Steven Todd Anderson in all of the military aspects of the use of military firearms." Judge Mann told Snow—who had trained Steven—that he had given bitter truth to the axiom, "As we sow, so shall we reap."

Judge Mann said he believed Steven had changed because he had lived for four months in the Anderson house. There, he suggested, Steven saw life in a new way. Affirming an optimism in the court's ability to educate, Judge Mann concluded that Steven's presence throughout the long trial "should now [make him] realize the immeasurable value our society places on human life."

Overlooking the most important fact that Steven's father was dead and not alluding to Steven's failure to confess or show publicly his remorse, Judge Mann nevertheless asserted that "the defendant is a much different person from the one who was on the so-called Jenkins farm on September 29, 1983."

Rejecting retribution as wrong but without faith in the prison's power of rehabilitation, Judge Mann believed that the only purpose of punishment was to confine and to segregate. Therefore, Judge Mann chose to segregate and confine Steven with a sentence of life in prison, allowing "proper authority to determine at the end of a seventeen-year period whether or not Steven Todd Anderson should be granted parole, or whether he should continue to serve what potentially may be confinement for life."

MORE STORIES

THE STATE OF MINNESOTA and Lincoln County invested considerable resources in the prosecution of Steven. Not counting the salaries of county attorney Michael Cable, the clerks of court, and the sheriff, nor the services donated by the attorney general's office and the Bureau of Criminal Apprehension, Lincoln County spent $40,000—3 percent of its annual budget—on the case.

In a May 30, 1984, Affidavit of Indigency, Swen Anderson surrendered Steven's case to a public defender to appeal it to the Minnesota Supreme Court. He claimed he could no longer bear the cost of the case. Without referring to the funds he received from author DiFonzo, he claimed that the case—which he had taken for free—had already cost him "in excess of $30,000 both for out-of-pocket expenses and for time spent without compensation."

Confident that he had laid the groundwork for a successful appeal, Anderson optimistically waited for the court's ruling. On December 12, 1985, the Minnesota Supreme Court let the lower court's ruling stand. It upheld the jury's right in first-degree murder cases to evaluate circumstantial evidence and denied that "a proof of motive is required to prove guilt." Furthermore, the court denied all claims about the impropriety of the trial, including the vital matter of the nonsequestration of the jury.

Predictably, Tom Fabel found the ruling to be "thoroughly meritied by the evidence." He hoped the ruling would have a "calming effect" on the people in rural areas, although he underlined that he did not see the Jenkins case as a typical rural reaction to the farm crisis. He believed an appeal to be unlikely and, if made, he believed the state's conviction was now "99.9 percent bulletproof."

Swen Anderson declared the ruling "a tragedy." He commented, "It's going to be hard on the kid." Swen knew Steven to be a terribly withdrawn boy who lacked confidence and who needed all the love and care he could get. Swen knew that Steven did not trust adults. He had seen Steven sit for two and three hours at a time and say only a handful of words. Steven, as Swen and Elizabeth observed, did not seem to know how to express his feelings. In one instance, irritated by the noise of one of Swen's children as he sat watching television, Steven was beside himself with frustration and anger, seeming not to know how to simply ask her to stop. In another instance, when in good-natured fun he gave one of the children a face-washing in the snow, he was afraid of the reprisal he would suffer for his action.

By the terms of his bail, Steven had to be with Swen when not at home or in school. (These terms were faithfully observed. The Granite Falls police chief did not recall receiving any complaints about Steven violating the agreement.) For much of Steven's stay with Swen, he was Swen's sidekick. One of Swen's attorney friends remarked that Steven was "Swen's little dogboy. He carried Swen's briefcase. He sat where Swen put him. The kid," the friend continued, "never said a thing." He specifically recalled a time when, in the course of a lengthy meal with Swen and Steven, Steven "did not say a single word."

On occasion, Steven tagged along with Swen on his circuit of restaurants, the courthouse, fellow lawyers' offices, and LuVern Hansen's and Kermit Ness's homes. Kermit Ness and his wife Lynn saw Steve as "never initiating a conversation." "He was a closed book, a wall," Kermit remarked. However, one time near the end of one of Swen's interminable monologues, Steven said to Kermit, "See what I have to put up with all day long."

"All the time Steven was in Granite Falls, he never felt safe," Kermit remarked. LuVern Hansen agreed with Kermit's observation: "While Steven might smile and talk a little, he was always afraid. He took friendship from any quarter given."

When he first came to Granite Falls, Steven was a celebrity of sorts. Young girls flocked to him, and in other towns, young girls were heard to say, "If he came to our school, I would be his friend. I would sit next to him." Romance was found in the publicity he had received.

The next-door neighbor girl, Laurie Kompelien, became Steven's steady girlfriend. The Andersons welcomed Laurie into their home, and the Kompeliens welcomed Steven into their home, so Laurie and Steven visited back and forth. Laurie gave Steven her senior class ring and Steven borrowed money from Swen to get her a gift. On the night of the jury's deliberations, Steven and Laurie wandered about the courthouse holding hands, sitting now and then with a small group of teenagers on the inside courthouse steps that led from the first and second floor. A few months after Steven went to prison, Laurie, whom Steven at least at one point expected to wait for him, got married. (Since then, she has divorced and remarried.)

During his stay in Granite Falls, Steven was confirmed at Swen's church, St. Paul's Evangelical Lutheran Church, which is affiliated with the Missouri Synod. Swen thought that getting Steven confirmed was important, and he let people in and out of court know about Steven's confirmation. Both Swen and Elizabeth believed a special bond existed between Steven and the minister, Leroy Urman, who confirmed Steven. They believed that Urman, who later visited Steven in prison, truly cared for Steven and that Steven felt true affection for Urman, who suffered severe bouts of depression. Several months after Steven went to prison, Urman—suffering from cancer—hanged himself in a hospital in the Twin Cities.

Swen, who faithfully visited Steven in prison—seeing him once or twice a month as well as telephoning him—feared for Steven. He worried about Steven being abused, going crazy, or even committing suicide. Swen was especially concerned when he saw Steven revert to his military dress and huddle in the corner of his cell. All along, Swen had believed Steven should get the best psychological counseling available. Elizabeth, Darlene, and psychologist Schwartz agreed. Nevertheless, Steven received no counseling either in Granite Falls or in prison. Somehow Steven, who was observed superficially to fit peacefully into the adult world, in truth existed beyond its touch.

When first imprisoned at Oak Park Heights—a maximum-security facility designed for reform and education, which was adjacent to Stillwater Prison—it was rumored that Steven had not only reverted to military appearance but that he considered himself to be a prisoner of war. According to Kermit Ness, Swen seriously worried about Steven's military dress and his relation to other prisoners. Swen and Elizabeth worried particularly about Steven's being victimized on one occasion when Steven joined what was described as "a prison motorcycle gang."

It was reported that once when he was first in prison, Steven had gone to pieces—"lost it"—shouting and screaming uncontrollably. On another occasion, he got into a fight and was punished with confinement.

Later reports to the family indicated that Steven was doing as well as could be expected. His spirits had improved. He wrote to his families, and he sent Christmas cards that he designed to his family in 1985. Under the tutelage and encouragement of Swen and Elizabeth, Steven started to become a serious reader, impressing them both with his insightful understanding of *Call of the Wild* and *Moby Dick,* the classic that preoccupied Swen in the last years of his life.

In the educational unit of the prison, Steven took college classes in art, algebra, drafting, and blueprint reading. As of Christmas 1986, he was at the end of his sophomore year in college. Later he started karate for exercise and began a class in computers. Steven still received no regular psychological treatment.

On May 27, 1986, the United States Supreme Court let stand without comment the ruling that Steven had received a fair trial. Fabel commented that this was "the last gasp. . . . Anything from this point forward would be of a truly extraordinary nature," he said.

Swen Anderson was silent this time. On February 2, 1986, he had been found dead in bed by his family. He had died at home of an apparent heart attack. He had had a history of heart trouble and high blood pressure, which may have been related to the rheumatic fever he had as a boy.

Swen Anderson's obituaries summarily reviewed his life and predictably spoke of him as "the colorful and controversial attorney" who, in the generous words of a fellow attorney was "unfailingly honest," "a bucker of the system," and a man who was a "mortal enemy for life against the establishment." Under the title "The Booming Voice of Allan Swen Is Stilled," Jane McKeown of the *Montevideo American-News* waxed eloquent in describing two Swen Andersons. There was the Swen Anderson inside the courtroom, who had "the respect of his attorneys and judges for his tremendous legal mind," and there was the Swen Anderson outside of the courtroom,

who sometimes could appear to be brash, talking loudly enough to be heard from one floor to the other of the courthouse. He had the habit of singing loudly in the men's room, and the sound would carry far through the building. . . . He was the champion of the underdog, and if he believed that you were innocent, he would go to great lengths, assuming some of the cost himself in your defense.

Unfortunately, none of the obituaries collected the bountiful stories about Swen that formed a veritable folklore. There was the time, one story began, when he waved at and cursed terribly the young girls in a boat that followed him down the river. He did not stop his foul cursing until he discovered he had hooked anchors with them.

Another time, he appeared in court in a snowmobile suit; when the judge told him he could remove it if he wished, Anderson confessed he had nothing on under it. On another occasion at a legal convention, Swen dragged a fellow lawyer to his room and showed him, in front of a mirror, what a fast draw he was with a six-gun.

One fellow attorney remembered how he and his client, who was charged with drunk driving, sat in Swen's office and watched him charge back and forth with musket in hand as if in a state of military attack, not stopping until they proposed an agreement that Swen, then Yellow Medicine County Attorney, would accept.

Another attorney recalled what Swen called the two-brassiere theory of the Luella Thompson case. According to Swen, the sheriff's wife had suggested that if Luella had been raped, the brassiere in her bedroom would not have been carefully folded and placed on a chair. Luella countered that she was not wearing that brassiere at the time of the rape because she had tried it on that morning and discovered it was too small.

None of the obituaries spoke directly of Swen's vanity. A detective who had once worked for Swen commented: "Police and lawyers are the two most egotistical professions. Swen was more egotistical than anyone I've ever seen. He was always talking about the great job he was doing." His wife Elizabeth assented to this eulogy: "Swen—an extreme of compassion and vanity. You could love and hate him, kiss and kick him."

Not one of the obituaries ventured to say that in losing Steven Jenkins's case, Anderson had lost what he himself felt was the most important case of his life. He saw—as he let his fellow attorneys know—the Jenkins trial as bringing him a national reputation. He spoke of himself in the company of great defense attorneys. At the end of the Jenkins trial, he bluntly asked Fabel if he was the best defense attorney Fabel had ever faced. Elusively Fabel replied, "All you guys give me a lot of trouble."

Swen Anderson had a second and last encounter with Tom Fabel in the summer of 1985. In Lake Wilson (a village approximately thirty-five miles south of Marshall), a fifty-nine-year-old man shot and killed his fifty-six-year-old wife and her ninety-two-year-old friend. Anderson enthusiastically took the man's defense. This case raised a stir throughout the region, yet it ended very differently than the Jenkins case had. It was uneventfully concluded with a plea-bargained agreement, with the defendant pleading guilty to two counts of second-degree murder. Swen Anderson—the obituaries did not note—had not vindicated his loss to Tom Fabel.

Even after Steven's verdict and sentencing, Swen Anderson's optimism abounded. He was confident that the work he had done on the appeal would win at the supreme court. He had more than jokingly asked Marshall attorney David Peterson which famous movie star should play him when DiFonzo's book on him and Steven was made into a Hollywood movie. (Swen himself proposed George C. Scott.)

Swen constantly talked to his regular attorney friends about the book and the film in which he would have a large part. He seemed won over by the idea that a well-known author, nominated for a Pulitzer Prize, had chosen to put him on stage, front and center. He never stopped fishing for compliments. "The book, the publicity," a friend remarked, "was the pot of gold at the end of his rainbow. The book never stopped being a big deal for him. . . . He was thinking books and bucks before the trial was ended." Another friend said after the trial, "Anytime you talked to Swen, about anything, it returned to the book. You had to hear about it eighty-six times. [With him] all returned to the book."

On the surface, the trial did not appear to discourage Swen. He was still heard from; his braggadocio was not entirely stilled. He was the region's premiere criminal lawyer. With some fanfare, in 1985 Swen affiliated himself with attorney Clarence Hagglund to form Hagglund and Anderson Trial Specialists Ltd. Having been recently certified by the National Board of Trial Advocacy in criminal law—as his new partner had earlier been certified a trial specialist—Swen could now claim that his firm was the first—not only in western and southern Minnesota but in the whole state—to have a certified criminal trial specialist and civil trial specialist. On the surface, Swen looked as ready as ever for business.

Swen's friends, however, noticed a deterioration in his health after the trial. One friend, a long-time fellow prosecutor, said, "After the trial Swen had one ailment after another. Frequently when he would show up in court he would appear ill and feverish. He once was seriously ill and went to Rochester." (Surely in Minnesota, and perhaps throughout much of the Midwest, the phrase "go to Rochester" is a synonym for going to the Mayo Clinic, which one does only when one is gravely ill—sicker than any local doctor can diagnose or cure.)

Another friend and fellow attorney said, "The trial took a lot of starch out of him. He went downhill, physically as well as emotionally. He was more withdrawn after the trial. This case, so unrepresentative of his earlier work, was one of his worst. He got all wrapped up in it. He didn't bounce it off anyone. . . . It was an ego trip for Swen." However, this same friend, who considered Swen to be potentially one of the best ten trial attorneys in the state, saw the onset of Swen's problems even earlier. "Even before the trial he was yelling and screaming less. He started wearing a hearing aid. He was talking more and more, and working less and less. Failure to prepare became his hallmark."

Others remarked on the decline of his abilities after the trial. A friend observed that on one occasion Swen went to court all confused about the names and issues involved in the case he was trying. An attorney friend remarked that Swen did things that did not altogether make sense, and he appeared—now as never before—ready to make the most money with the least effort on his client's behalf.

In one instance, a long-standing positive relationship Swen had had with a local law firm broke down. In the opinion of the lawyers of the firm, Swen became unjustly accusatory and abusive about actions one of its lawyers had taken, even though those actions were based upon what the lawyers took to be Swen's prior and express agreement. In their opinion, Swen no longer dealt with the merits of issues but increasingly made things a matter of personalities. The firm no longer accepted Swen's spoken word.

If for no other reason than the prominence of the Jenkins case in Swen's professional and personal life, it had to mark the high and low point of his career and the turning point in his fate. In losing the Jenkins case, Anderson lost the case of his lifetime. Kermit Ness said that this case was Swen's Gethsemane. In as profound a way as imaginable, this case became Swen and Swen became this case.

Swen gave the case its unique stamp. In the words of his partner, Hagglund, the Jenkins case belonged to what he called the realm of "Swen's world." The case was as eccentric as Swen himself. Not only did the case turn on questions about Swen's conduct of it and his adoption of Steven, but there also remained the puzzle of what Swen himself really knew about Steven's role in the murders and the death of his father.

There is much evidence to suggest that Swen Anderson firmly believed Steven was innocent of killing the two bankers. David Peterson, with whom Swen frequently spoke, said Swen "never deviated" even by inference or supposition (as he might in other cases) from his belief in Steven's innocence. Peterson added, however, that Anderson was "capable of making a snap judgment and then not changing his mind come hell or high water." Private detective Ken Nordin, who worked on this case, said in an interview that once Steven passed the polygraph examination, Swen never doubted Steven's innocence. Eric DeRycke and several other local attorneys agreed. Kermit Ness had no doubt that Swen considered Steven innocent.

Swen Anderson himself, testifying publicly to Steven's innocence, said: "I have children at home and I wouldn't have taken him into my home if I didn't believe that he was innocent."

In all probability, once Anderson decided Steven was innocent, he never found time or interest in reexamining his judgment. Swen knew that Steven had passed the polygraph test and, according to Kermit, Swen heard Steven describe a young willow at the corner of the garage, which he could only have known about if he had stood where he said he had been standing during the crime.

On more than one occasion, Anderson inferred to fellow attorneys David Peterson and Eric DeRycke, as well as to others, that Steven had killed his father upon his father's request. Swen repeated the idea that the father could not have killed himself with Steven's shotgun the way the Texas police hypothesized that he did. Whether Swen believed this or only considered it a real possibility—as he continually did in his speculations with Kermit Ness and LuVern Hansen—the inference amounted to a confession of his limited knowledge of Steven. (Kermit Ness believed Steven had to shoot his father to escape him.)

"He [Swen] was never able to get Steven to open up," LuVern Hansen remarked. No matter how Swen and Elizabeth tried, they never succeeded in getting Steven to tell them the story of the crime, the flight, and the death of his father.

The possibility that Steven killed his own father, for Swen found additional support in the Schwartz report, drove Swen to believe that Steven was "an absolute loser"—a victim of terrible evil. Swen did not conceive of Steven as a victim of the farm crisis or of class poverty, but of an awful father and a broken family. Abused and dutiful, the Steven whom Swen most pitied, had killed his own father out of filial duty. This was no farm story.

FAREWELLS

HANDCUFFED AND UNDER THE SUPERVISION of a Yellow Medicine County deputy, Steven went to the funeral home to pay his farewell to Swen Anderson. Swen had promised to love him and to free him. According to the deputy who accompanied him, Steven smoked a cigarette in the waiting room and then went into the adjoining room to view Swen's body. He returned a few minutes later and said without emotion, "You might as well take me back."

Darlene showed up at the funeral home with Louis, who had to be dissuaded by Elizabeth and her family from making this an occasion "to give a eulogy against the state." This caused "a small uproar."

Darlene, who appreciated the care and affection that Swen and Elizabeth had shown Steven, nevertheless had constantly questioned the manner in which Swen had tried the case. She focused particularly on the witnesses she thought he had failed to call. Darlene persisted in her questions and Swen, in time, grew tired of answering them. In fact, on the morning of his death Darlene had come to Swen's to ask him more questions about the trial.

Now Swen was dead, and Elizabeth, having to handle Swen's death, would have yet greater responsibility for her children at home. Darlene would have to try to make herself as close as she could be to Steven. This would not be easy. Steven had always been his father's boy, and for a long time his anger had been directed at Darlene and Louis. One of Swen's friends remarked that Steven was often upset after being with his mother. Darlene would do all she could. She visited Steven regularly, sometimes flying with Louis to Oak Park Heights and later flying Louis's plane herself.

Neither Darlene nor her daughter Michele nor Louis would accept the idea of Steven's spending his whole life in prison. To them it was wrong; the sentence was cruel and unfair. The state was making Steven pay for the killing. Steven had not shot. It was James who had gotten Steven into this mess. It was Susan Blythe who, they believed, had altered her testimony to help convict Steven. The state, they believed, had gone after Steven with all of its force.

They believed—each in their own way and perhaps with some guilt—that Swen Anderson, whom they had trusted, had failed Steven. Why this was they were not entirely sure, but they blamed Swen Anderson for not using more witnesses, including Louis himself, since he had known and had employed James. They blamed Anderson for not introducing the suicide note. They were convinced he should have done better—that indeed no public defender could have done worse. The more they mulled over the trial and the appeal, the more they became convinced that Swen had failed Steven. They even speculated in some more elemental way that Swen had sold Steven out. (Nina and Clayton too, according to their friends, had no love lost for Swen Anderson. He adopted their only grandson; he bungled Steven's case; and by not plea bargaining he cost Steven years in prison.)

Louis carried his ideas about Swen Anderson's failure to represent Steven adequately to the attorney general's office. Swen himself, according to his friends, believed Steven's conviction was ultimately the unexplained work of certain unnamed bankers. Louis had other theories. His first idea was that the state had somehow threatened Swen and made him throw the case. He saw Fabel's condolence note to Elizabeth as an expression of Fabel's arrogance: a way to rub his victory in. By letter and in person, Louis informed Fabel and his boss, Attorney General Hubert (Skip) Humphrey III, that he would reopen the case with the help of the best lawyers available.

Darlene and Michele also tried to gain Steven a new trial. They believed that the most promising line would be the charge that Steven had incompetent counsel. Darlene read about that in law books. Michele, now the mother of two children, shared the burden of Steven's fate with her mother. She too sought the help of attorneys. In June of 1986, with the aid of a lawyer friend, Michele tried to get a few lawyers together to explore Steven's case and to examine the issue of whether Steven had adequate counsel. This was Steven's last and only hope for a new trial.

Michele and Darlene continued to stick together. They share not only two grandchildren but a common hatred for James, a concern for Steven, and the results of a terrible family tragedy. They suffered from the things "their men" did.

Darlene, Michele, and Louis could not forget Steven and his case. They constantly puzzled over its outcome, repeatedly questioning why the trial went so badly. They were not alone in wondering whether Steven and his case did not get swallowed up by Swen's interest in DiFonzo's book, tentatively titled *A Good Place to Live and A Good Place to Die*. They asked whether DiFonzo's story—and what DiFonzo and Swen wanted to make it—did not become more important to them than Steven's trial itself. That DiFonzo's supposed book, once listed in *Forthcoming Books*, was never published, only heightened their speculation about DiFonzo's "real motives."

As extreme as such speculation might seem, it had some toehold in fact. Swen entangled himself and his personal and economic affairs with those of DiFonzo. Swen invited DiFonzo to his son Clifford's wedding. In turn, DiFonzo invited Swen and Elizabeth, with Laurie Kompelien, to visit his summer home in Maine to help in the completion of the book. Elizabeth and Swen even considered moving east, and DiFonzo took an interest in them and in their children.

According to friends, Swen, who was never prudent with his money ("spent it like a drunken sailor," one friend said), came to expect considerable royalties from the book and the movie. He put significant sums of his money under DiFonzo's control for what Swen took to be advantageous long-term investments.

In the aftermath of Swen's death, Elizabeth, confused and perhaps too willing to trust someone who was a professional writer, turned to DiFonzo for help in planning her future. She gave substantial parts of her insurance money and retirement savings to DiFonzo for his care. She also transfered some of her papers and records to DiFonzo. In the fall of 1986, after over six months of futilely trying to regain all her money from DiFonzo, Elizabeth began to discuss taking legal action against DiFonzo with Montevideo attorney Donald Maland, whom she had retained to handle Swen's estate. DiFonzo was no longer welcome in the Anderson household nor was he welcome to visit Steven.

A serious parting of the ways had come. Writer DiFonzo had in some sense been evicted from the story. Yet the storyteller, in truth, had become an inseparable part of the story, which constantly turned upon itself, adding question to question, story to story.

The lawyer and the boy, Swen and Steven—such opposites—were joined together in the story. One was loud and noticed; the other silent and almost invisible. One revealed almost everything, and the other hid almost everything. Nevertheless, lawyer and boy were joined together by the story they helped make, a story that will be told as long as the story of the father and son who killed together is told.

CHAPTER SEVEN

The Conspiracy:
They Told Each Other Stories

I touched the knife hilt at my side, and remembered that all men were once boys, and
that boys are always looking for ways to become men. Some of the ways are easy, too;
all you have to do is be satisfied that it has
happened.

—JAMES DICKEY, *Deliverance*

Mile after mile I followed, with skimming
feet,
After the secret master of my blood.

—STANLEY KUNITZ

T HE Jenkinses' last place at Hardwick has been knocked
down, and the land has been returned to corn and
soybeans. A young family with five children moved in
and redid the Jenkinses' Ruthton home. The weed-covered lawn, across which Rudolph Blythe made his last rush for
life, is now carefully cared for. It holds a large children's swing
and slide set and a video dish.

Farm protest has subsided. Even though the farm economy
has grown considerably worse—even disastrous by some accounts—and three years later there is still no sign of relief in
sight, farm protest in southwestern Minnesota and in the entire
Midwest has not turned to violence. Indeed, a March 1987
scholarly study of five midwestern states, conducted by the
Minnesota and North Dakota health departments, established
no significant connection between farmers, suicides, and the
farm crisis from 1980 to 1985.

This does not mean Steven and James Jenkins have been

forgotten here. Their crime is now a part of the region's consciousness. People still talk with passion about the crime. The very name Jenkins has for many a certain eerie ring to it. One person explained he did not buy the Jenkinses' farm because he saw the skull of a dead calf in the barn. Another cannot forget the sight of Steven standing outside the school at Lynd, repeatedly throwing his knife at a tree, trying to perfect his throwing technique. And then there is all the Swen lore. In Ruthton, one person summarized the case as having involved "one crazy kid and one crazy lawyer." Perhaps one day a folklorist will tell how southwestern Minnesota told the story of Steven and James Jenkins.

Others must tell the story of Steven and James Jenkins as part of their family histories. Lynette Thulin—who reestablished herself in Fargo, North Dakota, and is studying speech pathology across the river at Moorhead State University, in Moorhead, Minnesota—will tell her three daughters the story of their father's death. Susan Blythe—who successfully sold the bank and moved to the Twin Cities to begin a new life—will tell her son Rolph what happened to his father and what she thinks about the book she cooperated in the writing of.

Darlene and Michele Jenkins too must tell the story of James and Steven. Michele must ask why she escaped and her brother did not. So must Darlene. Darlene undoubtedly must ponder the matter of what could have been different. Both Darlene and Michele know they escaped the family that Steven did not.

Indeed, their family, like every other family, is captured in a set of stories—some of which are told, some hidden, some understood, and some confused. Their family story, however, became everyone's story when James and Steven did what fathers and sons rarely do: when they killed together.

The story of James and Steven Jenkins is a family story. It is the story of a homeless father and son who were tragically joined together. They were drawn to each other, and they could not separate themselves from each other. They turned upon each other like broken cogs as they found themselves without a woman and a home. They shared their frustrations, anger, madness, and illusions. They were destined to hurt themselves and the world.

Darlene knew how Steven was drawn to James. "James," Darlene said in her statement to the BCA, "was always getting Stevie," in her words, "into some big goddamn mess." Darlene tried to guide Steven away from James and his half-cocked ideas. The last time she spoke to Steven before the crime, she tried to persuade him not to hope for too much from his father and the dream of restarting a farm: "I said to Stevie, because I've been so many times with Jimmy and it has been one disappointment after another, 'don't get your hopes up. . . . I hope to God it works out for you, but don't get your hopes up that it is going to.' "

Clayton Jenkins too knew the madness that joined his son and grandson. He had heard too many of his son's stories to believe what James said. Long ago he had quit lending money to his son. It was like throwing money down a hole. He knew his son's temper tantrums. "His face would turn solid purple." And he knew his son was no good for his grandson.

Clayton also knew Steven was strange. He saw Steven make bombs, attempt to make a bulletproof vest, and train himself to be a soldier who belonged—and could belong—to no army. Clayton warned Steven that no good would come from all that "military stuff." Clayton told a neighbor who had known the family for many years—according to a Lincoln County sheriff department's investigative report—about a time when he was taking Steven to Ruthton and Steven suggested that they "take a gun along and shoot someone."

According to the same investigative report, Clayton said that another time he had seen James and his grandson Steven get into an argument in his yard. Steven had an army carbine and he gave a .22 rifle to James and suggested he and James have a shoot-out. James looked at the gun, saw it was empty, and handed it back to Steven. (Since Steven had the carbine, it meant that this had been a recent incident. Also not without implication is the fact that Steven kept the carbine and gave the .22 to his father.)

In the immediate aftermath of the murders, Clayton had not wanted either James or Steven to come back. To the question of a BCA officer, "Are you a little afraid of them?" Clayton had replied, "Oh, yes, I don't trust them at all."

What Steven was doing with all that military stuff—at least

in retrospect—appears evident. On the one hand, he was fleeing from a world that had hurt him so. On the other, he was hardening himself to meet the world on his own terms. Unlike his father, Steven had no dream of becoming a farmer or mechanic. He had no plans for the future except to become the soldier of his imagination.

By the time Steven went to Texas, he was totally dedicated to this fantasy. His friendships, his dates, even his most causal conversations turned to the subjects of weapons and killing. Back in Minnesota, Steven was alone and angry, living off of and for his self-made military regime. He was absorbed in his own fantasy of being an avenging soldier.

In retrospect, he appears destined to have collided with the world. There was no one who could have deflected him.

While James had a quick temper and at times a nasty will, he never appeared to be as cut off from people as Steven was. By most accounts, James had a social side. By the most superficial acquaintances he was often judged to be ingratiating; with people he got to know, he did what Steven apparently never fully or easily did: he openly shared his feelings and problems, although not always truthfully. This was especially so with women, to whom James constantly looked for friendship and comfort. Several women spoke of his openness, tenderness, and warmth.

When at the Ruthton farm, James confided continuously in Lynn Swanson, telling her the details of his deteriorating marriage. In Texas, James carried on a lengthy platonic relationship with Brenda Enlow. According to her, they shared their problems. She accompanied him to the hospital when he complained about his poor daytime vision and about the pain in his legs caused by broken blood vessels. She found James a compassionate person who was never angry.

Nevertheless, according to Enlow, James blamed his wife and her boyfriend for burning down his Hoffman barn. He also told her he had leukemia, which had been in a state of remission since he had had treatments in Mexico. On several occasions, James expressed his concern about Steven's infatuation with guns. He told Brenda that he "tried to talk Steven out of buying 'that gun,'" and he feared that Steven was plotting to get even with his mother and her boyfriend. Steven, in James's opinion, was "buttering them up" to get even for the divorce. When Enlow told him that Steven was going to get into trouble, he said, "I know, but there is not a damn thing I can do about it."

Another woman in whom James confided he met as he hitchhiked back to Texas in August 1982. Betty Jean Ginhardt of Pocola, Oklahoma, picked James up near Lincoln, Nebraska, and gave him a ride to her home. (James stopped there two times later, once in the early summer of 1983—when he spent a few days looking for work—and the last time when he and Steven went to Brownwood, Texas—where they had picked up their trailer camper and were on their way home to Minnesota.) Betty Jean Ginhardt described James Jenkins as "an extremely honest, hard-working, country-type person." According to her, James was upset with his ex-wife, whose running around had, in his opinion, caused James to lose his farm. He had told Ginhardt his ex-wife might try to kill him for his insurance policy.

James wore his heart on his sleeve. If a woman would listen, he would talk. Back from Texas, James made application for maintenance work at the Blue Mound Inn in Luverne, Minnesota. Impressed by James as a patient, tolerant, and hard-working man, co-owner Barbara Loosbrock spent almost an hour listening to James talk about his divorce. Among other things, he said—according to Loosbrock—that his former wife was not happy. His boy had taken the divorce badly, and he very much needed a family.

The evening before the crime, James and Steven visited Vicki Nelsen, a friend of James who once worked with Darlene at Bayliner Boats in Pipestone. He went to see Vicki "just to talk," according to Steven. There James did something that revealed the homeless condition that he and Steven suffered. James cruelly teased Vicki's two young sons—one was seven, the other six. "Jimmy," Vicki said, "was giving them a bad time about me running away . . . that I'd left [leave] 'em home by themselves, that I'd run away."

What James told everyone—especially women who would listen—was a family story: he had lost one family farm and he intended, if he had his way, to start another. He tried to sustain himself and Steven with that story. It was his dream, and it was his lie.

The story shielded James both against his failures in the

past and from his likely failures in the future. He had not failed. Darlene, Louis, and Rudy Blythe had cost him his first farm and family. He would succeed in resurrecting what, in fact, had never really existed: a thriving and successful farm. The story was more important to James than was reality.

It did not matter to him that people had treated him well in Texas and that he had done as well there as anywhere. Nor did it matter that he did not have enough money to start a farm, that it was a particularly bad time to start a farm, that a farm would not provide Steven the help he needed, and that ultimately it would furnish neither of them the woman and home they needed. What mattered to James was the story: he once had a good farm and he would have another.

There was no one left—not Darlene nor Michele nor Clayton—to contradict James except Steven; and Steven was lost in his own story. Indeed, this was the heart of their conspiracy. They agreed to believe each other's stories. They exchanged illusions. Steven believed—at least he did not contradict—his father's dream of returning to Minnesota to start a new farm. James tolerated and did not challenge—as any good parent would have—Steven's fantasies of being a soldier. Their dark reciprocity amounted to "a farm for you and an M-1 for me."

For years James and Steven pretended to one another. They did not acknowledge that they were losers. They insisted that they were not "nobodies"—and they did this in the face of poverty, poor jobs, and secondhand, broken-down things. They tried to find respect despite the fact that they had no place in the community and that, inside the home of James Jenkins, there would always be disorder.

Whoever lived with James Jenkins had to live around James Jenkins. He was suspicious and accusatory, bullheaded and impractical. A letter from Darlene's mother to Darlene reveals how difficult it was to live with James, even when the letter is discounted for its intention to help Steven and for what appears to be its rehearsal of shared memories:

I hope that the attorney can help Steve and prove what we know about Jimmy. I only want to remind you of the time Jimmy picked corn with the Allis picker for Dad and he deliberately ran Lassie . . . thru it. The poor dog was crazy and howled and Dad had to get the poor dog out of the rollers and shoot him, and Jimmy stood and laughed. (I don't know if you saw it but Dad and I did.) Then do you remember when James shot Mick and Stevie's police dog. . . . He got mad at Stevie and Mick because the pigs got out and he shot the dog. Do you remember how he cut the tails off the milk cows because they switched him in the face and he hit the cows with clubs, broke or dislocated one cows [sic] hip, and when he drowned the calf because it couldn't drink right. How he chased Stevie with the pitch fork and clubs, how he shoved me up on the road between our place and the Bernards [sic] when I checked on the loads when he combined our grain, how he came over like a mad-man at 5 o'clock in the morning, accused us of hiding Mick and Stevie over to Petersen's and accused us of hiding you. . . . Then he came over and told me you were crazy and I should put you in an insane asylum. He was so mad he was purple in his face. . . . Jimmy didn't have his head screwed on straight. Stevie should not be made to suffer for what Jimmy did.

Many things in the house of James Jenkins were pretended. Between James and Darlene much must have gone unspoken when the truth could have only meant more conflict and earlier divorce. Much must have gone unspoken as James, according to Michele and Darlene, fabricated story after story, and Steven himself was told to play along with his father. When Darlene did start the divorce proceedings in 1982, she and James had almost nothing to divide except the children. There was nothing left to say. They did not talk after the divorce.

Steven's sister Michele understood the need to dissolve the marriage. When asked how she got along with her father, she testified: "Sometimes we could, sometimes we couldn't, it just depended on what he was feeling, but I'd always be . . . con-fronting him because he lied so damn much and I would always, you know, catch him in lies then I'd confront him with it."

Steven, younger and male, was more willing to believe his father's stories. In fact, he probably believed what James said about Darlene—her "running around," her relationship with Louis, and the loss of the farm. He never understood the reasons for the divorce.

After James and Steven left the Ruthton farm, they were more or less poor migrants living off of stories about the family they once had. On more than one occasion, James sold his tools and wrote bad checks to survive from one week to the next. In their first days in Texas, they had nothing. They hitchhiked where ever they wanted to go, allowing every passerby to either take or leave them. On job applications in Texas, James had to write "no address" or give the address of a person he had just met. For references for jobs and credit, he also had to rely on people he had just met.

In Texas James and Steven depended entirely on the generosity and hospitality of others. Strangers took them in, fed them, showed them around, and made them as much as possible part of their families. They could do an occasional favor—work for free on Snow's farm or wire Beard's house for room-to-room stereo, as they once did—but otherwise they lacked the means to reciprocate. They had no home to invite guests to and no money to show their generosity.

James and Steven worked for minimum wages. Sometimes they even worked for free just to have something to do. At times Steven worked without pay alongside his father, because there was nothing else to do.

They could not hide their humiliating condition from each other. Walls so necessary between a father and son collapsed: they slept, ate, and worked together. With no sure roof over their heads, no woman to keep them both together and apart, and no fixed society to order their lives, James did not remain the father nor did Steven continue to be the son. They became, as more than one Texas witness reported, "buddies" and "equals"—something a father and son should not and cannot long be to each other.

One incident that occurred in Texas reveals just how close James and Steven had become. As a result of intervening in a teacher's disciplinary action in the schoolyard, James was called in to be disciplined by Brownwood superintendent James Lancaster. Lancaster told James that he would be terminated immediately if this type of activity happened again. Lancaster told BCA officer Berg that Steven accompanied James to the meeting and sat down on the superintendent's couch. When Lancaster asked Steven why he was there, Steven said he "came along for the show." When Steven was asked what that meant, he said he thought it might be interesting to observe what was going to take place. Lancaster, according to Berg, let Steven know there was not going to be any show and proceeded to give James a strong tongue-lashing in Steven's presence.

James and Steven were together too long and were too close

in Texas. They chafed each other by their very presence. Steven grew more and more angry and fixed on weapons. James, by contrast, was increasingly preoccupied with the idea of starting his farm. Two alien dreams were in competition, even at war, with each other. Yet so as not to lose each other, father and son accepted each other and each other's stories.

James saw Steven's tattooed body. He could not overlook the weapons that cluttered the pickup. He saw Steven's constant shooting and was aware of his continuous conversation about weapons. Yet James did not confront Steven about this. Instead, he condoned Steven's descent into angry and dark fantasy. Acting indulgently, as divorced parents sometimes do, James bought and let Steven keep the weapon with which Steven so confusedly and tragically identified. Back in Minnesota, James yielded once more to Steven's obsessions. James signed and purchased for Steven a used 12-gauge shotgun. Either as a gift for Steven's birthday (August 19th) or as an acknowledgment of their being back together, or both, James bought Steven another weapon.

In turn, Steven followed James, who was all Steven felt he had left of family. Steven could not say—perhaps could not even clearly conceive—that his father was a loser or that his father had cost him one family and would never secure him another. But no doubt Steven, at least at moments, suspected all this.

Much of Steven's anger and exaggerated male posturing was aimed at making himself the man his father was not. A son does not attack his father without wounding himself. Ultimately, therefore, it was easier for Steven to attack his father's enemies, Louis Taveirne and Rudolph Blythe. In this sense, Steven was only a boy caught in the web of his father's hate.

To have a family, Steven and James needed each other. Yet they could only deceive each other and bind themselves in each other's falsehoods and madness. They could live neither together nor apart. They were destined to victimize each other.

Things reached a crisis when James returned home from Texas in August. Steven—who claimed he returned home months earlier to see his sister's new baby (already a few months old)—was filled with anger. Louis Taveirne remarked to Virgil Veire a few days after the killings (as reported by the BCA) that he feared for his life. Steven was the most "militant" kid Louis had ever known. He shot, according to Louis, "whenever he had time. . . . He would do just the opposite of what [I] told him to do, and Steven . . . did not like accepting authority."

By contrast, James appeared to return home in an optimistic mood. He had some money in his pockets. Yet his appearance masked the fact that he was returning home to—indeed he was rushing headlong into—old problems. The divorce and the loss of the farm were still on his mind. Trying to start a new farm would only exacerbate his feelings of loss and anger. He not only had to look for a farm and credit, but he also had to look for another job. He had nowhere to stay but at Nina and Clayton's. He could not help but encounter memories of old failures.

After considerable difficulty, James found the place at Hardwick. For it, he bought a tractor and a grinder. He got his old flatbed truck out of storage at his father's.

The house at Hardwick was nothing like the place at Ruthton. It was, at best, only the promise of a new home. It had no curtains in it—only a table, a few chairs, and a big easy chair. James and Steven slept in separate bedrooms on mattresses on the floor. They ate at restaurants. It was, in the words of BCA officer O'Gorman, as if they were "camping out in a house."

James's dream was quickly coming undone. Locating the house and buying the few machines James judged essential to starting his operation consumed most of his cash—and there were still payments of $175.00 a month to be made on their pickup. To buy cows, more machinery, and so much else to make this place their new home, James needed credit. And who was going to give him credit—a man with only $15,000 in assets (if he counted everything to his advantage)? Who was going to lend money to a forty-six-year-old man without credit references who had just arrived in Minnesota from Texas? Aside from the fact that bankers and lending agencies were far more leery in 1983 than they had been a few years before, they had policies on the books to not lend to operations precisely like the one James proposed. James's application gave creditors additional reasons to say "no"—insufficient assets, weak credit references, and so on. And "no" they said—banks and lending agencies alike. If not deluded by his own story and driven by his own will, James could have foreseen all this. He knew what a farm cost and what sort of cash and credit record he had.

James's story came apart, credit denial by credit denial. By the end of September—in less than a month—not a shred of hope remained, even for James. His money from Texas was gone. Another failure, another screw-up.

This time Rudolph Blythe—whom James had used, along with Darlene and Louis, to explain his failure at the Ruthton place—became the first target of his hatred. James correctly surmised that Blythe's references were damaging his chances for the credit that, given his credit background and the economic times, would have been marginal at best. Moreover, James learned directly from cattle jockey Daryl Mammenga—James's "last hope"—that Blythe had given him a bad credit reference.

Blythe became the target of James's hatred—the scapegoat for his entire life. For James, Blythe was not just the banker who had denied him credit, but the man who had taken away one home and denied him another.

It was 1983, and James found himself no closer to having a home and respect than he had been three years before, when he had lost his Ruthton place. This time, however, he had gone down failure's road faster and further than ever before. He was forty-six and in poor health. His legs were going and his eyesight too. He could not keep living with his aged parents: he was too proud for that. The thought of returning to Texas or going somewhere else to get together a new grubstake was beyond his energies. That was a story too big for even his telling. It was 1983, and he was still a lifetime away from the farm, the family, and the respect that he—an only son of a poor family—wanted so badly.

It was easier "to go and get Blythe" than to rethink a life of failure—to conjure a dream he himself could believe. James was at the end of the road, and so was Steven.

Steven could not keep practicing forever. He had too much anger bottled up inside not to explode in some way or other. His father's dream had failed, as Steven probably surmised it would all along. Steven did not want to live with Darlene and Louis. While he stayed with his grandparents often, he never stayed for long. He had no plans for a future of his own. He made no additional efforts to join the army. His ruptured spleen had made that impossible. He could only continue to be the soldier of his imagination.

James and Steven had no home. They had no community. They did not belong to the class that, when in crisis, turns easily to a psychologist. They had no minister. And they had no woman who would hear them out and tell them to wait for a better day. No one implored them, in God's name, to forsake their anger. They could not hear women and children crying. They could only hear angry voices shouting within themselves—and they were men and they would act.

Blythe was at the eye of their anger. He had, they told each other, taken one farm away from them and stood in the way of their getting another. "Getting Rudy" became the new story they told each other.

The story did much for them. It gave them moral stature and right. Informally they could link themselves to all those farmers who—in increasing numbers—saw bankers as the enemy. James and Steven could hear this plaint against the banker—which they themselves had already issued in Texas—strongly echoed by the growing farm protest whose very epicenter was Lincoln County.

The story of "getting Blythe" allowed James and Steven to say that James had not failed but that he had been cheated. (It was not accidental that James began to say that Blythe was sleeping with Darlene.) Going out to confront Blythe together allowed James to pay Steven back for his own failure as a father. All along James had acted on his dream of being a farmer, and he had expected Steven to believe him. Now—and this was his gift to Steven—they would act on Steven's dream of being a soldier. They would go together, as buddies, comrades-in-arms, Jenkins menfolk, to revenge family honor.

As some fathers take their boys deer hunting to symbolize the passage to manhood, so James took Steven manhunting. Together they would get Blythe. James would let Steven bring his weapons, and he would allow Steven to use his military skills. James surrendered himself to Steven's dream of "military action."

For Steven, the story of "getting Rudy" gave him the chance to be a man and a soldier, which were one and the same in his mind. Now he could finally show his stuff. As his father's eyesight worsened, Steven increasingly saw the world through the narrow sight of his M-1.

Steven had long conceived of himself as his father's helper and caretaker. By going with his father to get Blythe, Steven would help avenge his father's shame. He would help pay back the world that had so hurt him and his father.

In Texas, Steven spoke of avenging the two businessmen who murdered his mother. (Were the two businessmen Taveirne and Blythe?) According to Vicki Nelsen, whom James and Steven visited the evening before the crime, Steven believed that the Ruthton foreclosure had been "a raw end of the deal . . . that his [Steven's] folks got the raw end of the deal."

It is possible that Steven returned to Minnesota not to see his sister's baby but to prepare his revenge. He may have returned to find a target for the diffused anger that filled him. With his father's encouragement, Blythe became that target.

The conspiracy to get Blythe was another story father and son told each other. It revealed that they would tell each other false stories until their destruction.

They both knew—they had to know—that, whatever their specific plans, this story amounted to a farewell. They knew they could not point a gun at a banker, rob him, kidnap him, hold him for ransom, murder him—or whatever they confusedly planned to do—without risking either death or prison.

As they completed their plans at their last supper together at the Mayfair Cafe, they were saying goodbye to each other. They were giving up on the nurturing myth of the family farm for a belief in the magic, curative power of violence: the deed transforming the world.

Implicit in their farewell was the mutual admission that they had failed. They had tried and lost. They had nowhere to go and nothing else to do. They could not save each other. They had reached the point where they would test the devil's luck. They would throw themselves off of the cliff and see what happened.

The crime against Blythe was a way for James to call it quits. It was an alternative to suicide. He would not have to pick up his gun and shoot himself. The crime against Blythe was James's confession to everyone—to his son, to his parents, to Darlene, to Michele, and even to Louis—that James Jenkins had lost. He was through. He was not working anymore. "A guy just as well be dead."

James acknowledged that he would no longer try even to be Steven's father. He would start no farm nor refound a family. He would not even spare his son by abandoning him. Instead, he would take his only son along with him on a crime that could only mean death or prison. James's story about getting Blythe was a story of great despair and filicidal treachery.

In accompanying his father, Steven too surrendered himself to their story. He went along with his father, taking all his weapons and knowing that only wrong could come from what they were doing. He had no one but his father; this story was the last thing left between them. With this story, they said good-bye and confessed their homelessness.

By acting on this story, they did what they could never openly admit: they acknowledged that they could not go on together any longer. The time had come for them to part. James had bucked reality as long and hard as he could, and he had failed. He was never going to be a father of a family again. Steven really did not have a father. He could not play soldier forever. One day he had to grow up and be free of James. Rather than face these realities, father and son chose their story—and they left the consequences of the deed itself to say their fare-wells.

For James, time had run out. For Steven, time was full and at hand. James would now have his last confrontation with a world that had defeated him at nearly every turn. Steven, who had yet to try his will against the world, was ready for his first test.

That day, they were both seeking something profoundly out of the ordinary. Their wishes were, in some terrible way, granted them.

Their crime was a violent commemoration of their home-lessness. They returned to the farm where they had last been members of a family. Using their own home site as the stage, with a single act they told the world how much they had lost. They screamed out against what the divorce had meant to them, what it meant for a father and son to be without a wife, a mother, and a home.

We cannot know from where inside any person shoots, nor do we know the particular sequence of events that occurred that foggy morning on that weed-infested farm. But we do know the shots that rang out that day were long in preparation. They were inseparable from—and exploded by—what two lifetimes had put together.

Human flight is never pure. The terror and the desire that propel it are not constants. When two people flee together, flight is even less calculable. All the differences between them come into play; they ride different waves of adrenalin. James and Steven were not equals in flight. James, the father, was tired and was not well. Steven was young, trained, and energetic. One had shot, and one had seen the other shoot; that alone separated them in some unbridgeable way.

Nevertheless, they were in some sense equals in the crime. They had murdered together. They were fugitives. They had killed the myth of family. They were now homeless and unable to save each other.

Once in Texas, they knew there was nowhere to go. There was no one there waiting and willing to take them in and to protect them from the law. The way back home—to Darlene, to Clayton and Nina's place, to childhood, to the dream of a family—was forever blocked. They were two lost boys.

At an abandoned farm near Paducah, Texas, James and Steven reached the end of the road. This was the last place they would ever be together.

The site was desolate. It barely showed on Texas's dry and flat October landscape. This was not rich, foliant-covered, harvest-time Minnesota. The place was an ill-defined, weed-covered lot; at its rear stood a few pines, a couple of clumps of small trees, a telephone line, an abandoned feedlot pen, and an empty garage. In front of the garage, about halfway back to the main road, there was a small concrete slab. This was where James and Steven spent their last hours together. This was their last home, their last stage.

On the slab of concrete, the police found a quart plastic Coke bottle half-filled with water and two coils of metal baling wire. At the edge of the slab in the undergrowth, they found a discarded can of Van Camps pork and beans that the police surmised constituted James and Steven's last meal.

James had nothing left but a pickup, a flashlight, and what the Texas police found in his pockets: nineteen .22 shells, one soapstone, one screwdriver, two keys, one pair of eyeglasses, one Timex watch, thirteen pennies, and one ballpoint pen—not a pencil—from a Pipestone lending agency.

If the jury was correct, James had seen his own son run down and kill two men. In the trap he had set for Blythe, he had snared his own son. No rationalization—and James, if true to character, tried many—could have stood against his own self-accusation. To paraphrase the New Testament, he had given his son a stone when his son asked for bread, a snake when he asked for a fish. He had destroyed his only son—all that was left to him.

Exhausted, his body worn, seeing no way forward or back, James's mind was filled with thoughts that cut like broken glass; never before had the idea of suicide comforted and seemed more appropriate. Yet suicide itself was not without its considerations for James. Should it be a dual suicide? Should each kill himself, or should he kill Steven or Steven kill him?

In this realm of dark conjecture, one hypothesis demands attention. Was James's suicide his last gift to Steven? With his death, did James try to secure Steven's innocence? Did he even try to command Steven's innocence, making his death itself a blood-will, by which he compelled Steven to swear himself to be forever innocent? Was this the last story they agreed to tell the world?

If this was the damning sacrament of James's suicide, by which he pledged Steven to a life of lying, how bitterly sad were Steven's last words to BCA investigators Berg and O'Gorman: "I have got my responsibility, okay?"

Yet James left no suicide note—at least he did not leave one at the scene of the crime for the police to find. If his intention was to leave a note, he did not even get that right.

The Texas police assumed that James's death was a suicide. The top and back of his head were blown off by a single 12-gauge shotgun blast of double aught buckshot through his cheek. According to the Texas police, only a single set of tracks, presumably James's, led to the spot where his body was found. The ground under James's body was less damp than the ground around his body. For local county sheriff Frank Taylor, there was no way James's death could have been anything other than a suicide. Sheriff Abe Thompson—who went to Texas with Minnesota BCA officers Berg and O'Gorman—agreed with the Texas authorities that James's death was a suicide.

However, BCA officers Berg and O'Gorman questioned whether James's death was a suicide. Even though they did not have a chance to examine James's body and the ground around it (which the Texas police did not rope off), some things did not add up. The shotgun, according to Officer Berg, was under James's body; usually in such cases, though not always, the body is thrown back. James had his flashlight with him, even though he would not be going anywhere if he were planning to commit suicide. James's body was not found in the vicinity of the garage where, according to Steven, his father was when Steven left to turn himself in. Instead, James's body was found 150 to 250 yards away at the mouth of the farm road. Directly contradicting Steven's testimony, the tire tracks—according to a Texas police officer—led from the slab directly to the road, not back to the garage area. What Officer Berg considered to be most significant was what happened when Steven was returned to the site by the Texas police. Just as they entered the farm road, Steven, who until then had been slouched down in the back seat of the police car, popped up and asked, as if to instruct them where to look for his father, "Do you see my Dad?" According to the story one Texas officer told Berg and O'Gorman, apparently Steven knew what he could not have known according to his first statement: where his father's body was.

Was it murder or suicide that finally severed the tie between Steven and James? Did Steven kill his father? If he did, was it because his father had asked him to, or was it because Steven blamed his father for the murders? It is possible that Steven—as Swen seemed to envision—was an obedient son who did everything his father wanted him to do. Another possibility is that Steven was angry. He became more and more disgusted with his father, who wallowed in despair, thereby denying Steven either a chance for an escape or a shoot-out. And there is yet another possibility, the cruelest of all: that Steven coolly calculated that his innocence depended on his father's death.

Like so much else about their lives and their relationship, Steven and James's final parting itself is a matter of uncertainty and conjecture. And so it will remain, unless Steven speaks out; and the time for that is perhaps forever gone. Maybe Steven is pledged, either as a soldier or as the son of his father, not to tell their true story. But some facts do speak by themselves.

Symbolic of his whole life was the fact that James's body

was found at the road's edge. Contradicting what he resisted his whole life, he was buried in a public grave, at public expense, at Paducah's Garden of Memories Cemetery. The family did not bring his body back. They were quoted in the paper as saying they did not have the money to bring him back to Minnesota.

As if he were a character in a Greek tragedy, James's fate led him to destroy everything—even his own son. Only death in exile was left to him. And even his body was not returned home, where he had always willed to be.

Steven turned himself in. He said he had to get back to his family, to Darlene, Nina, and Clayton. He returned to Minnesota in police custody. For less than a year, he lived with the lawyer who offered him a new home and a new life, and who promised him freedom. Then Steven was sent to prison, with the true story locked within himself.

The story of James and Steven Jenkins is a story of terrible homelessness. It is about a father and a son who did not survive the destruction of a family. Outcasts, migrants, fugitives—they fought against and were defeated by a world in which they found no home.

Their story is a story of abuse. The father totally failed the son. He did not spare the son from the father's dream of refounding a farm, nor did he even deflect the son from his own violent fantasies of being a soldier. The father did not teach the son reality. Instead, he gave himself and his son over to the worst that was in them and between them.

This is also a story about men who found themselves without community and with only hard ideas of what their masculinity required. Men who are alone are often not kind to themselves.

In yet another sense, this is a strange story about a father and son who became closer than ever a father and son should be. Abdicating all responsibility for his son, the father allowed the son his violent fantasies. The son—who over the years had transformed himself into his failed and angry father—became the terrible instrument of his father's revenge.

Together, this father and son were lost. They were caught in the web of the stories they had told themselves and each other. And so it is that they came to do what fathers and sons rarely do: they conspired and killed together.

We Tell Each Other Stories

Though the two enmesh
Like gears in motion, each with each conspires
To be at once together and alone.

—J. V. CUNNINGHAM,
Strong Measures—Contemporary American
Poetry in Traditional Forms

THINGS happen, and we tell each other stories about them. And, in our stories, we come to know ourselves. We tell stories to love and hurt, to prosecute and defend, to get rich and famous, and sometimes because there is nothing else to do. Storytelling is fundamental human business. It seems even that stories are all we have, so we had better tell good ones. At least, that is the conclusion to which this story led me.

As soon as it was reported that two bankers were murdered by a farmer and his son on their former farm, it was predictable that there would be a story linking the murders to the contemporary farm crisis. The nation was in the beginning phase of an extremely serious farm crisis, which was centered in the Midwest. Even prior to the time of the murders, the darkest prophecy had already been announced: this crisis, as serious as that of the 1930s, would mark the end of the family farm.

Two common assumptions about all crises, shared by the political left and right, assured the creation of a story that would make the murders an expression of the farm crisis. First, it is assumed that crises give rise to violence. Second, to complete a circular argument, it is assumed that violence—either domestic or public—reveals the existence of a crisis.

With such widely accepted but dubious assumptions as these—assumptions that are challenged by a striking absence of violent protest, despite the seriousness of the present crisis—it was certain that the killings by the Jenkinses would be described as the story of the unfolding farm crisis. Farm advocates, politicians, and writers could not resist this story. Murder is a dramatic, violent, and personal way to tell one part of the nation about a crisis in another part. Here was a good story to tell the Atlantic and Pacific coasts about the American heartland.

On the surface, there appeared to be an indisputable basis for describing the murders as a story of the farm crisis. Bankers were murdered. James Jenkins was—at least for a good portion of his life—a farmer. He murdered two bankers on his old farm site. He murdered the banker he had planned all along "to get." On this basis, more than a few reporters—Andrew Malcolm most notably—christened James as the representative of every farmer and treated the killings as the quintessential revelation of the contemporary farm crisis.

There was a similar yet more subtle social-cultural story of the killings to be told. James Jenkins could be made to typify the nation's rural poor—not the Midwest's failing family farmers, but all the poor of the American countryside who persist in trying to make it where the odds are against them. James lived his life in poor counties—counties in which most cannot and do not make it. James quit school and, while he had a variety of mechanical skills, he did not have an education or requisite skills for a good job in contemporary society. James tried many things, including his own heavy machinery business and an impossibly small diary farm. He worked, as did his wife. He often worked at low-paying and temporary jobs. His life was inseparable from working with broken things and never having enough money. James did not migrate to the cities. He persisted in finding a place in the countryside he knew. Over decades—not by the experience of one credit denial—his life became one of failure, lies, and anger. Against all common sense, he tried to make it on his own terms where almost no one could have succeeded. Finally, well into middle life and confronted with failure that could not be reversed, he despaired and lashed out violently. He did this—if we accept this story—not as a separate individual but as a member of the class of the independent rural poor. His frustration, anger, and violence were theirs.

From the moment Steven Jenkins, the son, turned himself

in, however, a dark shadow was cast over any sociological telling of the story of the murders. With Steven, the story became inescapably psychological—irrepressibly about the irrational. Steven, eighteen, never in the military, was dressed like a captured American war prisoner. His father was dead, allegedly by suicide; Steven was alive and was not telling a complete and honest story. In all likelihood, Steven, not James, did the shooting. Once Steven is considered to be the shooter, or to have gone along for more than the ride, only a false story can say the bullets that flew that day were "fired" by the farm crisis or rural poverty.

Once Steven enters the story, it takes an irreversible turn in the direction of the individual, the irrational, and the psychological. What cannot be suppressed, or treated as only incidental, is the particular relationship of this father and son and the broken family from which they emerged. How did a father and mother allow their son to go so far down the road toward military and violent fantasies? What pain must have been in that family for the son to have taken up an identity as a soldier and maintained it until the murders themselves? Finally, what kind of father would take his son along on a crime that could only spell their mutual destruction—prison or death. What was between them? These questions made this story.

If myth were bred bone deep in us, the way it was in ancient Greece, the story of James and Steven Jenkins would have told itself. The myths would have told us that fathers devour sons and that sons castrate and kill fathers. Fathers and sons are not equals—comrades in adventure; equals in friendship, affection, and intimacy; nor contemporaries in experience. We would have known that fathers and sons do not fly together, that their flight together—like that of Daedulus and Icarus—must end in destruction. Right from the start, we would have known that tragedy awaited them. Primal laws are violated only at the price of disaster.

Steven and James did what fathers and sons should not do: they became equals. The father, doing what any divorced father might be tempted to do, degraded the mother and cursed the world to the son. The son, drawn to the father instead of the mother, believed the father and took the father's point of view.

Together, but womanless and homeless, they came to share

a terrible anger. Ultimately, they conspired to revenge themselves against the world that had hurt them so. They were lost men. They were adrift in their fantasies, frustrations, and anger. They no longer had place or community. They were like boys who had become angry about their condition; they were like wild men who, without hearth, had become uncivilized.

More than typical dispossessed midwestern farmers, James and Steven resembled fifty-four-year-old Don Nichols and his twenty-year-old son, Dan Nichols. In 1984, this mountain-man father and his son—seeking to make it alone by living off of the land in the Montana wilderness—abducted a young woman athlete who strayed onto their path. The elder Nichols—who, like James, did their talking—said he and his son had lived for more than a year in the wilds and had become lonely; they "hoped to begin a mountain family with Miss Swenson." Nichols, who had succeeded in eluding the police for several months as he and his son hid in the high mountains, commented after their arrest, "As long as you have an address, you are not free."

Unlike Nichols, however, James never surrendered himself to "the wild." He persisted in believing he should have a place on the land and respect in a community. He was like the prodigal son. While away from home, his thoughts focused on returning to southwestern Minnesota. He would have a farm again. A farm for James meant far more than making a living feeding and milking cows. A farm for him meant independence and respect, place and family. It was his metaphor for restoration, for the return of wife and family, and for being the father he should have been. In short, it was his idealization of the best days at the Ruthton place.

Returning to the farm was James's sustaining story. When his belief in the story died, there was nothing left for him. It was at that point that he surrendered himself to his son's belief in weapons.

Steven's dream of weapons was antithetical to James's dream of the farm. Steven's dream was about shooting, bombing, and killing. In his dream, there was no place for farm or family.

Out of despair, the father surrendered his dream to his

son's. He led the son on a mission of vengence. The son accepted the mission.

Here the story of James and Steven Jenkins had its terrible center. The conspiracy was an agreement between the father and son to destroy themselves. James relinquished his fatherhood to his son. He gave his son what he knew to be wrong for himself as well as for his son. In agreeing to go along, Steven joined his hatred and his shooting skills to his father's madness. In conspiring to get Rudolph Blythe (and perhaps Louis Taveirne), they despaired of ever again having a place, a woman, a home, a family, or even each other. Homelessness destroyed them both; to homelessness they sentenced themselves.

This story is a moral story far more than a farm story. Indeed, it lends credence to some of the oldest moral truths about human behavior: control your temper; tell the truth; don't aim too high; don't despair; keep your family strong; and don't lose contact with others. Above all else, this story, as a moral tale, says: "Men, be fathers to your sons."

In this story the tragic consequences of lying, deceit, and willfulness speak for themselves, as does the perennial need that all men and women have for love, respect, and a place they can call home. This story is also about the tragic things we humans do to one another in our homes. Indeed, where we are closest to one another—flesh to flesh, heart to heart—we often do the worst things. Our abuse outrages even the gods.

The story of this father and son, who could not live apart nor together, is a story the Greeks told long ago. Fathers and sons were not created to fly together. The gods do not permit it.

AFTERWORD

THE night before the trial began the prosecution's trial team members, Mike O'Gorman, Bob Berg, Mike Cable, and myself, were holed up in a motel room in Marshall, Minnesota, much like we would be for the next three weeks. We were elbow deep in the remaining tasks of trial preparation, and we all felt the added pressure created by the notoriety this murder of two bankers in southwest Minnesota had attained. In short, we were in no mood for interruption.

Then the phone rang. I answered and soon found myself on the listening end of a most improbable conversation. My caller identified himself as a local college professor. He wanted to share with me lines from a poem he was composing about the relationship between the murder defendant, Steven Jenkins, and his deceased father. While interesting, the unfinished poem was neither short nor exactly what I needed to hear.

Patience born of a thousand telephone calls from disgruntled, confused, or just plain curious citizens—the daily diet of a state attorney—was being tested. My mind was on the relevant questions, how, who, and why. I had scant time or, at that moment, scant interest in the poetic ruminations of an academic observer. Yet I found myself somewhat intrigued by this man for whom a farm yard murder was becoming a vehicle for many questions remote from our prosecutorial focus.

In the three years since that introduction to Professor Amato and the opening of that trial in the Ivanhoe Courthouse my curiosity about that ruminating man has been converted to respect, to affection, and to high esteem.

In a sense I was right on that first night. His inquiries and his passion for understanding an event far transcend the relevant, as that concept is understood by the law. But the legal rule of relevancy, the rule that evidence is admissible only if it has a logical nexus to the ultimate issue in a lawsuit, is itself a terribly confining straightjacket for the inquiring human mind. A well-known jurist once noted that the rule of relevancy is a concession to the shortness of life. Fortunately for the life of letters, the same concession is not required of historians, and it was wisely abandoned by Joe Amato in this book.

If there were but a single phenomenon to be observed in this book, it would have to be the extent to which interpretations of reality—stories, as Amato would say—themselves become reality. And if there is a single irony, it is that in this book Amato has not artificially created one of his own stories. He imposes no editorial slant, no forced interpretation of the events. Rather, he has allowed the events and the people to speak for themselves. The reader is therefore left, not with answers, but rather with questions, and questions on top of questions.

In this way is the professor our teacher. He has suggested and documented the multifarious influences which bore upon the lives in this human tragedy, but he has not insisted upon the causality of any one as an explanation for the denouement. We are left to ponder the role of historical imperative, the role of personal shortcoming, and the role of blind misfortune.

The advocates in this chronical were never so circumspect as Professor Amato. Through some combination of training, personality, and professional obligation the lawyers became the ultimate storytellers. We each had a story to convey, one consistent with the verdict we each sought.

The single interpretation of reality presented by the prosecution was that on that morning in 1983, everything that was perverse about Steven Jenkins came together in an outburst of life-shattering violence. The self-imposed isolation of that young man, the anger, the symbiotic relationship with a desperate and dispairing father, the fascination with guns, the absorption of a fantasy military life, the desire to be someone—something big, even for a moment—and of course the training and physical ability to put all this perversity into action became one with the moment.

The defense vision, Swen Anderson's creation, was that all the evil in Steven was but a pale reflection of the vast evil embodied in his father, which itself explained both the crime and any minimal role that Steven may have played. The detached reader, and all who cringe at the artificial simplicity of lawyer's arguments, may have noticed that there is no logical exclusivity between these two visions. One could assume, if only for the sake of argument, that James Jenkins was the more perverse individual on that awful morning. One could also assume that Steven's conduct was the direct and proximate result of his father's perversity. Neither of these assumptions, however, negate the plethora of physical and circumstantial evidence placing Steven's finger on the trigger of the M-1 carbine.

Storytelling is really the essence of a trial lawyer's responsibility. In telling their stories, however, the lawyers inevitably (perhaps regretfully) become part of the story itself.

Public curiosity often focuses upon the lawyers and their relationship with one another. Are they like embittered opponents in an ugly divorce, each seeing nothing but evil on the other side? Usually the answer is no, sometimes the answer is yes, and sometimes you really don't know. The Jenkins case was of this last variety. To this day I am uncertain as to how Swen Anderson viewed the prosecution, or as to how he viewed his own case. My only certainty is that Swen would be pleased by my ignorance.

Swen Anderson, who died suddenly less than two years after the Jenkins trial, was the most singular person I have ever met. If Hollywood ever put him on the silver screen, no one would believe it. Everything would seem exaggerated—his size, his volume, his mannerisms, his profanity, his zeal, his righteous indignation: his singularity. Swen was an American original. I found him honorable, trustworthy, and even delightful in his own peculiar way. I grieved his passing.

Swen Anderson occupies my memories from the Jenkins trial but he does not dominate them. Overshadowing Swen are my memories of the heroism that emerged from the ashes of the catastrophe. There was the dogged heroism of my colleagues and close friends, Bob Berg, Mike Cable, and Mike O'Gorman. And there was the quiet heroism of the widows and their children.

Bob and the two Mikes constituted 75 percent of the effort that went into this prosecution for the better part of six months. Mine was 25 percent, at best. I presented their work in court and I received the credit due them. They received scant attention and ample abuse. We should all have such friends.

The war analogy is often applied to long, difficult trials. When a group is involved on one side of the struggle, there often develops the type of camaraderie typically associated with war—at least in its romanticized form. The common opponent elicits warm bonds, tireless devotion to duty, even bravery and self-sacrifice. Anyone who has played a team sport or worked on a political campaign has experienced some of this.

A high-stakes trial delivers this experience in pure form. The team members are engaged in an intellectual, emotional, and physical struggle of great intensity. I have experienced this many times in my sixteen years of public lawyering and have always emerged from such trials with a heightened sense of human potential.

Good fortune has joined me to many outstanding trial teams. It would be unfair if not impossible to single out one as greater than all others. Still, it is hard to imagine better teammates for the particular problems posed by the Ruthton killings than Bob and the Mikes. The Berg-O'Gorman team is famous in law enforcement circles throughout Minnesota. O'Gorman is spitfire and inspiration. Berg is common sense and perspiration. Both are tenacious, tireless, and trouble if you are in their way.

A trial lawyer is never better than his facts. Facts are seldom better than the investigators who assemble them. That is especially true in a case so dependent upon circumstantial evidence as this one was. The very existence of the most compelling evidence establishing the guilt of Steven Jenkins was due to the intelligent and tireless investigation conducted by Berg and O'Gorman. Just a few examples of their heroic efforts need be noted.

The best evidence of James Jenkins's poor eyesight was the testimony of Dr. Theodore Fritsche, a Marshall opthamologist who examined James's eyes two years before the murder. The very fact of that examination was discovered only because of a cold contact made by the agents with Dr. Fritsche in an effort to obtain interpretation of other eyesight evidence. The contact itself was effort above and beyond the call of duty. During the ensuing conversation Dr. Fritsche vaguely recalled that he had examined a patient named James Jenkins, and from this came the motherlode of eyesight information.

Was the discovery of the Fritsche examination a lucky strike? Perhaps so, but powerful evidence of Steven's skill with an M-1 carbine was not. One of the first shots fired from the farm yard left a small hole in the windshield of Rudy Blythe's station wagon. The initial opinion provided by the Crime Bureau Laboratory was that the hole evidenced a deflected shot, which could lead to an interpretation of wild shooting. Berg and O'Gorman would not accept that opinion. Instead, they set up a re-creation of the shooting episode, complete with three new windshields for the station wagon and shots fired at the windshields from the same distance and angle as the farm yard shot. There were no deflections, as the lab had hypothesized. Rather, all three shots carried straight through the windshields and into a target mounted on the driver's door of the wagon—just the spot where Rudy Blythe would have been as he fled the vehicle. In this manner the windshield shot was tied to a shallow wound directly in the center of Rudy's back—powerful evidence, not of wild shooting, but of precise shooting by a trained marksman. Powerful evidence, produced by a powerful pair of investigators.

Like the heroism of the Crime Bureau investigators, the heroism of Lincoln County Attorney Mike Cable was also evidenced by tireless effort and personal sacrifice. Even beyond that, and even beyond the excellent legal work that Mike contributed to the effort, there was yet another form of heroism. Mike's willingness to accept and perform his public responsibility as local prosecutor in this case was a courageous act.

The prosecution of Steven Jenkins was not politically popular in Lincoln County, at least in the early weeks following the murders. Between the early publicity suggesting that the killings were part of the farm crisis and the early focus upon James Jenkins as the long time antagonist of Rudy Blythe, the prosecution met a chilly public reception. This coolness extended all the way east to St. Paul where my mother-in-law, a dear friend, expressed personal dismay over my involvement in the case.

As a rural county attorney in Minnesota, Mike Cable occupies a part-time position. When not engaged as county attorney he pursues a private law practice in Ivanhoe and Lake Benton. His private enterpise is an economic necessity and is very dependent upon the day-to-day good will of the local citizenry. An unpopular prosecution can jeopardize that livelihood.

I have seen local prosecutors duck their public responsibility under similar circumstances, including an instance in which a county attorney resigned and left the office vacant to avoid public controversy. Not Mike Cable. Mike never shirked, not in the early days when public sentiment ran against us, and not in the ensuing months when the trial demands left his private practice in shambles. Mike employed a succinct, well-worn profanity to dismiss the concerns of local politics that occasionally confronted us. By his willingness to do so and to take the attendant heat, Mike enabled us to put on a major league prosecution right in Steven Jenkins's own back yard.

Last, let me reflect upon the heroism of the survivors of this tragedy. Those closest to me have been the widows of Rudy Blythe and Toby Thulin, and through them, their children.

People who lose loved ones to murder suffer two of life's most agonizing experiences. First and most obviously, they experience the wrenching separation brought on by unexpected and premature death. The depth of that pain can never be known by those who have not suffered the same, but one can easily imagine that it is awful, very awful.

Compounding this misery is the anguish suffered by all crime victims. This pain is less imaginable because the experience is less universal, but it is very real and very predictable. Crime victims are struck by a sense of helplessness due to the randomness and irrationality of the event and by a sense of outrage over the human agency involved. The misery induced by victimization is increased by the subsequent misery induced through the sudden immersion into the criminal justice system.

Thus, the survivors of a murder victim must contend at once with unsurpassed grief, massive anger, frustration, and hostility. When legal proceedings ensue for months and years after the murder, which is common, these emotions remain present and hot for the duration. All this is further amplified by the isolation that society imposes upon those for whom there are no adequate words of comfort.

Considering all this, it is a marvel that human beings survive this unthinkable ordeal. That they do survive is something that I have witnessed many times, always with a measure of awe. There is, it seems, a remarkable resiliency in people that enables most murder survivors to emerge from the long night and to resume the necessary task of living. I can think of no human power that makes this possible.

And so it has been with Sue Blythe, Lynette Thulin, and their children. Their suffering has been as great as I have ever witnessed, their ordeal as extended, and their survival as heroic. In them I have seen the resiliency of life and the grace of God. Both widows have now established new homes far from Ruthton, both are successfully preparing their children for brighter days, and both are increasingly active in human service–type activities.

My list of heroes from this tragedy would not be complete without reference to Darlene Jenkins, the mother of Steven. Her loss, while very different from the other widows, was nonetheless staggering: her family responsible for two innocent deaths, her ex-husband dead in Texas, her son convicted of murder and sentenced for life, her family surrounded by infamy.

My only conversations with Darlene occurred when she was providing courtroom testimony, first in the grand jury and later at trial. I know nothing of her present circumstances. Thus, my only real impressions are based upon watching her in court day after day as she shared the travail of her only son.

Darlene did for Steven what I hope my own mother would have done for me in the same circumstance. She was a constant presence, she appeared to be a constant comfort, and she appeared dedicated to rescuing her son from this calamity, perhaps at any price. There was heroism in that dedication and heroism in surviving beyond it.

It seems necessary to conclude this afterword on a tale of death with words of life. There was nothing good or meaningful or even symbolic about the shooting in Ruthton. Lives were lost, others were destroyed, and still others were forever diminished by the tragedy. There is scant inspiration to be drawn from the deaths. But from the lives of the survivors and from those summoned to this crime by professional obligation, I have drawn great inspiration. The goodness and heroism of those lives is a better legacy for this case than the manifest evil of the crime.

THOMAS L. FABEL

St. Paul, Minnesota

ESSAY ON SOURCES

THE PRIMARY SOURCES for this work have been legal and public documents. Prior to, during, and after the trial, I had full access to the abundant materials at the Lyon and Lincoln county clerk of court's and attorney general's offices in St. Paul.

The written materials pertaining to the trial are gathered in four files, are titled and indexed as volumes, and are now held in the court administrator's office (formerly the clerk of court's office) at the Lincoln County Courthouse in Ivanhoe, Minnesota. These four volumes, containing 102 documents, are registered under Appellate Court File No. C4-8 #964, Case No. K-83-254.

Some important materials in volume one include: the indictment; a notice of affirmative defenses; a request for evidentiary hearing; a memo in support of state's motion to suppress psychiatric opinion testimony; the bail order; and the report from Carl Schwartz. In volume two there are fourteen petitions for witnesses outside the state, a variety of defense and state motions on the admissibility of types of evidence, as well as motions and memos regarding the use of a lie detector test and the validity of the suicide note of James Jenkins. Volume three includes a range of actions pertaining to instructing the jury and supplying it with definitions; the verdicts of guilty; a range of motions seeking to vacate judgment and requesting a new trial. Volume four includes the sentence (partial transcript); the notice of appeal to the supreme court; an affidavit of indigency; a request for a total transcript; a motion for the substitution of counsel; supplementary findings of fact and order (regarding the crime victims reparations board); and the judgment of the supreme court.

Additionally available at the Lincoln County Courthouse are the original and a copy of the four-volume, bound transcript of the trial as well as all of the material evidence used during the trial. The evidence includes James's eyeglasses, Steven's weapons, the clothing of Blythe and Thulin, and bullet fragments. Also, there are photographs, slides, and overheads used to identify the possessions of Steven and James Jenkins and to establish the scene of the crime, the nature of the shooting, and the wounds of the victims.

What proved even more important for this study were the working files of Deputy Attorney General Tom Fabel. These files, which presently remain in the attorney general's office in St. Paul, Minnesota, will eventually be turned over to the state archives. While Fabel's working files, which carry internal number 35. 733M. 0241, do not include correspondence from citizens to Judge Mann or to the Lincoln County clerk of court, correspondence on sentencing, the pre-investigation report, or the confidential pre-sentencing investigation report, nevertheless Fabel's files are immensely important because they contain all other materials including some (especially interviews) that never became part of the trial record.

Fabel's files include the following: correspondence about the case; press clippings; Steven Jenkins's seven statements prior to going to court; the transcript of the grand jury proceedings (which is confidential except for Steven's testimony in volume two); notes on jury selection; information about the trial proceedings; miscellaneous police reports; a range of evidentiary materials and expert testimony; a subpoena list; Fabel's opening statement and final arguments; instructions to the jury; notes about the court appeals, including the appellant's and respondent's briefs; and information from and about approximately 175 witnesses and potential witnesses.

Upon the basis of so much material generated by prosecution and defense alike, I could give specific direction to my own research.

Some additional evidence I sought was already revealed in public records. Matters of property, marriage, and divorce were found in Lyon and Lincoln County courthouses.

Newspaper articles and reporters provided useful background material for the case as it developed. *Minneapolis Trib-*

une reporter Paul Levy's background articles on James Jenkins and Swen Anderson after the arrest and during the trial were noteworthy. *Marshull Independent* reporter Steven Olson justly won an award for his thorough coverage of the trial. Occasional articles in the *Worthington Globe* were also very useful.

Andrew Malcolm's book, *Final Harvest* (New York:: Times Books, 1986), proved to be useful at several points. Written in close cooperation and partnership with Susan Blythe, Malcolm offered an intimate portrait of her and her husband's lives. Malcolm also offered sensitive portraits of Deems and Lynette Thulin. Malcolm's unjustified insistence that the murders be made to reveal "the farm crisis in the heartland" did not blind him to the telling detail of personality and locale.

Oral interviews played an indispensable part in this work. They were used to establish and verify information and point of view on such matters as James's alleged suicide and the suicide note itself; to understand technical and specific points of law that exceeded my understanding; to reconcile contradictory points of view and interpretation of intentions that surrounded the actions and the intentions of the principals of this case; to corroborate opinions found in the newspaper or in police interviews; and to develop my understanding of Steven and James, their characters, and their family background. On a few significant points, interviews opened new perspectives on fundamental matters.

I conducted over one hundred interviews, and this number excludes a great number of casual conversations I had in the course of my everyday living and teaching here in southwestern Minnesota. Many of the interviews were short telephone interviews, whereas other interviews approached what could best be described as ongoing conversations. In almost all cases people generously and even enthusiastically shared their opinions. They had a story they wished to tell.

I had several lengthy conversations with state prosecutor Thomas Fabel from the time of the trial in the fall of 1983 until the spring of 1987. I also talked with Lincoln County prosecutor Michael Cable several times during that period.

I interviewed BCA officers Robert Berg and Michael O'Gorman during the trial. I also interviewed Berg several times during 1986 and O'Gorman in December 1985.

I interviewed several other law enforcement officers in the region. Among them were Deputy Fred Durfey (following the crime); Lincoln County sheriff Albert Thompson (spring of 1987); Yellow Medicine sheriff Richard Rollins (fall of 1986, spring of 1987); and former Lincoln County deputy Vernon Dahl (spring of 1987).

I learned a great deal about the case and the people involved in it from attorneys in the area, including David Peterson (fall of 1985); Eric DeRycke (spring of 1986); Thomas Kramer (fall of 1985, spring of 1987); Clarance Hagglund (fall of 1986); Elizabeth Anderson's attorney, Donald Maland (fall of 1986); and Steven Jenkins's public defender, Robert Maunu (spring, 1987). Information about legal terms and procedures was shared with me by attorneys Kevin Stroup, Adam Bavolack, and Donald Marshall.

Extensive information about Swen Anderson was obtained in interviews with his friends Kermit and Lynn Ness and LuVern Hansen (spring and fall of 1986).

It should be mentioned that, while I never spoke to Steven Jenkins, I did interview several principals in the case; a few chose not to talk to me. I also interviewed approximately twenty-five neighbors and friends of the Jenkins family.

During the trial I spoke briefly with Luigi DiFonzo and Susan Blythe. After the trial I interviewed Judge Mann; jury foreman David Koster; state parole and probation officer Andy Doom; and prison social worker Fred Holbeck. I also interviewed Gary Brosz, the principal of the Tyler school.

Additional background information was provided by David Putnam, former owner of the *Granite Falls Tribune*; Duane DeBettignies of the *Buffalo Ridge Gazette*; Jane McKeon of the *Montevideo American-News*; and John and Marcia Neely, current owners of the *Granite Falls Tribune*. Conversations with several reporters were useful. Among those I spoke to were Paul Levy of the *Minneapolis Tribune*, Jim George of the *Pioneer Press*, Steve Olson of the *Marshall Independent*, and Kevin Black of KSFY-TV, Sioux Falls, South Dakota.

Other sources of information about the region included Lincoln County recorder of deeds Kenneth Toft, Clyde Pedersen (former owner of the Buffalo Ridge State Bank), Val Whipple of

Ivanhoe, Pat Andrezejek of Ivanhoe, and Henry Jacobsen of Tyler.

Many publications shed additional light on the issues involved in this story. Specifically useful for understanding the region are the following works: Joseph Amato, *Countryside, Mirror of Ourselves* (Marshall, Minn.: Venti Amati, 1980); Theodore Blegen, *Minnesota: A History of the State* (Minneapolis, Minn.: University of Minnesota Press, 1975); June Drenning, ed., *They Chose Minnesota: A Survey of the State's Ethnic Groups* (St. Paul, Minn.: Minnesota Historical Society, 1981); Paul Gruchow, *A Journal of a Prairie Year* (Minneapolis, Minn.: University of Minnesota Press, 1986); Bill Holm, *The Music of Failure* (Marshall, Minn.: Plains Press, 1985); Don Martindale and R. Galen Hanson, *Small Town and the Nation: The Conflict of Social and Translocal Forces* (Westport, Conn.: Greenwood, 1975); and David Nass, ed., *Holiday: Minnesotans Remember the Farmer's Holiday Association* (Marshall, Minn.: Plains Press, 1984).

Useful for understanding the present farm crisis and its impact on the region are the following books and reports: Julie Bleyhl, "Farm Financial Analysis" (report for the Minnesota Farmers Union, December 5, 1985); Gilbert Fite, *American Farmers: The New Minority* (Bloomington, Ind.: Indiana University Press, 1984); "Minnesota Farm Financial Survey, 1985" (report of Minnesota Department of Agriculture, February 3, 1986); William Pratt, "Midwest Farm Protest—Then and Now," in *Plowing Up a Storm: A History of Midwestern Farm Activism* (Nebraska Educational Television Network, 1985), 21–25; "Propping up the Farm," special issue of the *Minneapolis Star and Tribune* (1985); and Jonathan Rauch, "The Great Farm Gamble," *National Journal* (March 29, 1986), 13–16.

For an introduction to the poverty of the American countryside and to the material and psychological condition in which the poor find themselves, see Frederick Buttell and Howard Newby, *The Rural Sociology of the Advanced Societies* (Montclair, N.J.: Allanheld, 1980); R. T. Coward and W. M. Smith, *The Family in Rural Society* (Boulder, Col.: Westview, 1981); ibid., eds., *Family Services and Opportunities in Contemporary Rural America* (Lincoln, Nebr.: University of Nebraska Press,

1983); R. Craycroft and M. Fazio, eds., *Change and Tradition in the American Small Town* (Jackson, Miss.: University Press of Mississippi, 1983); National Rural Center, *Rural Poverty* (Washington, D.C.: National Rural Center, 1981); and Lillian Rubin, *Worlds of Pain: Life in the Working-Class Family* (New York: Basic, 1976).

For introductions to the vast and growing literature concerning the modern family, see *Inventory of Marriage and Family Literature* (published annually by Family Social Science, University of Minnesota); *American Family History: A Historical Bibliography* (Santa Barbara, Calif.: ABC-Clio, 1984); John Crosby, ed., *Reply to Myth: Perspectives on Intimacy* (New York: Wiley, 1985). Also of general use are Talcott Parsons, *Family: Socialization and Interaction Process* (Glencoe, Ill.: Free Press, 1955), and Letha Scanzoni and John Scanzoni, *Men, Women, and Change: Sociology of Marriage and Family* (New York: McGraw, 1976). Of specific use for themes of family study that intersect with my study are two important works by Jules Henry: *Pathways to Madness* (New York: Random House, 1971) and *On Sham, Vulnerability and Other Forms of Self-Destruction* (New York: Random House, 1973).

The majority of material on father and son relationships that I surveyed is divided into two groups. Taking its impulse from Freud, one part of the literature examines the father-son relationship as a matter of the deepest psychological conflict; an equally abundant amount of literature stresses the importance of a father as a role model and guide for the son. Indicative of some of the materials found are Donald Bell, *Being a Man: Paradox of Masculinity* (Lexington, Mass.: Greene, 1982); Leonard Benson, *Fatherhood: A Sociological Perspective* (New York: Random House, 1968); Henry Biller, *Father, Child and Sex Role* (Lexington, Mass.: Heath Lexington Books, 1971); Arthur Colman, *Earth Father/Sky Father: The Changing Concept of Fathering* (Englewood Cliffs, N.J.: Prentice-Hall, 1981); Maureen Green, *Fathering* (New York: McGraw-Hill, 1977); Daniel Levinson, *The Seasons of a Man's Life* (New York: Knopf, 1974); David Lynn, *The Father: His Role in Child Development* (Monterey, Calif.: Brooks/Cole, 1974); Ignaz Maybaum, *Creation and Guilt: A Theological Assessment of Freud's Father-Son*

Conflict (London: Vallentine, Mitchell, 1969); Lorna McKee, ed., *The Father Figure* (New York: Methuen, Inc., 1982).

For information about the condition of males in contemporary mass industrial society, see Christopher Lasch, *Haven in a Heartless World: The Family Besieged* (New York: Basic, 1977); ibid., "Why the Survival Mentality is Rife in America," *U.S. News and World Report* (May 17, 1982): 59–60; Zick Rubin, "Fathers and Sons," *Psychology Today* (June 1982): 23–33; Richard Sennett and Jonathan Cobb, *The Hidden Injuries of Class* (New York: Random House, 1972); and Peter Stearns, *Be A Man: Male in Modern Society* (New York: Holmes and Meier, 1979).

For information about homicide, a most useful bibliographic guide is *Homicide: A Bibliography of Over 4500 Items* (Augusta, Ga.: Pine Tree, Inc., 1982). Also useful is *Encyclopedia of Crime and Justice*, Vol. 2 (New York: Macmillan, 1983); J. Gaute and Robin Odell, *The Murderers' Who's Who: Outstanding International Cases from the Literature of Murder in the Last 150 Years* (New York: St. Martins Press, 1979); and James Wilson and Richard Hernstein, *Crime and Human Nature* (New York: Simon and Schuster, 1985).

Specific works that, while not offering definitive analogies, throw light on psychological elements and themes of the Jenkins case are Eric Ambler, *An Ability to Kill* (London: Bodley Head, 1963); Andrew Henry and James Short, *Suicide and Homicide: Some Economic, Sociological and Psychological Aspects of Aggression* (New York: Ayer Publishing, 1977); Angela Browne, "When Battered Women Kill" (unpublished manuscript, Denver, 1983); H. A. Bunker, "Mother-Murder in Myth and Legend: A Psychoanalytic Note," *Psychological Quarterly* 13 (1944): 198–207; Ann Burgess, "Family Reaction to Homicide," *American Journal of Orthopsychiatry* 45, 3 (April 1975): 391–98; Michel Foucault, *I, Pierre Reviere, Having Slaughtered My Mother, My Sister and My Brother: A Case of Parricide in the Nineteenth Century* (Omaha, Nebr.: University of Nebraska Press, 1982); Ernest Jones, "An Unusual Case of Dying Together," *Essays in Applied Psychoanalysis* (London: International Universities Press, 1912); J. W. Mohr, "Violence as a Function of Age and Relationship with a Special Reference to Matricide," *Canadian*

Psychiatric Association Journal 18 (February 1971): 29–32; Alex Pokorny, "Human Violence: A Comparison of Homicide, Aggravated Assault, Suicide and Attempted Suicide," *Journal of Criminal Law, Criminology and Political Science* 56, 4 (1965): 488–497; L. H. Rubenstein, "The Theme of Electra and Orestes: A Contribution to the Psychopathology of Matricide," *British Journal of Medical Psychology* 42 (June 1969): 99–108; Carol Stearns and Peter Stearns, *Anger: The Struggle for Emotional Control in America's History* (Chicago: University of Chicago Press, 1986); Emanuel Tanay, *The Murderers* (Indianapolis: Bobbs-Merrill, 1976); ibid., "Reactive Parricide," *Journal of Forensic Science* 21, 1 (January 1976): 76–82; L. S. Tucker, et al., "Mother-Son, Folie Deux: A Case of Attempted Patricide," *American Journal of Psychiatry* 10 (October 1977): 1146–7.

Two worthwhile studies of murder are Truman Capote, *In Cold Blood* (New York: NAL, 1965), and Peter Davis, *Hometown: A Portrait of an American Community* (New York: Simon and Schuster, 1982).

Two recent incidents of homicide and violence in the countryside have also been popularly related to the farm crisis and pressure of debt. For information about a Nebraska farmer who died in a shoot-out in 1984, see Calvin Trillin, "I Have Got Problems," *The New Yorker* (March 18, 1985): 109–118. For information about a farmer in Iowa who killed his banker, his neighbor, his wife, and himself in December 1985, see Kay Miller, "An Iowa Farmer's Day of Death," *Sunday Magazine, Minneapolis Star and Tribune* (February 23, 1983): 12–16.

For a specific study that suggests that there is no correlation between the farm crisis and suicide in the farm community, see "An Analysis of Suicides Among Those Who Resided on Farms in Five North Central States, 1980–1985," a 1987 collaborative report of the departments of health of Minnesota, Montana, North Dakota, South Dakota, and Wisconsin.

For a nonpsychological study of a father and son involved in a violent kidnapping and murder, see Johnny France and Malcolm McConnel's study of Montana mountain men Don and Dan Nichols: *Incident at Big Sky* (New York: Norton, 1986).